IMAGES
of America

BRAMWELL
A TOWN OF MILLIONAIRES

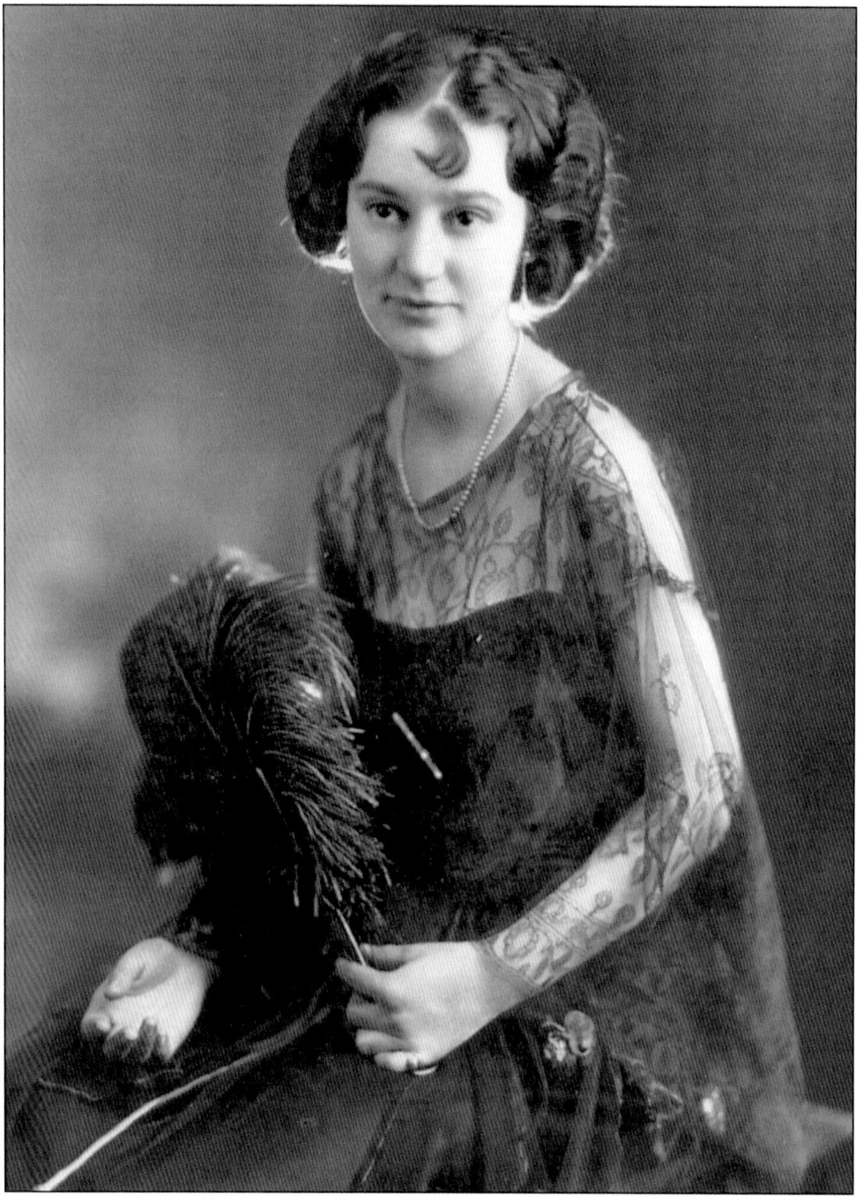

Golden Girl. Miss Goldie Rickmon lived for almost a century—and all of it in Bramwell. Born just before 1900, she experienced the Great Fire of 1910, the Great Depression, the Great Flood, two World Wars, the heyday of the famous Bank of Bramwell, and the transition from horse and buggy travel to motor cars to jet planes. She watched Henry Wade push the cart filled with bags full of cash down the middle of Main Street to the train station every payday. She saw the grand parties and elaborate weddings. Goldie watched as hard working men became millionaires and then lost it all, "going from shoestring to shoestring in three generations." On attending the sale at auction of everything in a 24-room mansion, she cried as she said, "I can't bear to watch this. I saw her come here to this house as a bride, and now this." It was Goldie who shared her memories and made stories of luxury and hard work and wealth and poverty come alive in imaginations of her students of all ages. She was Bramwell's "Golden Girl of Living History."

IMAGES
of America

BRAMWELL
A TOWN OF MILLIONAIRES

Louise Dawson Stoker and
Dana Stoker Cochran

ARCADIA
PUBLISHING

ISBN 978-0-7385-1826-8

Published by Arcadia Publishing
Charleston, South Carolina

Printed in the United States of America

Library of Congress Catalog Card Number: 2005923385

For all general information contact Arcadia Publishing at:
Telephone 843-853-2070
Fax 843-853-0044
E-mail sales@arcadiapublishing.com
For customer service and orders:
Toll-Free 1-888-313-2665

Visit us on the Internet at www.arcadiapublishing.com

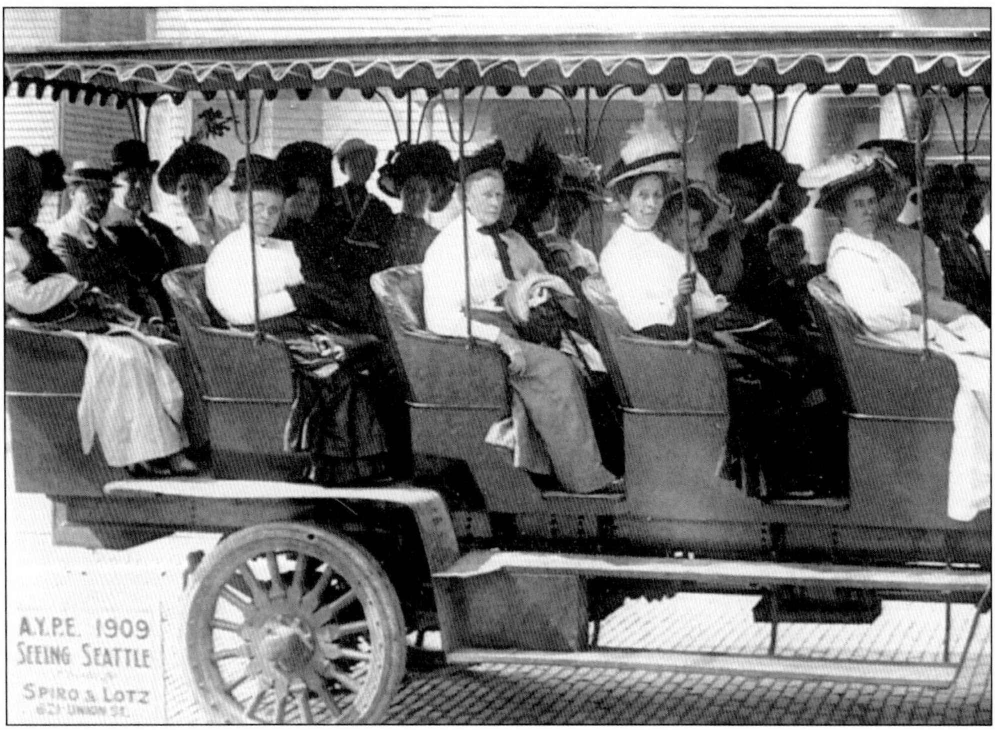

HONEYMOON TRIP. In 1909, Martha "Mattie" Wheeler got off the train at the Bramwell station and walked down Main Street past the Bluestone Inn. C.W. "Wes" Freeman was sitting on the veranda with friends. He took one look at her and said, "That one's mine, boys. I'm gonna marry her," and he did. Their honeymoon trip took them by train from Bramwell to New York to Seattle and back again. They toured Seattle in this open carrier. Mattie and Wes Freeman are the couple in the back row on the right. (Courtesy of Sunny Freeman.)

CONTENTS

Acknowledgments

We extend gratitude to all who have shared memories and memorabilia through the years. In addition to those recognized in photograph captions, we would like to thank everyone who aided and encouraged us in this publication. Heartfelt thanks are extended to those whose stories of the past have helped us write the words for the future. The list includes, but is not limited to, the following: the late Bill Becker, Harry "Beef" Bennett, Ansley Carter, Mildred Mitchell Cooper, Mamie Hill Bailey, C.W. "Sunny" Freeman Jr., Hattie Holley Heath, Dea Peraldo Hughes, Bill Jameson, Vester and Margaret Johnson, May Llewellyn Jones, Dwight W. McCormick, Frances "Penny" Witt Morgan, Evelyn Cooper Murphy, Helen Shupe Painter, Eleanor and Richard Painter, Leo C. Peraldo, Mauro Peraldo, John B. Perry Jr., Lillian Hill Pierce, Goldie Rickmon, Glenn Scott, Hazel Shultz, and David Sims.

A special thank you goes to the following, who shared snapshots from their past or provided assistance in this project: Ennice Hill Allen, Alma Mahaffey Anello, Fred Armstrong, Ellen Goins Bailey, Katharine Hewitt Barringer, Debra Basham, Linda Keesling Beggs, Sandra Martin Beggs, Lenora Jean Bolen Bennett, Camille Peraldo Brunner, Joan C. Browning, Joan Bange Buchanan, Virginia and Ruth Buckner, Edith Harris Butt, Warren Butt, Kate Cosby Cardwell, Mary Staton Carter, Josephine Dunagan Carver, Margaret Fitzko Carver, Thomas A. Colley, Sandy Collins, Mary Helen Painter Cornett, George Craft, Ken Davidson, Bonnie Dawson, James "Buzzy" Dawson, Henry N. "Skipper" Edmunds, Kelly Murphy Eller, Vernon Fields, Bill Foster, Dorothy Tabor Edmunds Graham, Shirley and Randy Gibson, Judith Davidson Gilley, Kelly and Vickie Goins, Melvin Goins, Steve Goins, Jim Graham, Debbie and Wanda Graves, Betty Ann Bennett Hamilton, Elbert "Dizzy" Harris, Dwight Hill, Cris Hill, Eva Yon Hill, Marlene Moran Houchins, Patricia Freeman Hudson, Bill Keller, Edna Cook Keller, Janet Buckner Mabe, Mantini's Photography Studio, Thomas Marshall, Edris Henry Miller, Jeanne Hamilton Monte, Alma Yon Murphy, Kim C. Murphy, John Nelson, Leo Peraldo, Cynthia Pitzer, David Richardson, Vickie Painter Rushbrook, Charlotte E. Sacre, Frank Sexton, Harman "Corky" Sexton, Kathleen Palco Sexton, Lois Sexton, James Shrader, Elva Mae Wright Skaggs, Bibbi Dawson Sigmon, Jeannine Hall Smith, Lava Yost Staton, Bob and Marianna Hughes Stoker, Polly and Elbert Street, Dr. Marvin Wilson Tabor, Betsy Perdue Thomas, Betty Jeane Thompson, Tiny Thompson, Daisy Walker, Wade Wilburn, Evelyn "Sissy" Williams, Sharon Scott Workman, Wayne Wright, and the Bluewell Rite Aid Pharmacy employees.

Photographs not credited in the captions are from the private collection of the authors.

Introduction

Bramwell is located on the southern tip of West Virginia. Sections of the town were named to the National Register of Historic Places in 1983, 1992, and 2005.

Bramwell was international from its beginning, built by men from 15 different countries. It was an intelligent and artistic community. In his unpublished memoir, Rev. Norman F. Marshall said, "At Bramwell, there was an unusually gifted set of parishioners . . . Bramwell, next to Carlsbad, New Mexico, had the most attractive social set of any place I have ever ministered in."

Bramwell was the place a future poet spent her impressionable early years. Anne Spencer, famous Harlem Renaissance poet, lived in Bramwell from age three or four until she went to school in Lynchburg, Virginia, at age 11. She spent her summers in Bramwell and returned there to live after her graduation in 1899. During those childhood years, Anne experienced no racial inequality and freely enjoyed a long friendship with a young white girl, Elsa Brown. The extent to which she valued her years in Bramwell is evidenced by the fact that she chose not to correct sources listing her birthplace as Bramwell. Anne's reason for letting the inaccuracy stand was explained by her son, Chauncey Spencer, to the author in 1993: "My mother was of strong character. She wished to say she was from the free state of West Virginia rather than the slave state of Virginia." Annie Bethel Scales and Edward Spencer were married May 15, 1901, in Bramwell, and her best friend Elsa was maid of honor. The marriage was performed by Rev. Norman F. Marshall, rector of Bramwell's Holy Trinity Episcopal Church, who also included in his memoir, "Bramwell was an unusually beautiful small town, almost unimproveble (sic) in beauty, nestling in the mountains 2,500 feet above sea level and saturated in dampness. The mountains around it were much higher still. They gave ample chance for long hikes . . . Magnolia-like rhododendrons scattered in nearly every direction."

The Bluestone River, flowing the length of Coopers/Shinbrier, Bramwell, and Freeman/Simmons, relates to the town in many ways. Bridges for different uses have existed. The horse-and-buggy bridges were replaced by new automobile bridges for millionaires who always bought the latest of everything. Railroad trestles crisscrossed the river. There were swinging bridges (pedestrian footbridges) that sometimes gave the only access to a few houses. Everything had to be carried over them, including furniture. As a recreation site, the river serves fishermen and children. There was once a large swimming hole at Shinbrier called "Blue Hole" and another behind the Bluestone Baptist Church. They were used for early-day swimming lessons. "That's where my brother threw me in and said, 'Swim or drown,' and here I am, so I learned," a former resident reminisced. Summer and winter, the river was a playground for young and old. In winters, it froze over and was a perfect place for ice skating. Long lines of people formed and skated the two miles to Shinbrier and back. Their favorite sport was "crack-the-whip." A granddaughter of the first mayor remembered "always being on the end of the line when they cracked the whip."

Bramwell's history appears to be the subject of a work of fiction. However, no exaggeration is necessary. The community sprang up almost overnight. Men followed a rainbow with black gold—coal—at its end. It was an Appalachian Mountain coal rush that supplied fuel for the Industrial Revolution. Men seized the moment, made their fortunes, and became millionaires. Money seemed to flow through the streets as the Bluestone River flowed around the bend. Indeed, Bank of Bramwell employee Henry Wade pushed a wheelbarrow full of cash down the middle of Main Street to the train station every payday. He was never robbed. When a prominent man passed away, black horses and a black hearse were brought in by rail to carry him to the local cemetery in style. For Bramwell's most extravagant wedding, the groom's party traveled from St. Louis by private coach. It was sidetracked behind the train station until the wedding revelry was over. When guests left their coach for the ceremony, white linen cloth covered the sidewalk from the railcar to the church one block away. Elaborate parties catered by Washington, Richmond, or Cincinnati firms were held. The very finest Furnas ice cream was brought by rail from Cincinnati to please the palates of the newly rich. Ice cream cones created a game for a dog named Pepper. Each day, he was given a nickel to carry into the Bryant-Newbold Pharmacy where the soda jerk sold him a cone of cream. Across from the drug store, people relaxed on the veranda of the Bluestone Inn and watched the scenario play out. One elderly man remembered Pepper with these words: "When I was a boy, I hated that little white dog because he had nickels for a cone of cream and I didn't!"

Bramwell's story has yet another side—the one of hard-working coal miners who made the millions for coal mine owners and operators. The families who "crossed the ocean to the promised land," or who traveled from other states to the southern West Virginia coal fields, exhibited a pioneer spirit and determination that enabled them to survive the hard times and enjoy the good. They lived through two world wars, the Great Depression, major fires and floods, and came out of each experience with a renewed desire to succeed. Knowing the great equalizer is education, they passed the dream of a better life along to their children. From this legacy, the descendants of Bramwell natives continue to achieve. Bramwell has given its resources to the world: scholars, engineers, doctors, nurses, lawyers, pilots, research scientists, educators, musicians, and yes, coal mine owners.

The mist rises from the Bluestone River on a warm, humid summer morning, giving a feeling of protection and peacefulness. Driving a mile to the top of Pinnacle Mountain puts one high above the river. A vivid imagination pictures Shangri-La below the mist. It is called Bramwell.

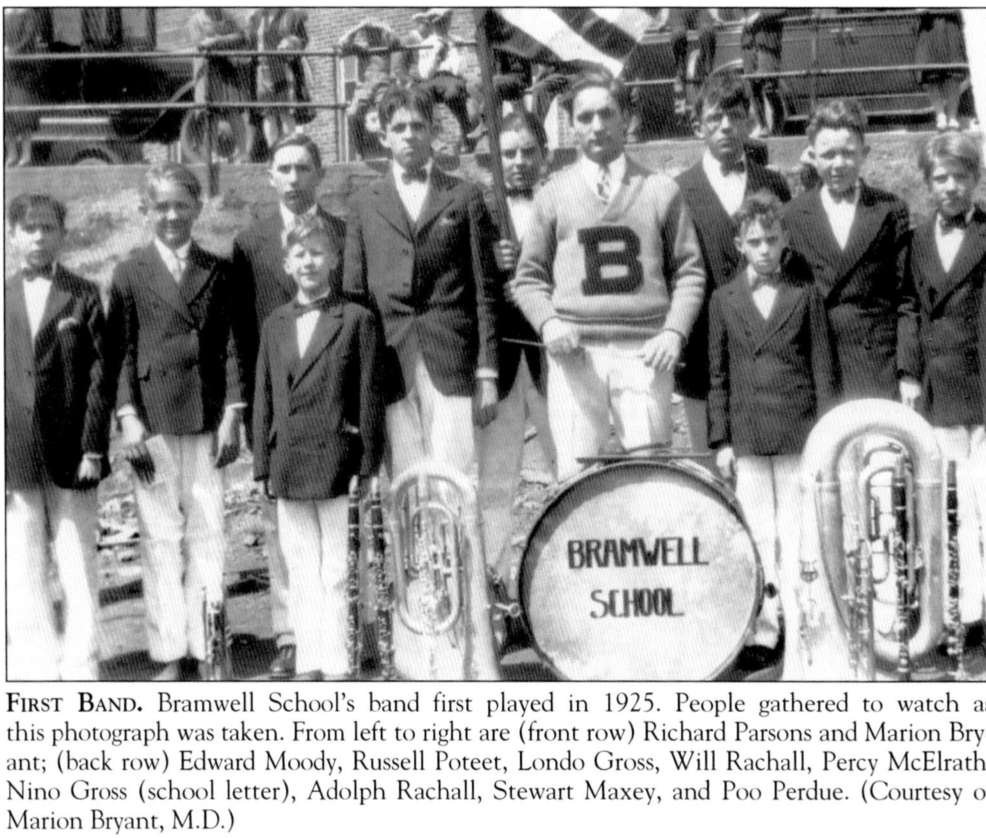

First Band. Bramwell School's band first played in 1925. People gathered to watch as this photograph was taken. From left to right are (front row) Richard Parsons and Marion Bryant; (back row) Edward Moody, Russell Poteet, Londo Gross, Will Rachall, Percy McElrath, Nino Gross (school letter), Adolph Rachall, Stewart Maxey, and Poo Perdue. (Courtesy of Marion Bryant, M.D.)

One

The "First" and "Only" Chapter

Every little baby has a name,
This little town should have the same.
So now, if you will all agree,
I choose to name it after me.
— J.H. Bramwell, November 20, 1888

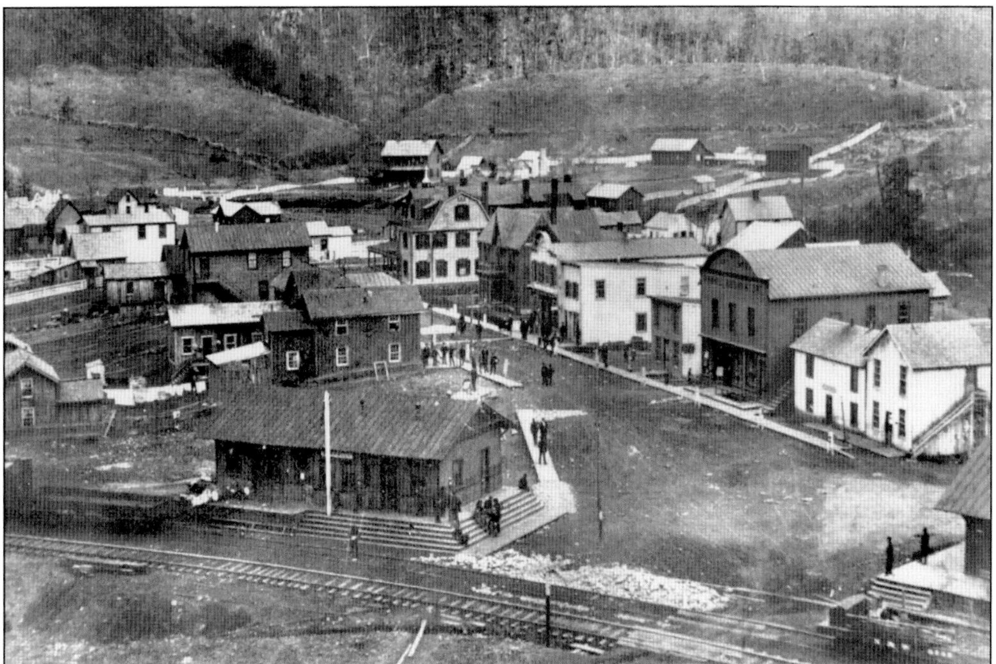

March 24, 1888. The first postmaster, J.H. Bramwell, designed the business district pictured above and acquired the first lot on Main Street. When the Bank of Bramwell was chartered in 1889, J.H. Bramwell was elected its first president and remained in that position until his death in 1894.

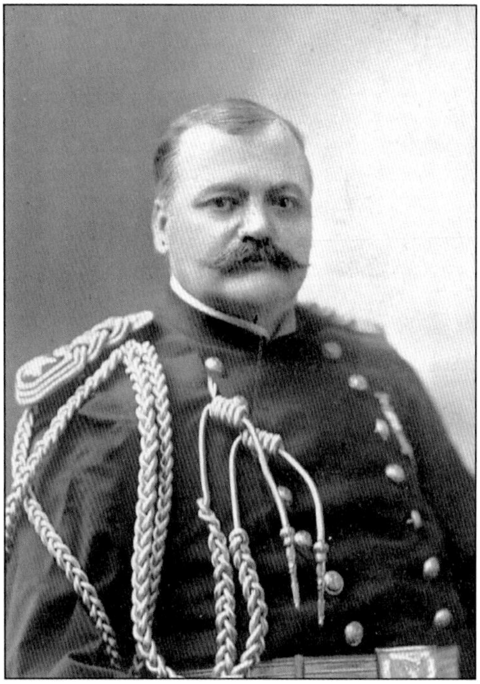

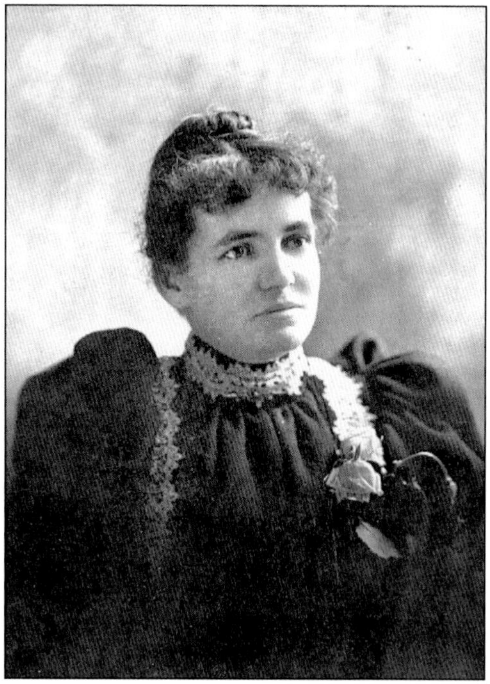

FIRST MAYOR, FIRST FIRST LADY. Bramwell was incorporated as a town November 20, 1888. The first election was held the following January. English-born John Davis Hewitt was elected mayor and served a one-year term. He and his wife, Katharine "Kate" Reedy Hewitt, moved from Pennsylvania to Bramwell. (Courtesy of Katharine Barringer.)

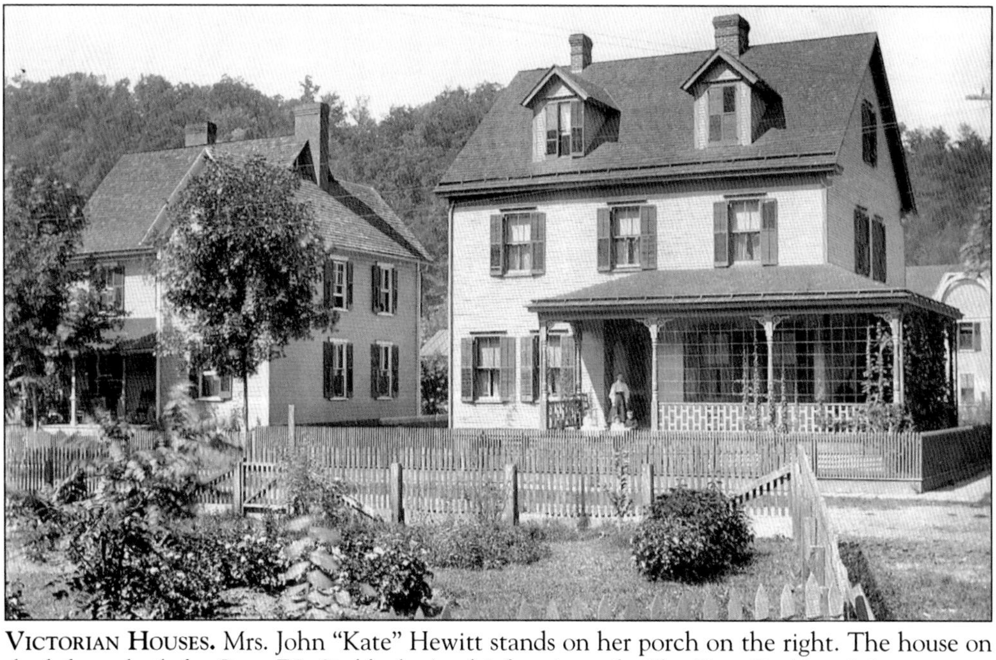

VICTORIAN HOUSES. Mrs. John "Kate" Hewitt stands on her porch on the right. The house on the left was built for Capt. F.L. Paddock. As chief engineer for Flat-Top-Coal Land Association, he designed the public water and storm drainage system in the new town. (Courtesy of Katharine Barringer.)

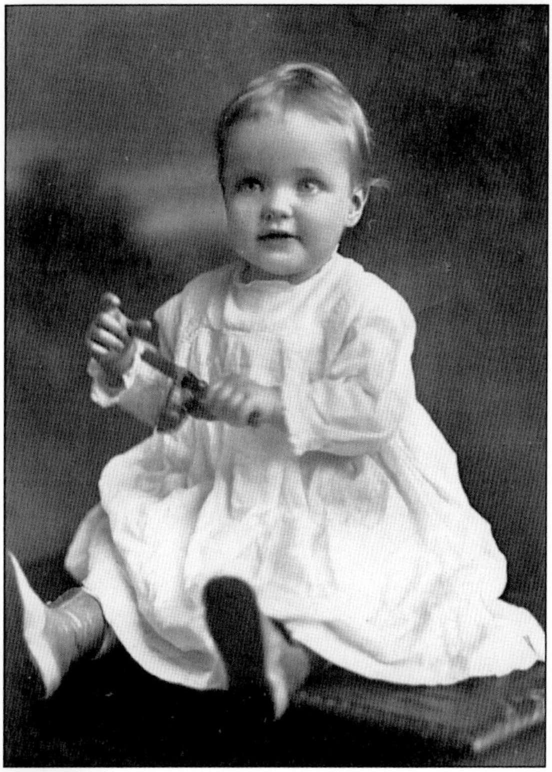

Hewitt Granddaughter, 1917. Katharine Hewitt was the granddaughter of the town's first mayor. She grew up to be Katharine Barringer, the first woman elected to the Bramwell town council. She retired from teaching at Bramwell High School, then served as the town clerk. After many years, she was again elected at age 86. (Courtesy of Katharine Barringer.)

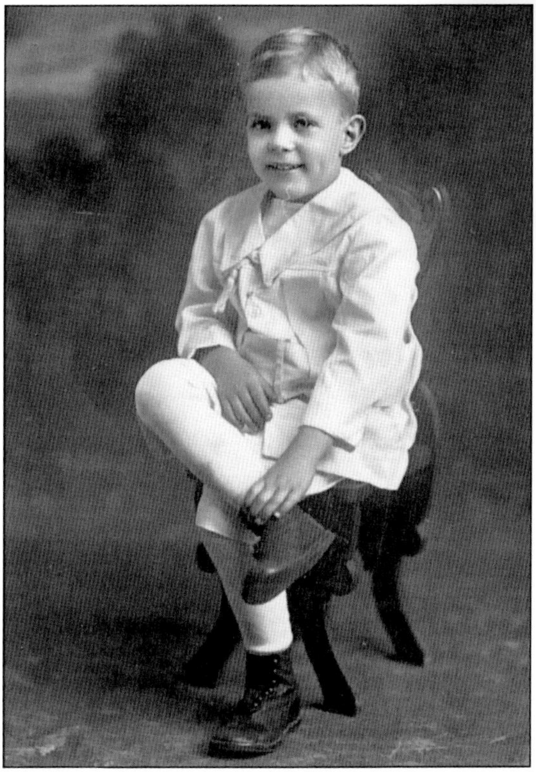

Hewitt Grandson 1917. John D. "Jack" Hewitt III and his sister, Katharine, were born in their new house beside the high school. (Courtesy of Katharine Barringer.)

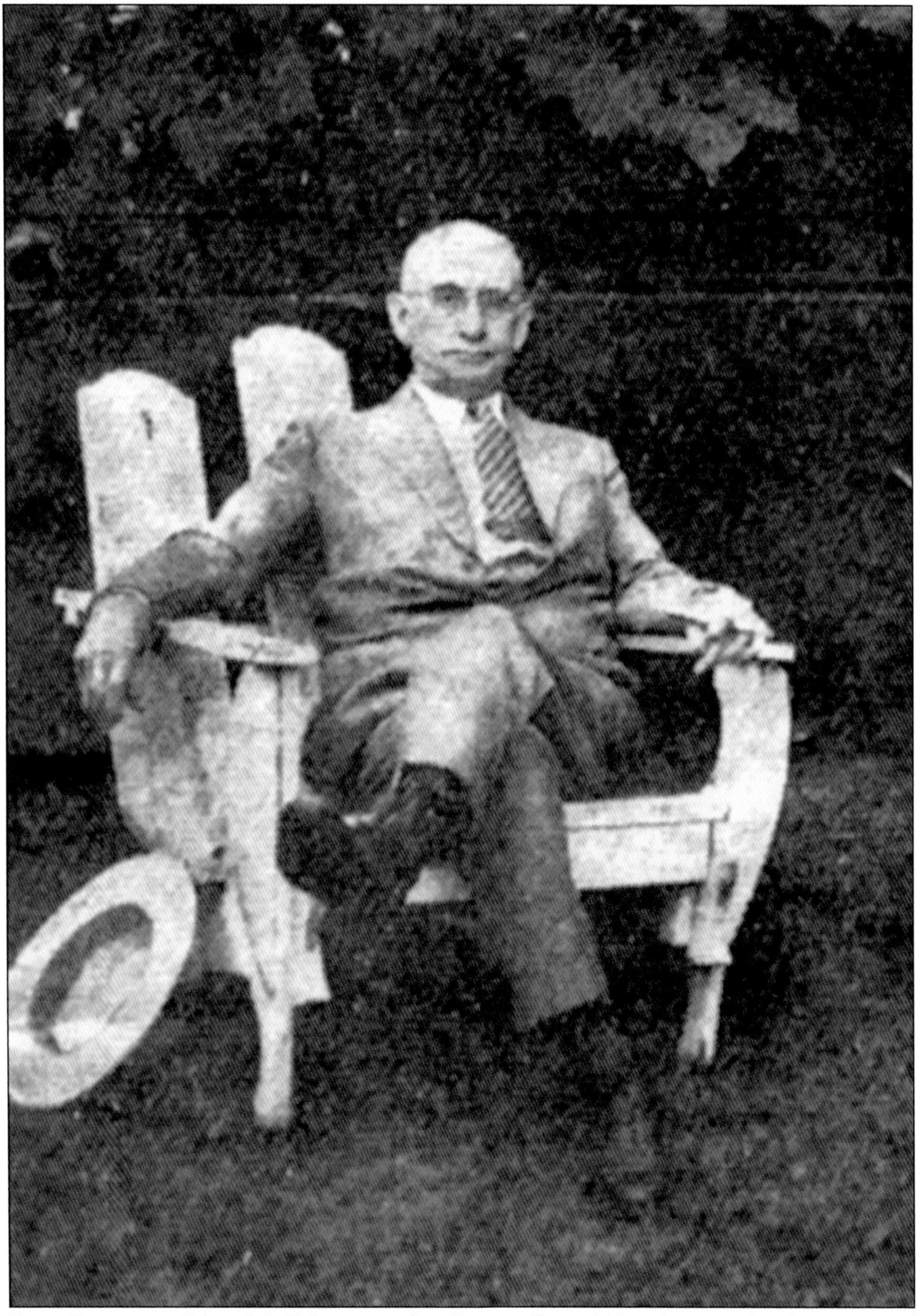

First Principal. Edward S. Baker moved to Bramwell in 1895 to become the first principal of Bramwell High School. The Bank of Bramwell soon employed him, and through shrewd investments he became a millionaire. Baker was the only Bramwell person to serve as a West Virginia state senator.

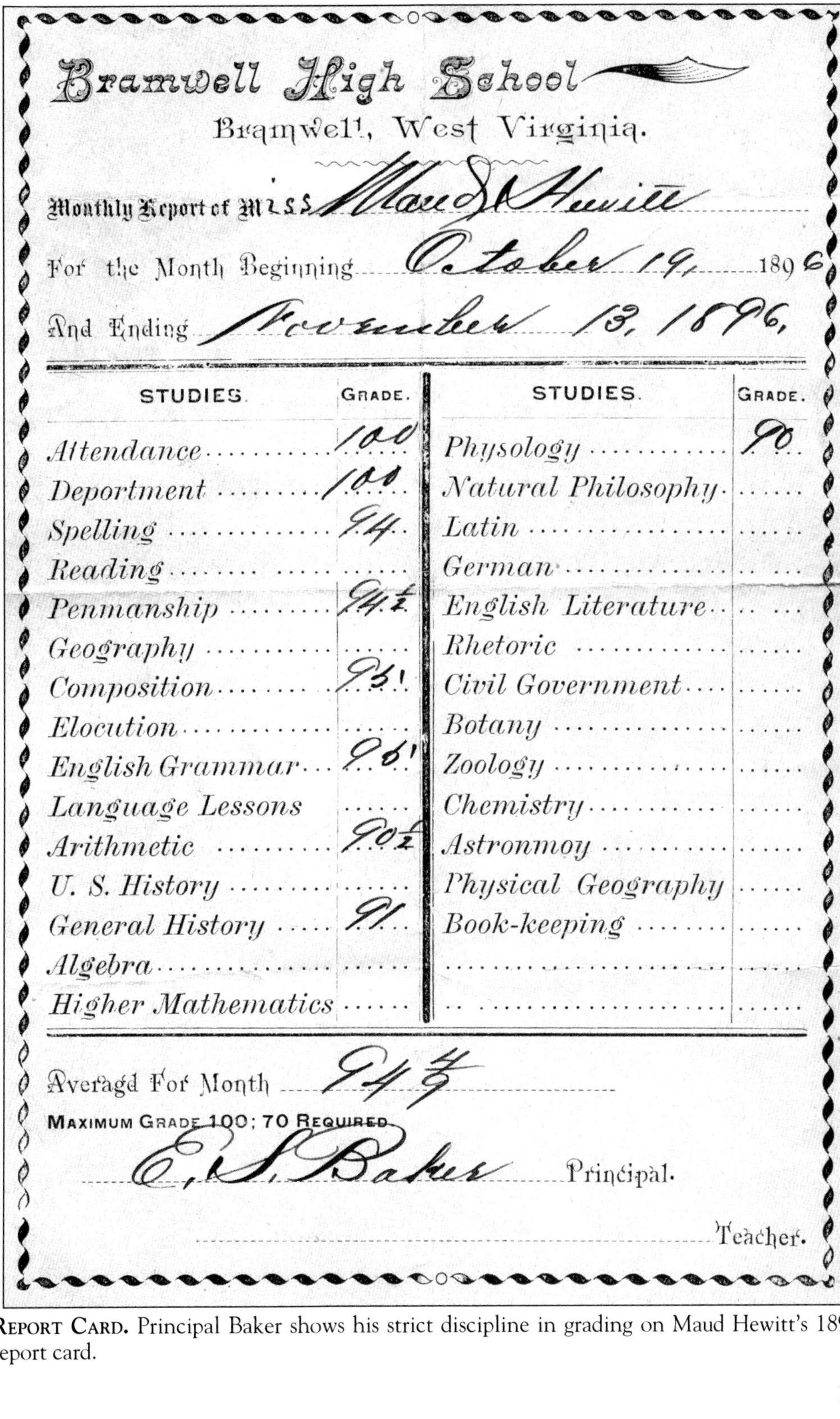

Bramwell High School

Bramwell, West Virginia.

Monthly Report of Miss Maud Hewitt

For the Month Beginning October 19, 1896

And Ending November 13, 1896.

STUDIES.	GRADE.	STUDIES.	GRADE.
Attendance	100	Physology	90
Deportment	100	Natural Philosophy	
Spelling	94	Latin	
Reading		German	
Penmanship	94½	English Literature	
Geography		Rhetoric	
Composition	95	Civil Government	
Elocution		Botany	
English Grammar	96	Zoology	
Language Lessons		Chemistry	
Arithmetic	90½	Astronmoy	
U. S. History		Physical Geography	
General History	91	Book-keeping	
Algebra			
Higher Mathematics			

Averagd For Month 94 4/9

MAXIMUM GRADE 100; 70 REQUIRED.

E. S. Baker Principal.

Teacher.

REPORT CARD. Principal Baker shows his strict discipline in grading on Maud Hewitt's 1896 report card.

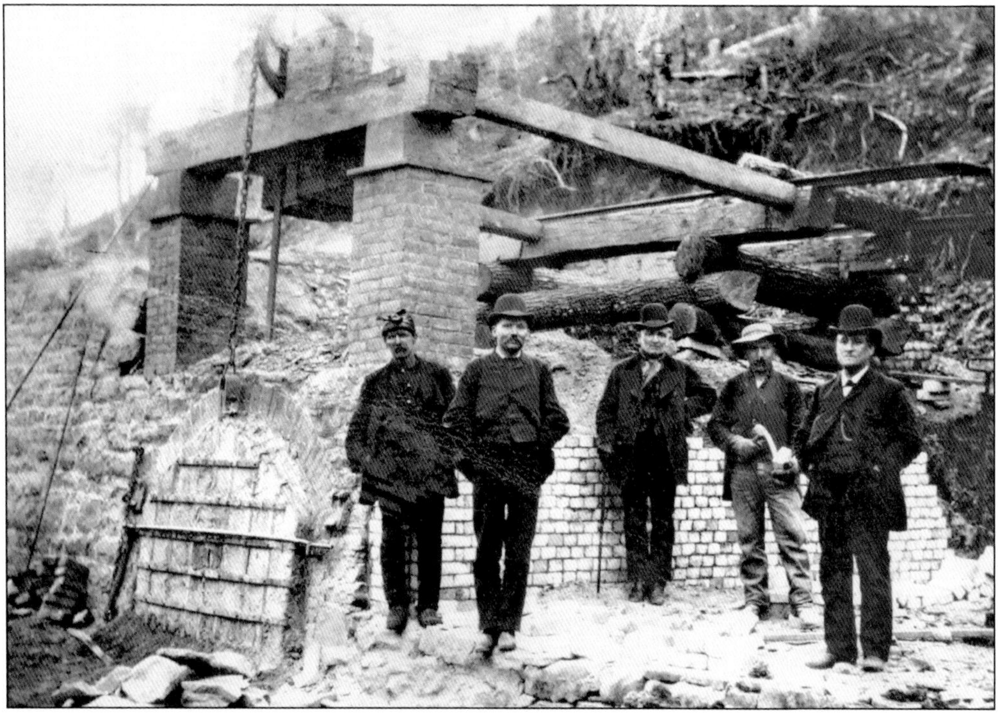

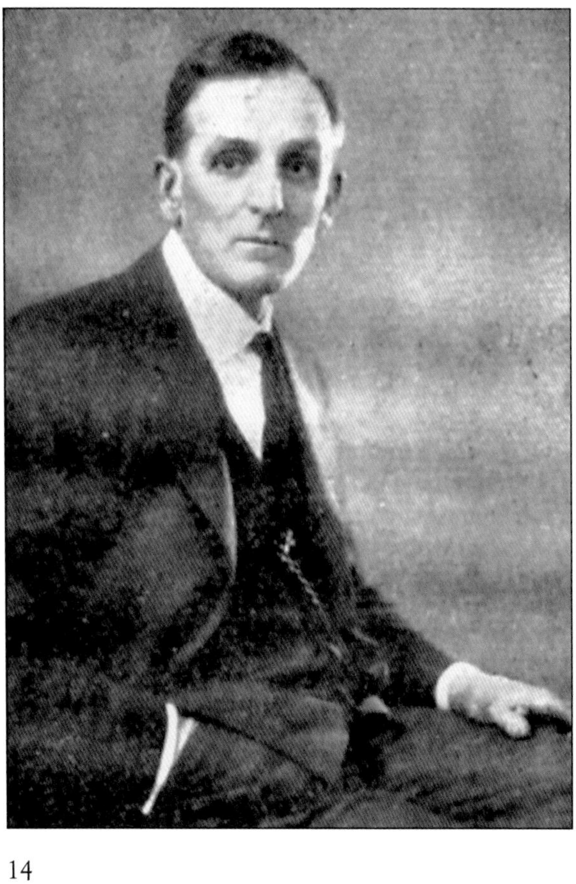

First Mine Owner. On November 4, 1884, John Cooper opened the first coal mine on the West Virginia side of the Flat-Top coalfield. His first job in mining had been in England when he was six years old. At his death in 1899, he was the second president of the Bank of Bramwell. John Cooper is on the right, sporting a derby hat. The second man from the left is Thomas Cooper, John's older son. (Courtesy of Eve Cooper Murphy.)

Only Congressman. Edward Cooper Sr. was the only Bramwell person to be elected to the U.S. Congress, serving two terms in the House of Representatives beginning in 1914. Just as his father, John Cooper, he was an avid Republican. (Courtesy Kelly Murphy Eller and Kim Murphy.)

First Black Councilman. In the 1950s, Sherman Graves was the first black man to be elected to public office in Bramwell. A spokesman for the people and an advocate for community progress during his tenure, he also served the town as vice-mayor. (Courtesy of Debbie and Wanda Graves.)

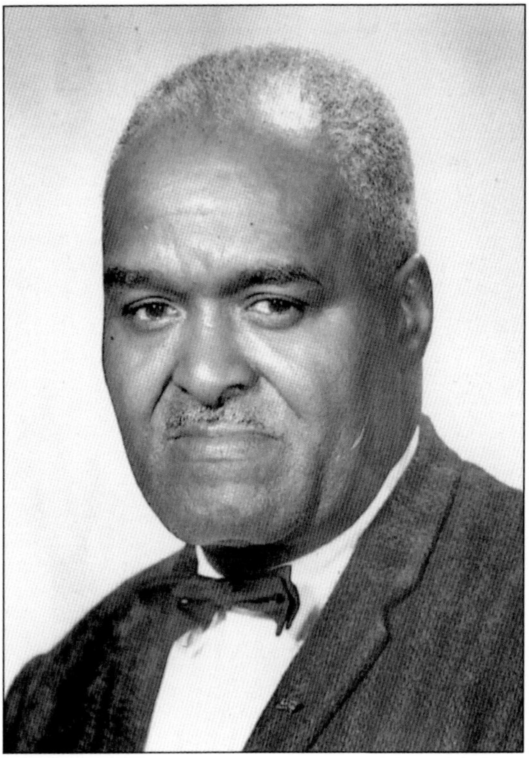

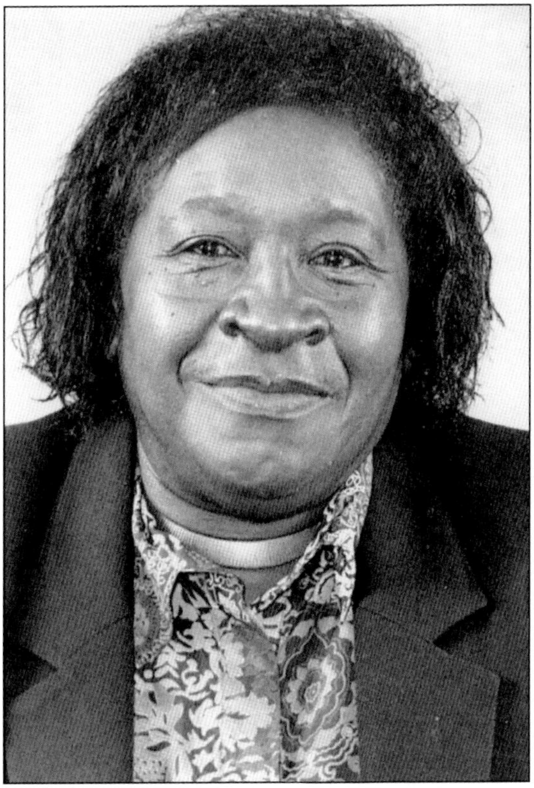

First Black Councilwoman. Edris Henry Miller, third-generation Bramwell resident, was elected to the town council in 1987. She taught at both Bluestone and Bramwell schools. (Courtesy of Edris Henry Miller.)

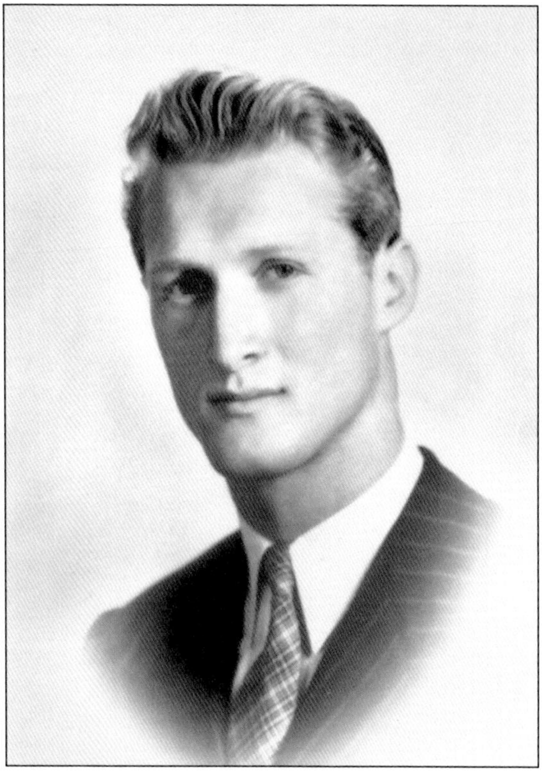

First With NASA. Robert Hutch "Bobby" Wright grew up on top of Jones' Hill. As a young pilot in 1943, his goal was to work with airplanes. He accomplished that and more, as the only Bramwell native to become a NASA engineer. (Courtesy of Elva Mae Wright Skaggs.)

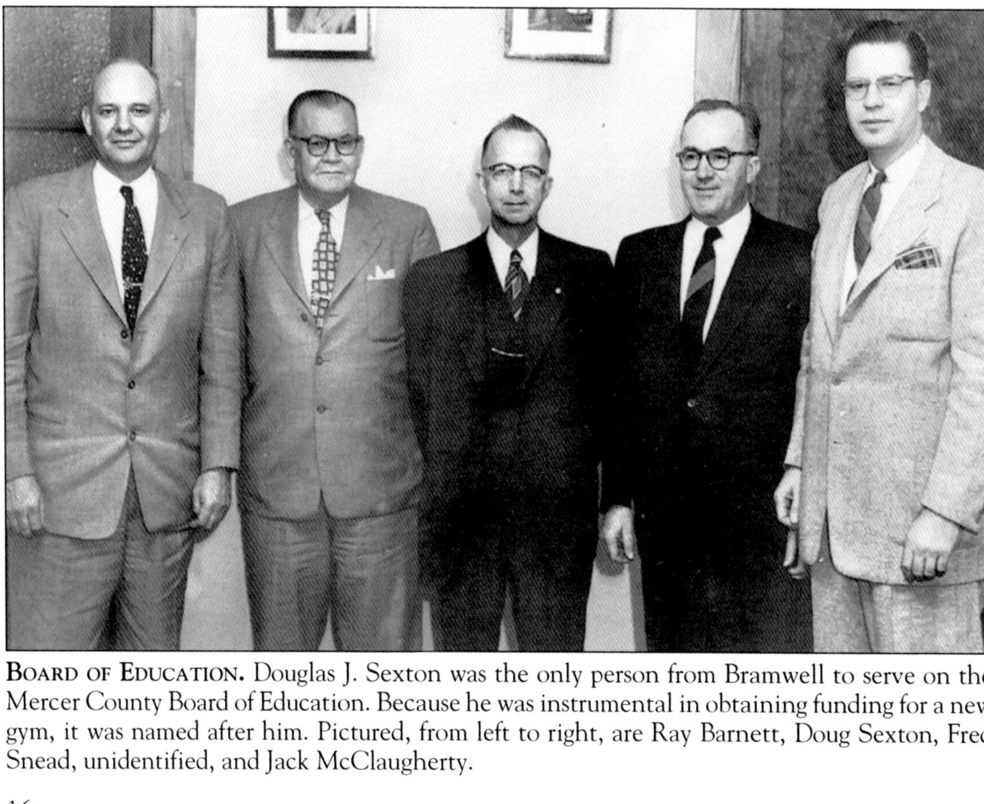

Board of Education. Douglas J. Sexton was the only person from Bramwell to serve on the Mercer County Board of Education. Because he was instrumental in obtaining funding for a new gym, it was named after him. Pictured, from left to right, are Ray Barnett, Doug Sexton, Fred Snead, unidentified, and Jack McClaugherty.

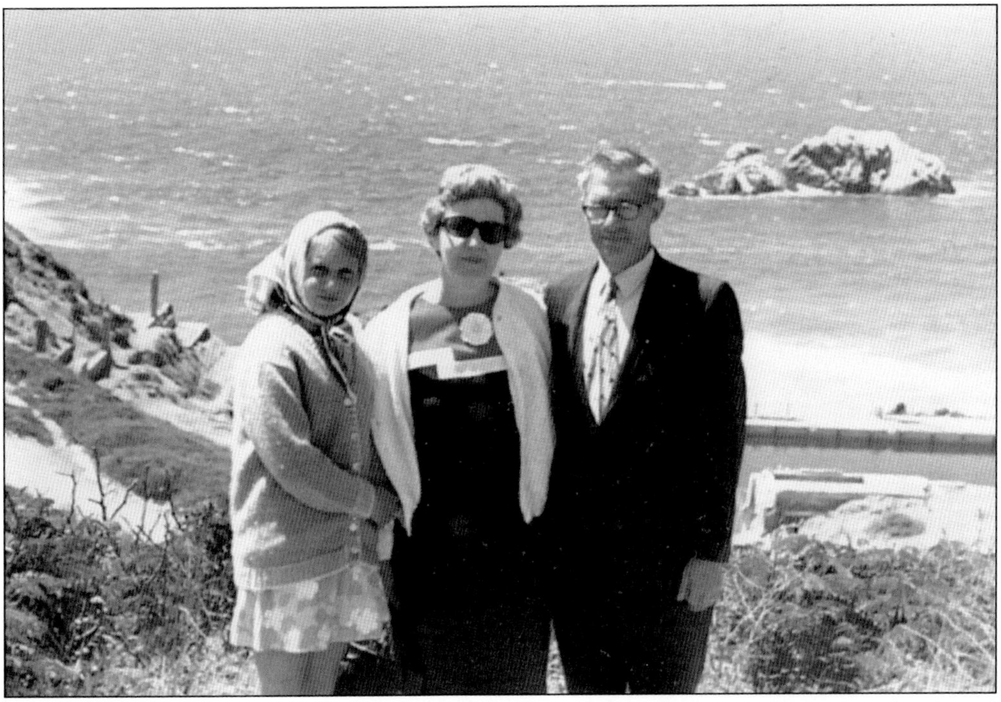

First Delegate and Commissioner. Donald Anello was the only Bramwell citizen to be elected to serve on the Mercer County Commission and later, the West Virginia House of Delegates. The 1969 photograph shows Don with his wife, Alma Mahaffey Anello, and daughter, Carrie Jo. (Courtesy of Alma Anello.)

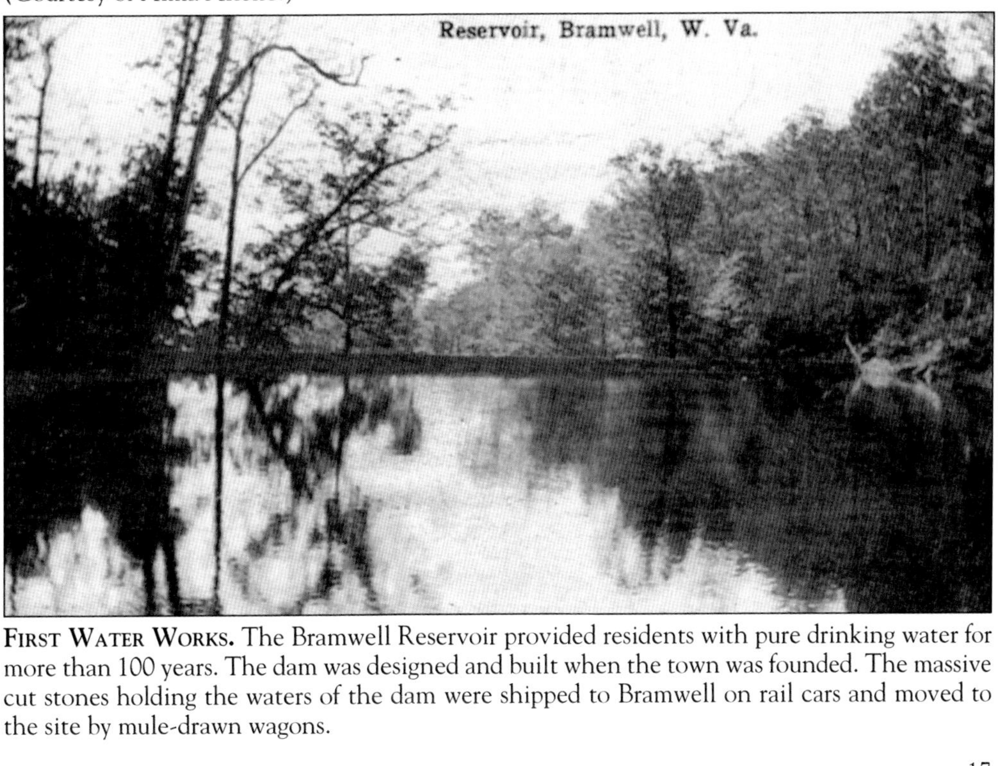

First Water Works. The Bramwell Reservoir provided residents with pure drinking water for more than 100 years. The dam was designed and built when the town was founded. The massive cut stones holding the waters of the dam were shipped to Bramwell on rail cars and moved to the site by mule-drawn wagons.

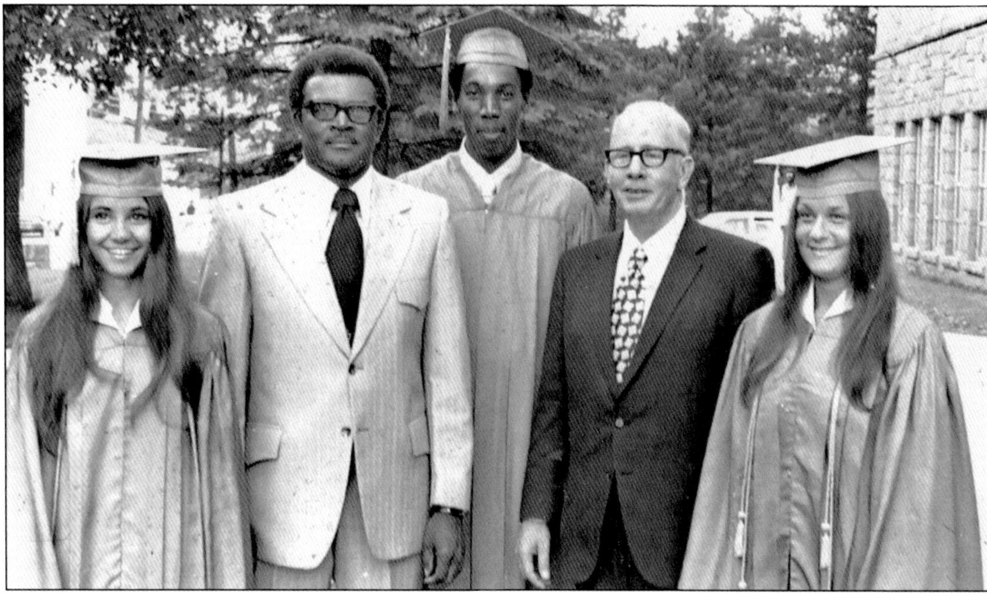

First Black Principal. Dr. M.B. Guyton was the first and only black principal at Bramwell High School. Posing for the 1972 graduation are, from left to right, salutatorian Rodi Honeyak, Dr. Guyton, class president Robert Williams, graduation speaker Judge Howard Jarrett, and valedictorian Lois Ann Dudash. Dr. Guyton had been junior high principal and coach at Bluestone High School in Bramwell.

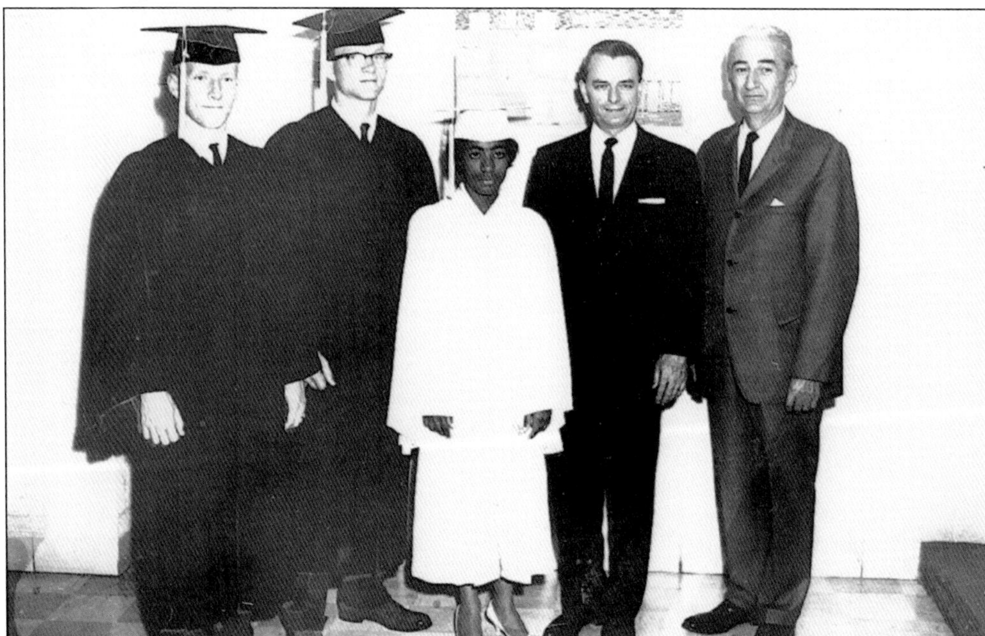

First Black Honor Student. The first black honor student to graduate from Bramwell High School was Sally Gravely in 1965. She is shown here with other honor graduates, guest speaker, and principal. From left to right are salutatorian Herman "Butch" Hill Jr., valedictorian Donald Pierce Jr., Sally Gravely, U.S. Sen. Robert C. Byrd (speaker), and Bramwell High School principal Dwight W. McCormick. (Courtesy of Lillian Hill Pierce.)

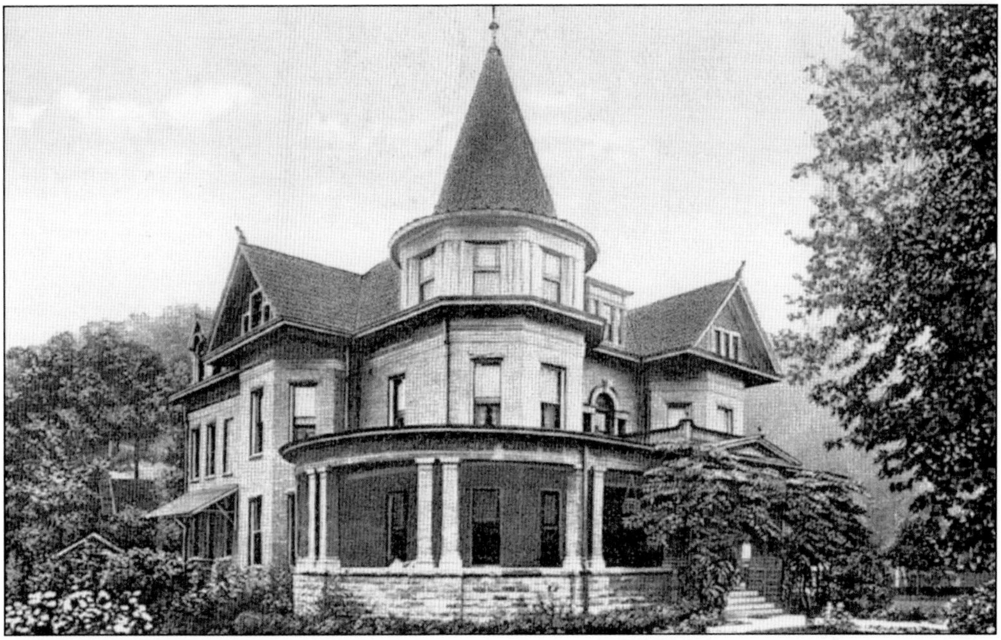

First Copper Roof. This stately mansion was built in 1910 for Edward Cooper Sr. It is the first house in the country to be entirely roofed in copper. The golden bricks were hand-fired in England, and the wrought-iron fence was crafted in Germany. A separate building on the grounds houses an indoor swimming pool. The Cooper house is one of only six in Bramwell owned by descendants of the original builders.

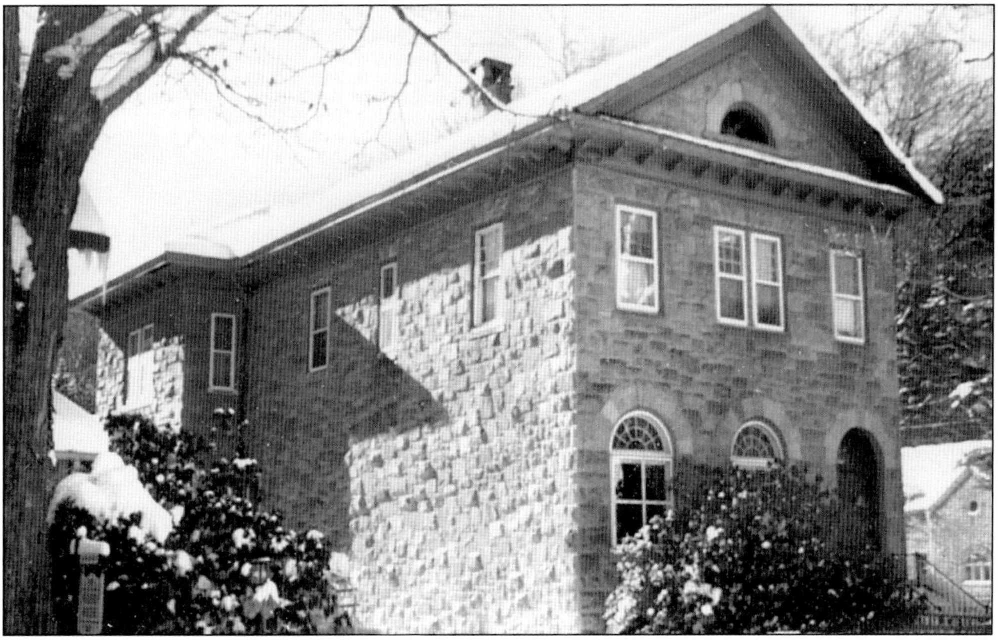

First Bank. The famous Bank of Bramwell had more millionaires per capita than any other in the country in its heyday. Chartered in 1889, it was in operation until 1933. Constructed of native bluestone, with carved oak and mahogany woodwork throughout, the exterior remains unchanged. (Photo by Dana Cochran, used with permission of Wanda Dillon.)

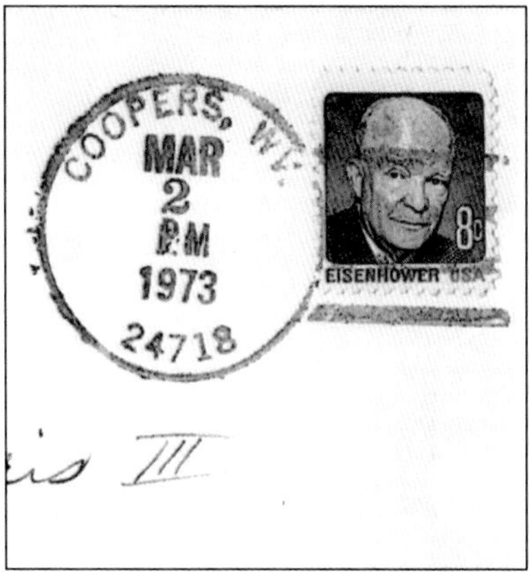

ONLY TOWN WITH THREE POST OFFICES. Three different zip codes in one small town was written about in *Ripley's Believe it or Not*. The communities of Bramwell, Coopers (Shinbrier), and Freeman (Simmons) were separated by almost four miles of winding Bluestone River. The original incorporation in 1888 was Bramwell only. Coopers had the largest population of the three towns in 1900. Each had its own train station and business area. After the other two were brought into the "town proper," their identities were maintained with the post offices. Coopers post office closed March 2, 1973. The last day for Freeman post office was August 7, 1997. Only Bramwell's post office remains as a center for mail service and daily news. Roy Cook and Arthur Goins Jr. visit at the post office in this 1993 snapshot. (Coopers postage cancellation courtesy of Edith Butt and Elbert "Dizzy" Harris.)

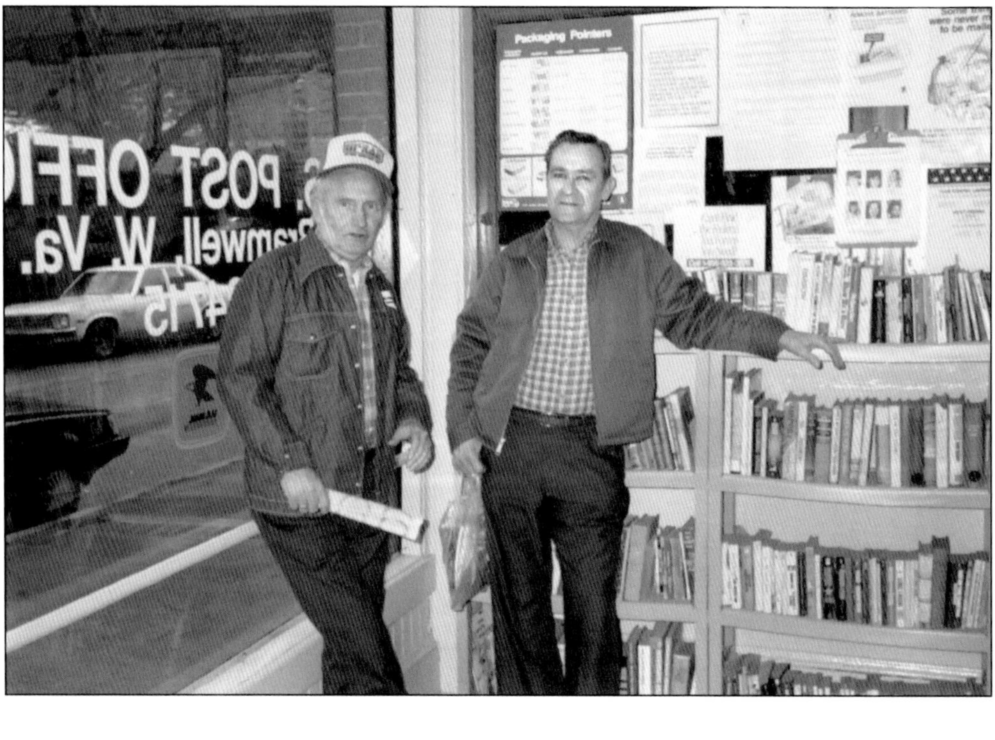

Two

Bramwell

Fleeting impressions of all our past
Of sight, sound, taste, touch
A song
Reminder of a moment
That could only last
In a heart.

—Lou Stoker

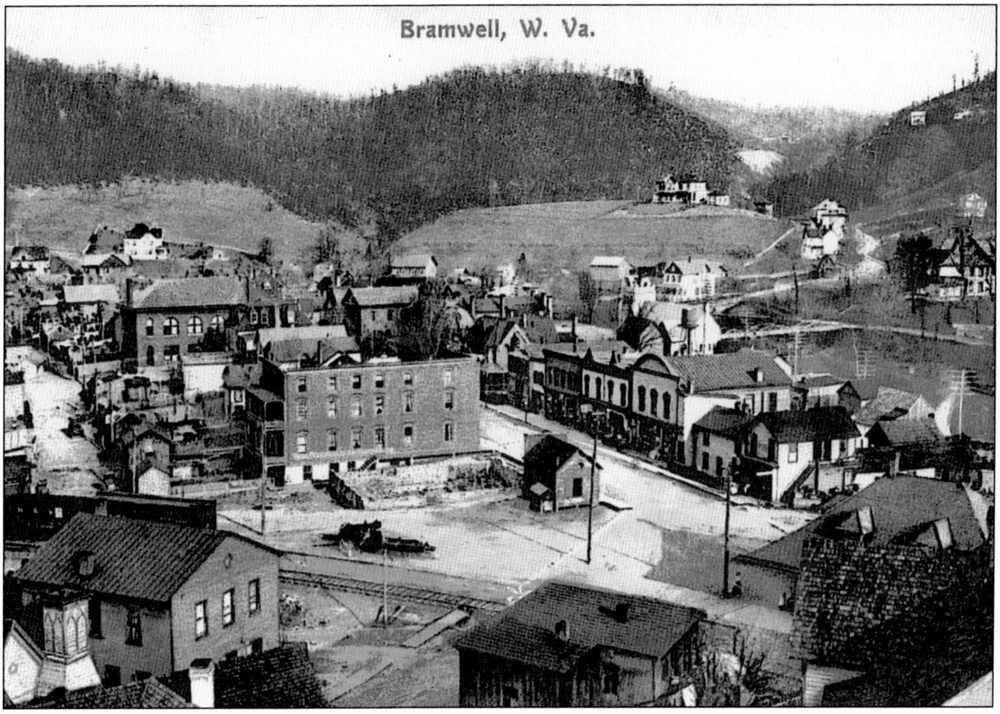

Bramwell 1896. Only 12 years after the first coal was shipped from the Mill Creek mine at Coopers, Bramwell was the center of coalfield business, with a train station that had dozens of steam engines passing through each day. There were two large hotels and a boarding house on Main Street. Electric service was available, and some of the mansions were built. Signs of prosperity were visible everywhere.

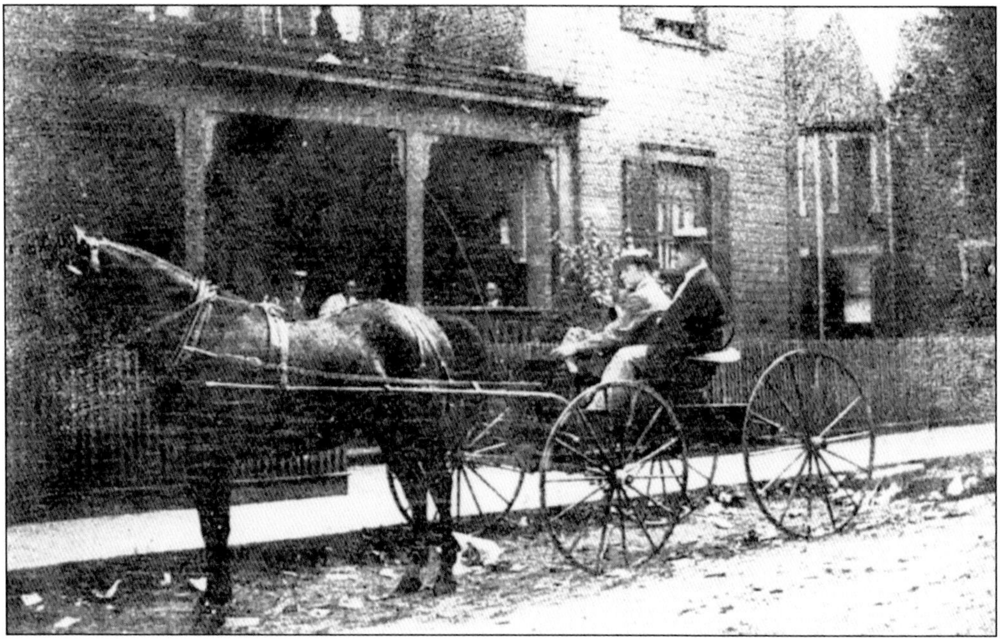

Sunday Drive. C.W. "Wes" Freeman (on right) and his driver make a stop on a dirt street in front of the Bluestone Inn. He lived in Freeman at the time the photograph was made, *c.* 1905. On the right is the turret of the Welch/Cooper house. (Courtesy of Sunny Freeman.)

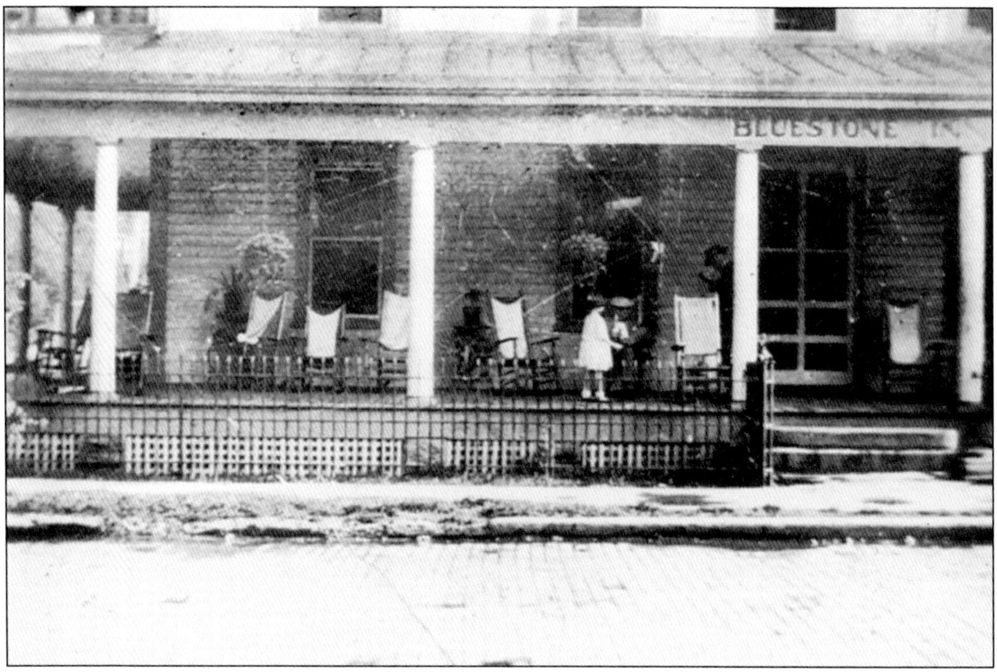

Bluestone Inn. The Norfolk & Western Railroad built large hotels throughout the coalfields. This hotel was constructed in the center of Bramwell in 1886. It served as a gathering place for social activities, with a favorite spot being the L-shaped veranda. It was a survivor of the Great Fire of 1910 but not the Great Depression and was razed in 1933. This photograph was made in 1909.

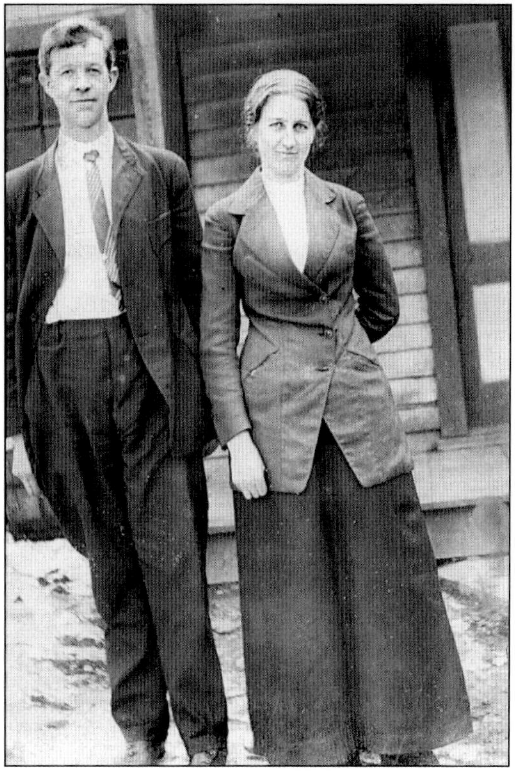

Bramwell Hill. George Robert and Mattie Cowan lived in their house on Bramwell Hill. It overlooked the comings and goings of the town. (Courtesy of Glenn and Louise Scott family.)

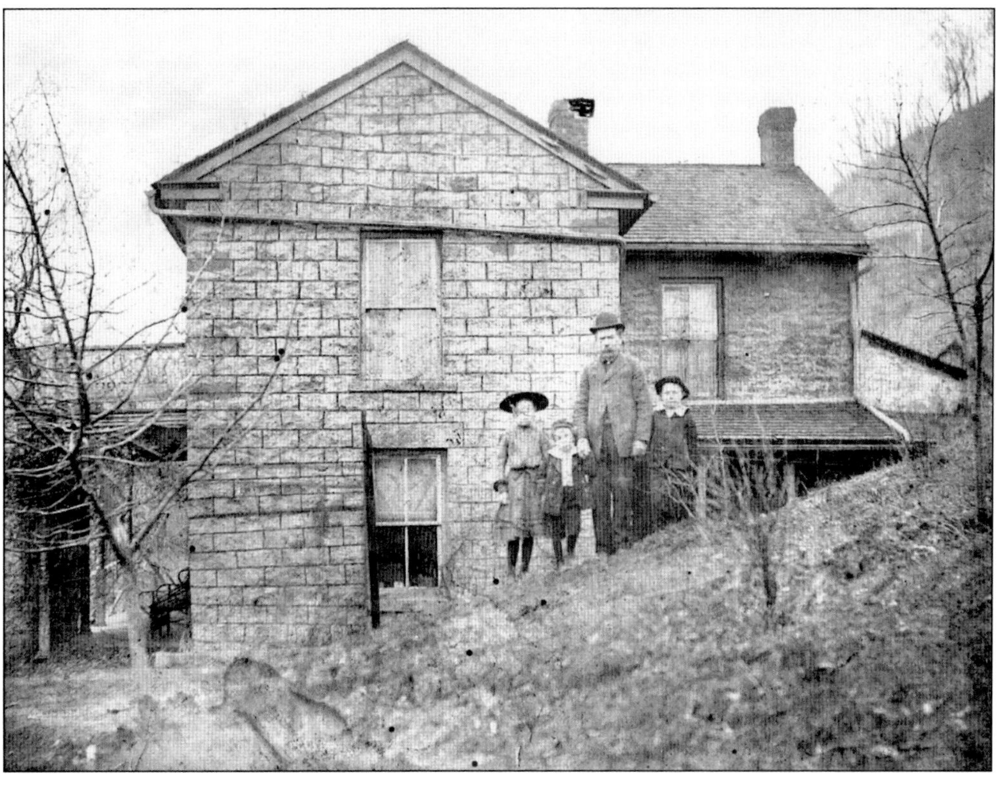

Scott House. Early resident Andrew Scott built his homeplace on Bramwell Hill in the 1890s. His family, from left to right, are Emily Scott, Glenn Scott Sr., Andrew Scott Sr., and Andrew Scott Jr. The house is still in the original family. Its current residents include the great-granddaughter of Andrew Sr., Sharon Scott Workman, and her family. (Courtesy of Glenn and Louise Scott family.)

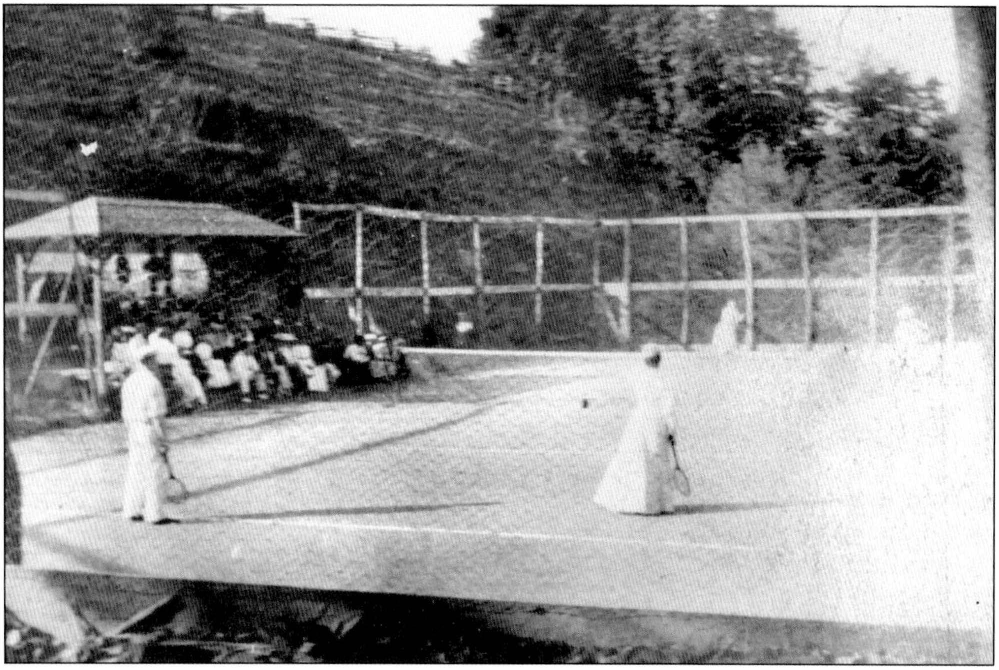

Tennis, Anyone? The Bramwell Athletic Club built and maintained a private tennis court. In true millionaire fashion, the base of it was red clay, imported from France. For the comfort of spectators, there was a covered shelter.

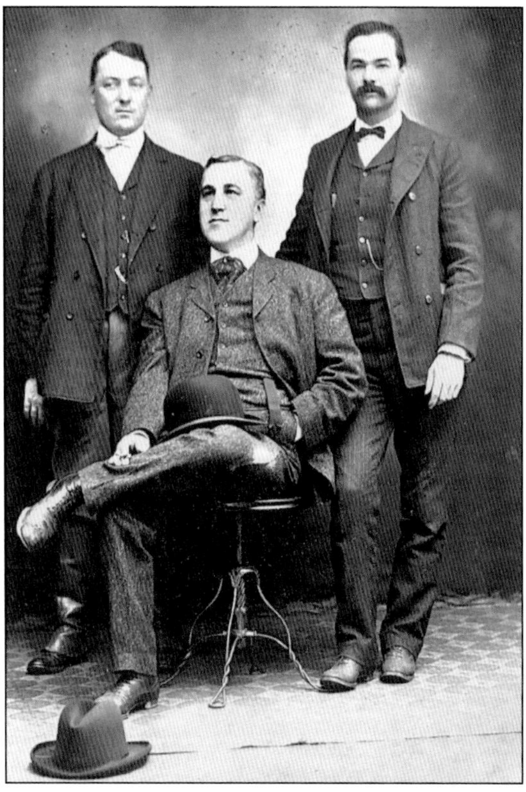

Looking Dignified. C.W. "Wes" Freeman is seated with his cousins in this undated photograph. (Courtesy of Sunny Freeman.)

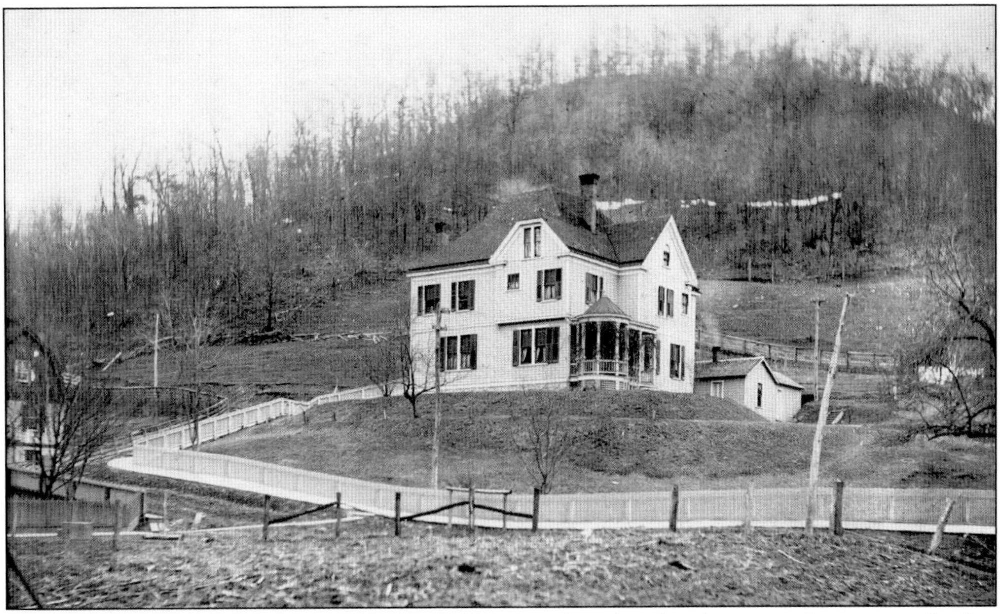

Freeman House. In 1909, C.W. "Wes" Freeman bought this house and property for his bride, Martha "Mattie" Wheeler. He spent a fortune and the next 20 years creating the Freeman estate.

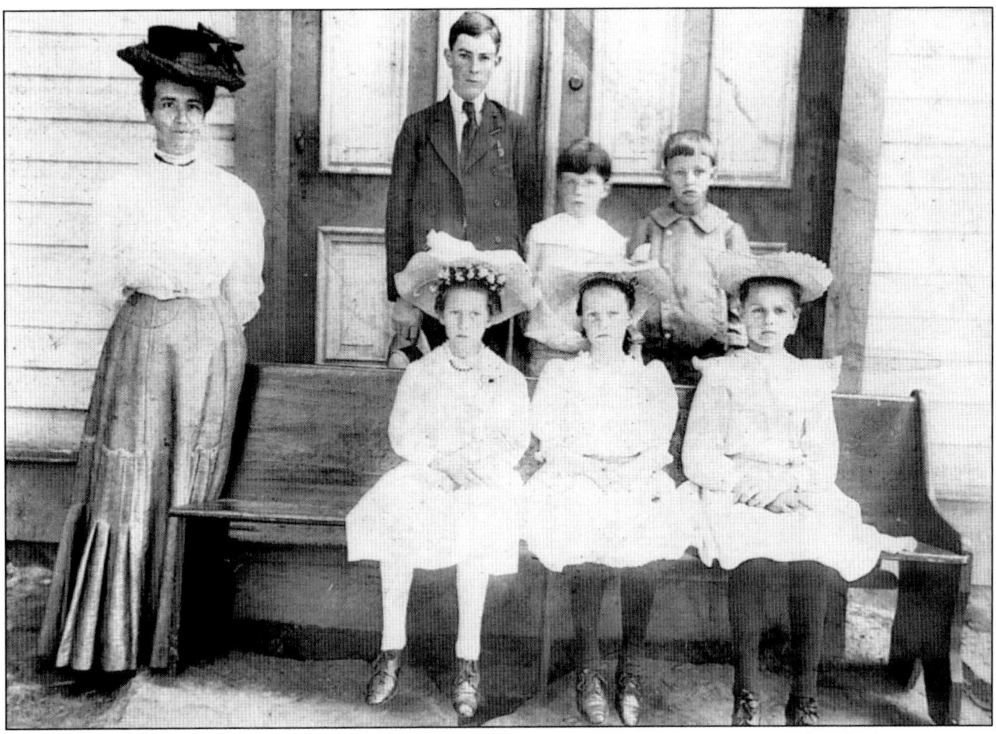

Sunday School. In a picture taken before 1903, Mrs. J.C. Pack's Sunday School class poses at the front door of the original Methodist church at Simmons. The church was later sold to the Baptists. Boys, from left to right, are Wyatt Harmon, Nester Perdue, and Dewey Hilton. The girls are unidentified.

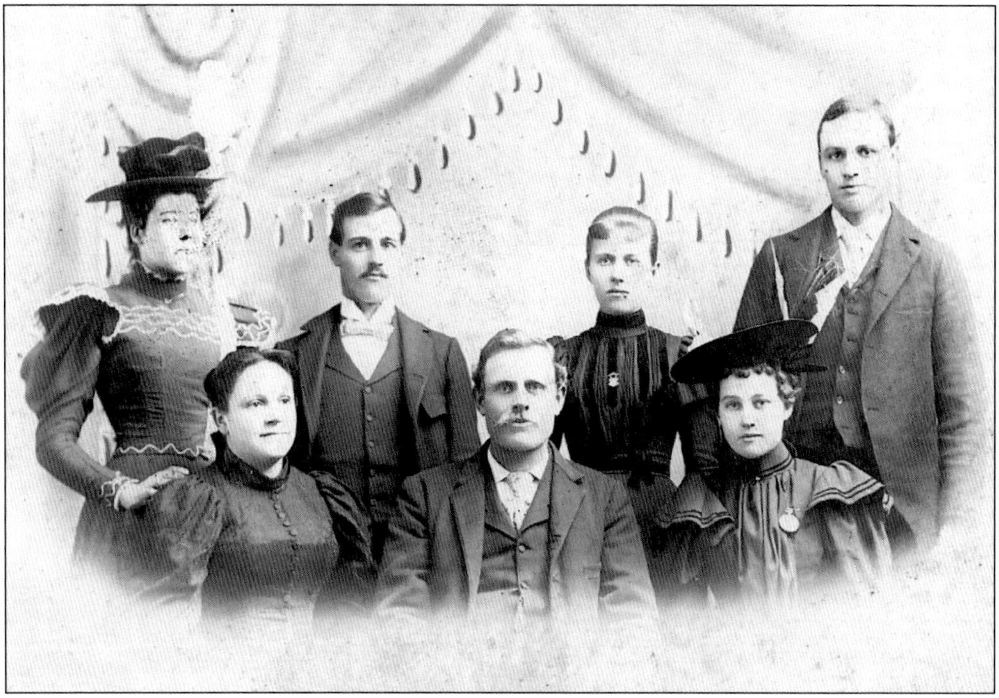

Faces of 1900. Members of the social whirl are these turn-of-the-century Bramwell residents. From left to right are (seated) Mrs. C.H. Sturm, C.H. Sturm, and Ella Motley; (standing) Cora Motley, Henry Craft, Mollie Craft, and John Tolbert.

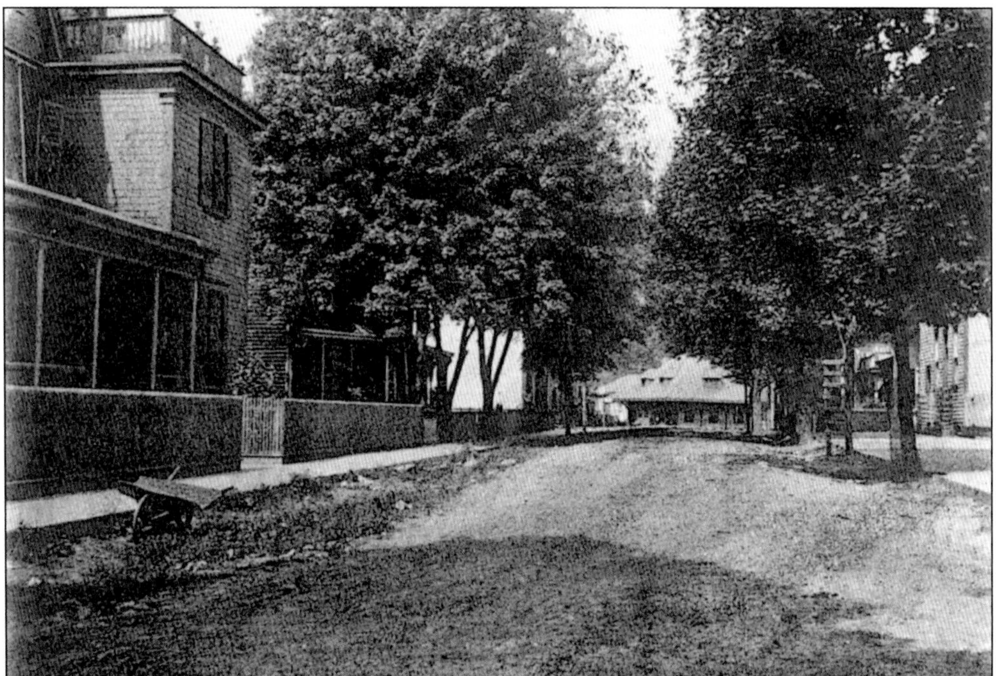

Street Scene. Looking west on Main Street before 1909, the dirt streets were tree-lined with board sidewalks and hitching posts.

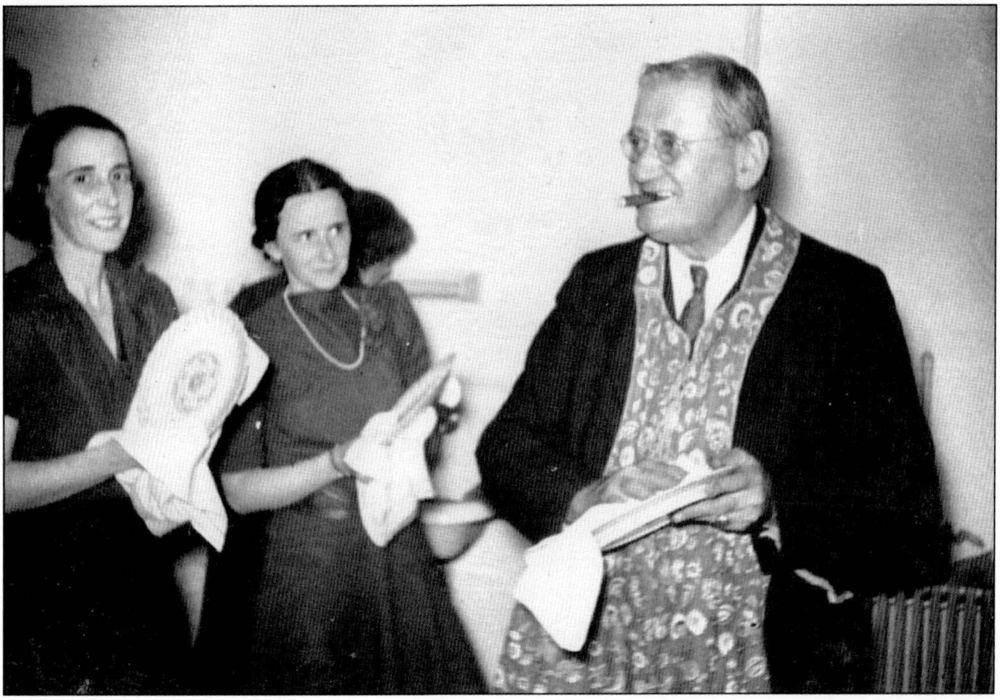

You Wash, We'll Dry. W.A. Jameson helps his daughters, Margaret and Edith, dry dishes. He was secretary to millionaire banker, Isaac T. Mann. When Mann went to Washington, the Jameson family moved also. Both families kept their homes in Bramwell. (Courtesy of Bill Jameson.)

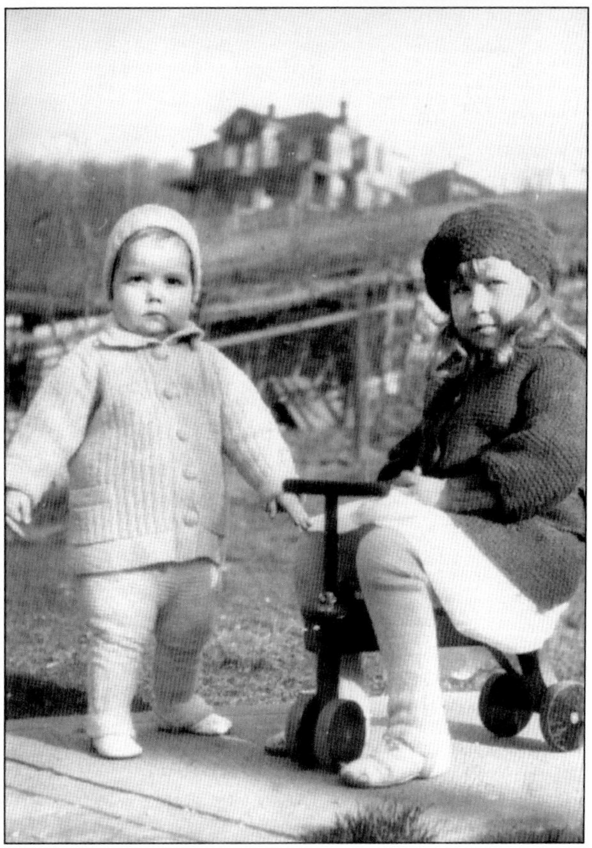

Trike Riding. Dowell and Suzanne Smith, pictured c. 1919, lived in the Schoew house located on the Bluestone River and Duhring Street. In the background is the Stuart Buck house, later owned by the W.H. Bowen family. (Courtesy of Eve Cooper Murphy.)

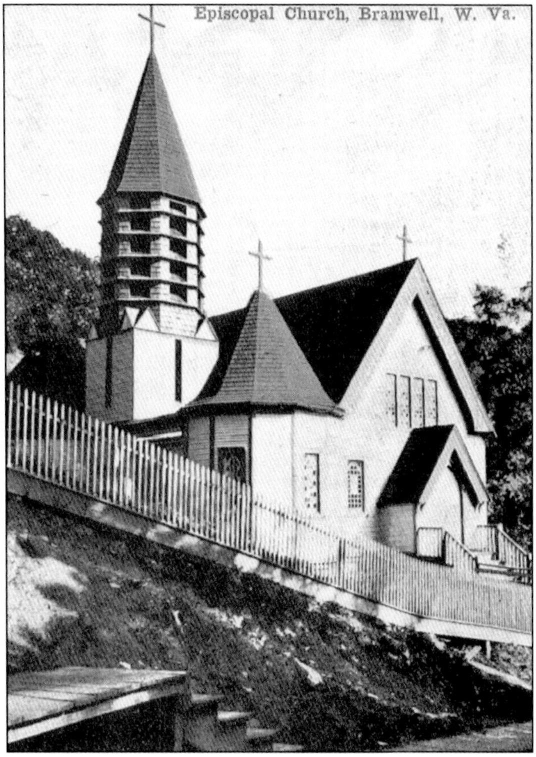

HOLY TRINITY. Businessmen who settled in Bramwell founded the Holy Trinity Episcopal Church. The church interior was elegant cherry and stained glass. Early members felt they were the elite of the town. In 1903, a member wrote back from Philadelphia, referring to Bramwell as "a roving community" and added, "All the new families who are coming in seem to be Presbyterians."

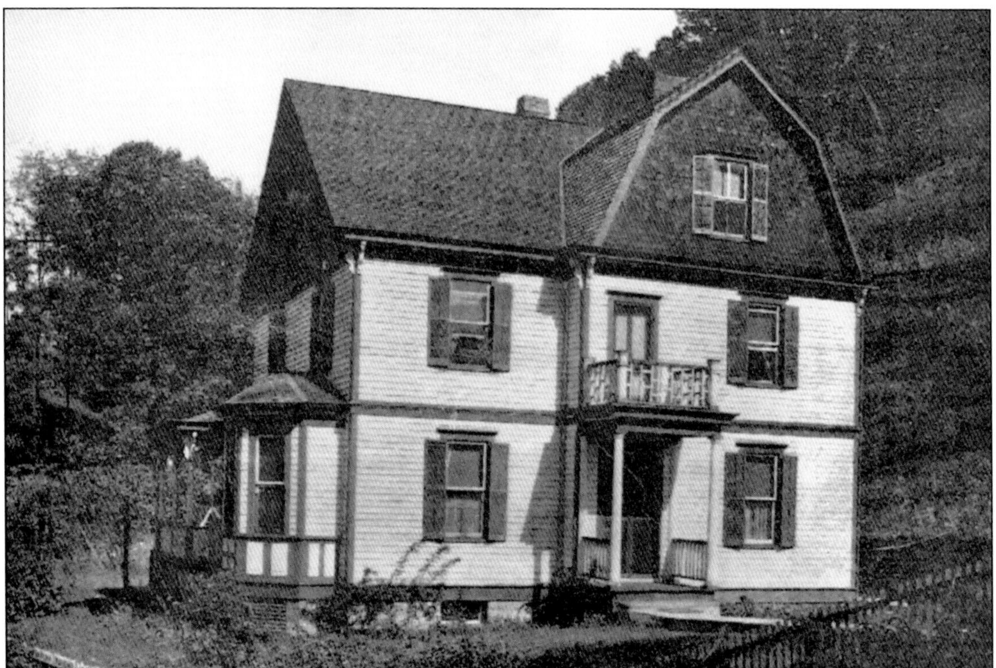

RECTORY. The Episcopal church rectory was finished in 1898 at a cost of $4,200. This three-story dwelling allowed for large families and frequent guests in the early days when visitors traveled by rail.

CHURCH INTERIOR. Built in 1893, the Episcopal church was a beautifully appointed frame building, with solid cherry cross beams. Capt. Fred Paddock was the organist, and B.F. Keller was the choir director, of whom a former rector wrote, "He conducted as good music as a city choir would do."

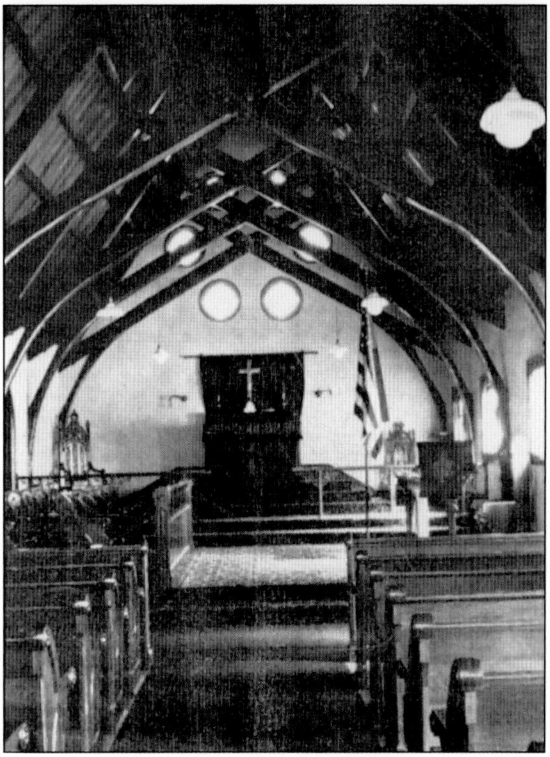

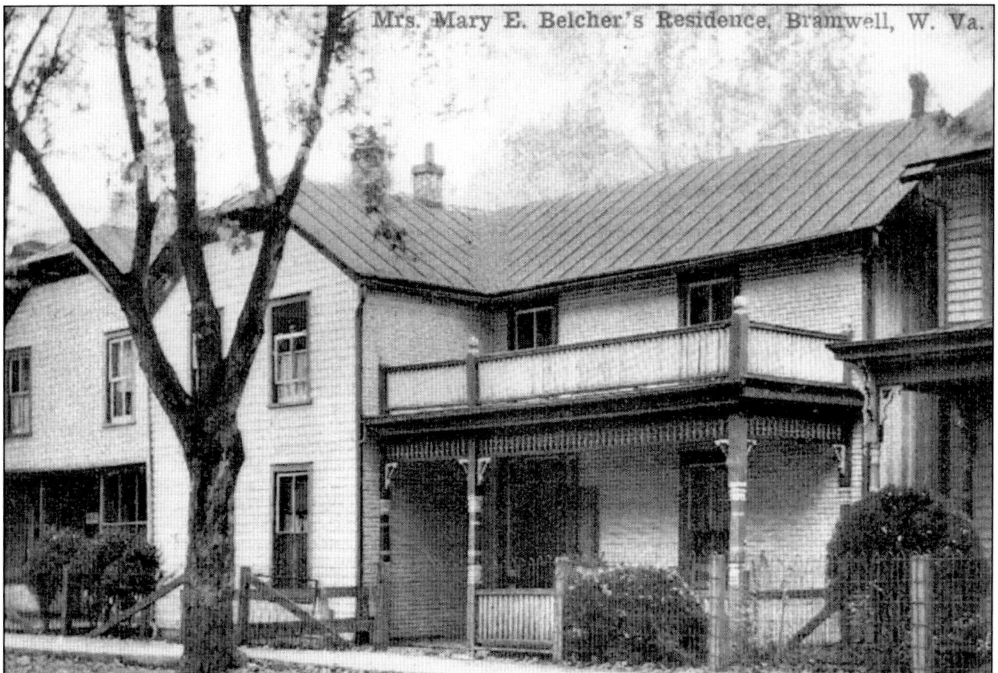

BOARDING HOUSE. This Main Street photograph, taken before the turn of the century, depicts Mary Belcher's Boarding House. The building was destroyed by fire in 1910. (Courtesy of Vester Johnson.)

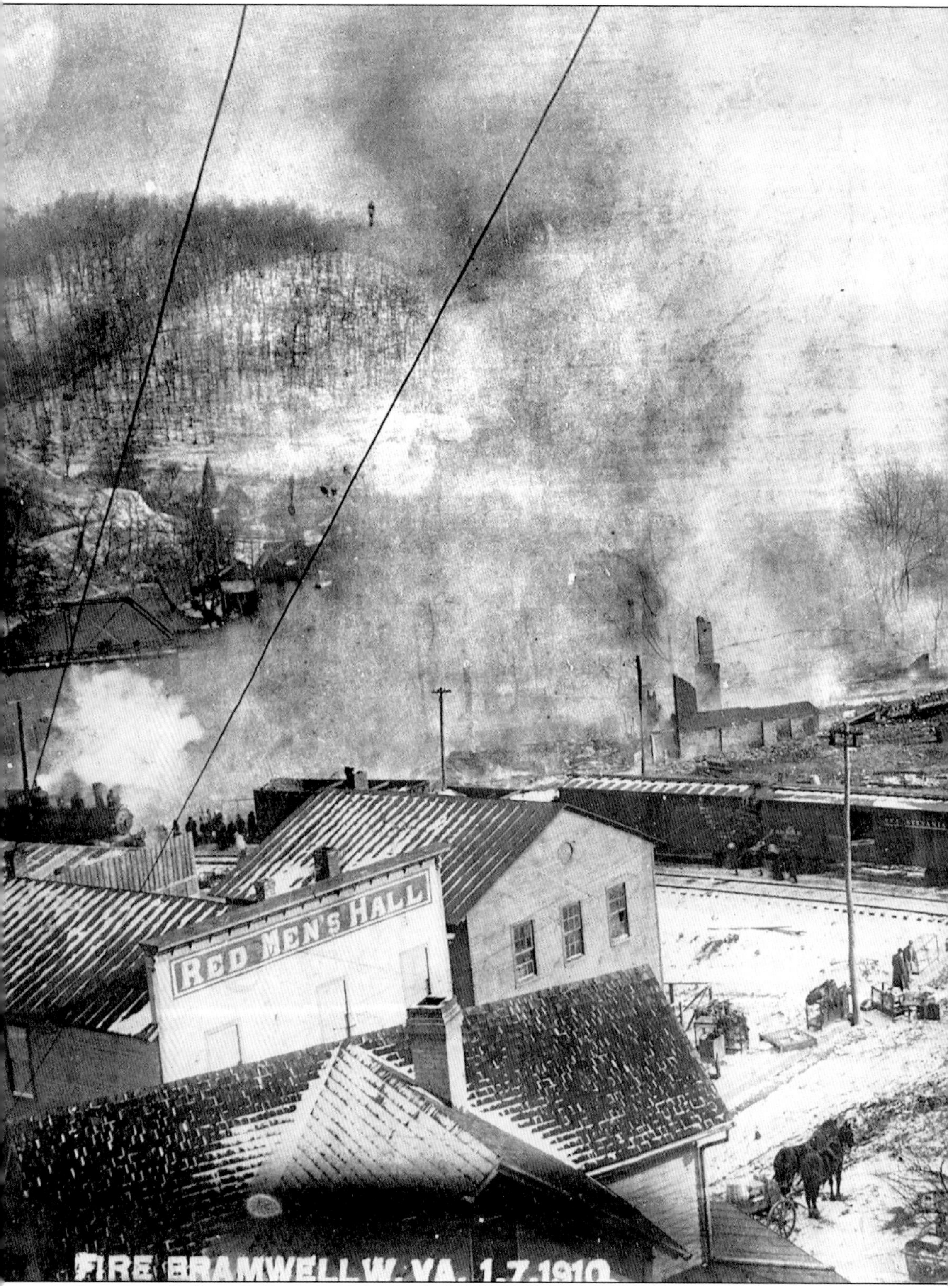
RED MEN'S HALL
FIRE BRAMWELL W. VA. 1-7-1910

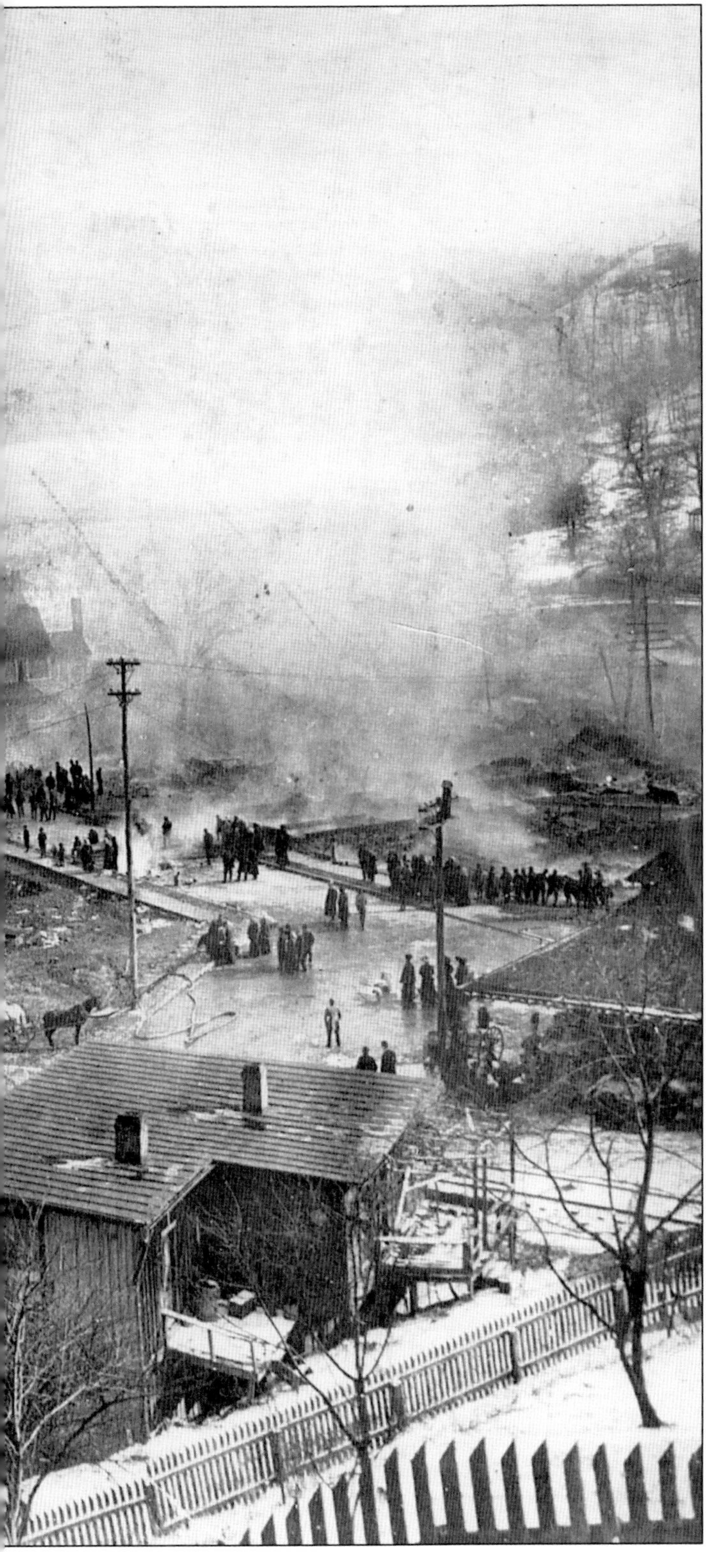

Disaster Strikes. On an icy, windy January day in 1910, the course of Bramwell was changed. Fire broke out in Smith & O'Conner's Poolroom. Before the flames had been doused, every business except one on South River and Main Streets had been destroyed or too badly damaged to save. Speculation regarding the cause of the fire ran the gamut from an overheated flue to a match-chewing mouse in a coat pocket. Barely visible through the smoke is one house standing on Main Street. It was a grand Victorian house built by pioneer land agent Capt. I.A. Welch and then sold to Edward Cooper Sr. at the end of the 19th century. Damaged by the fire, Cooper decided to raze it and build a new one. The resulting structure is pictured on page 19. (Courtesy of Glenn and Louise Scott family.)

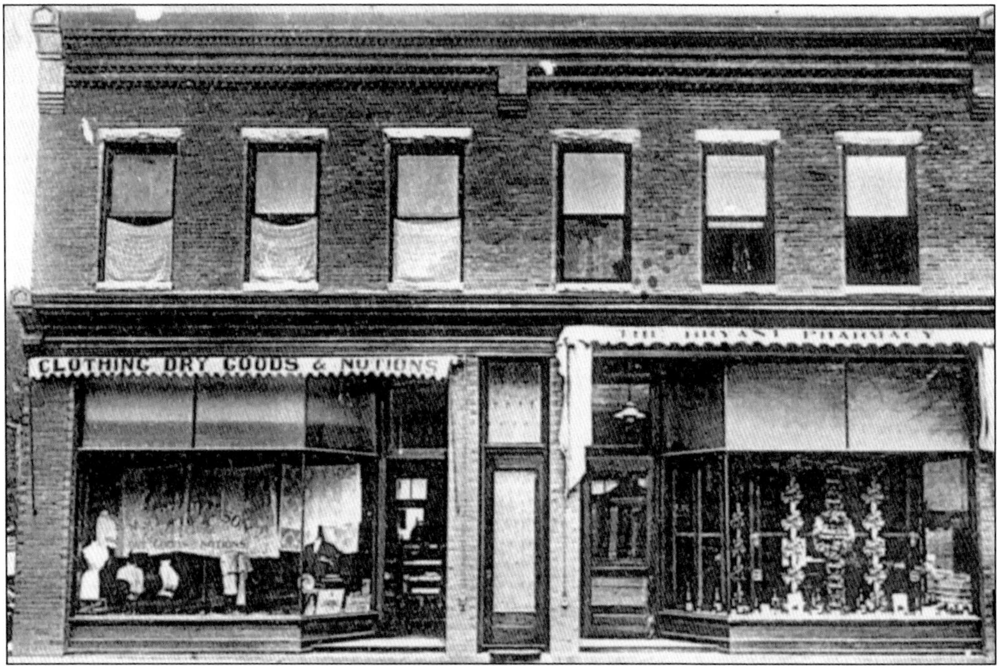

New Pharmacy. There was a building frenzy in 1910. The new Bryant Pharmacy on the corner (in later years, the Corner Shop) opened for business just before Christmas in time for ladies to buy Chanel #5. It was the third drug store in the nation to stock the fine French perfume.

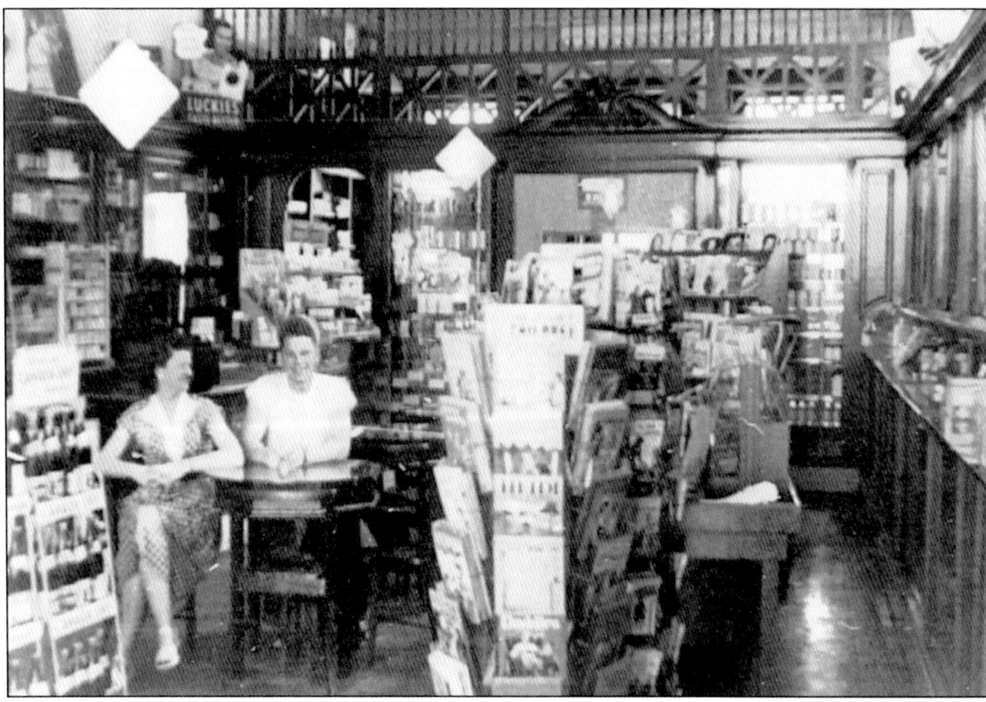

The Store. Forty-four years after the Bryant Pharmacy opened, Virginia Lee Byrd McGrady takes a break from behind the counter to have a soda. (Courtesy of Virginia McGrady.)

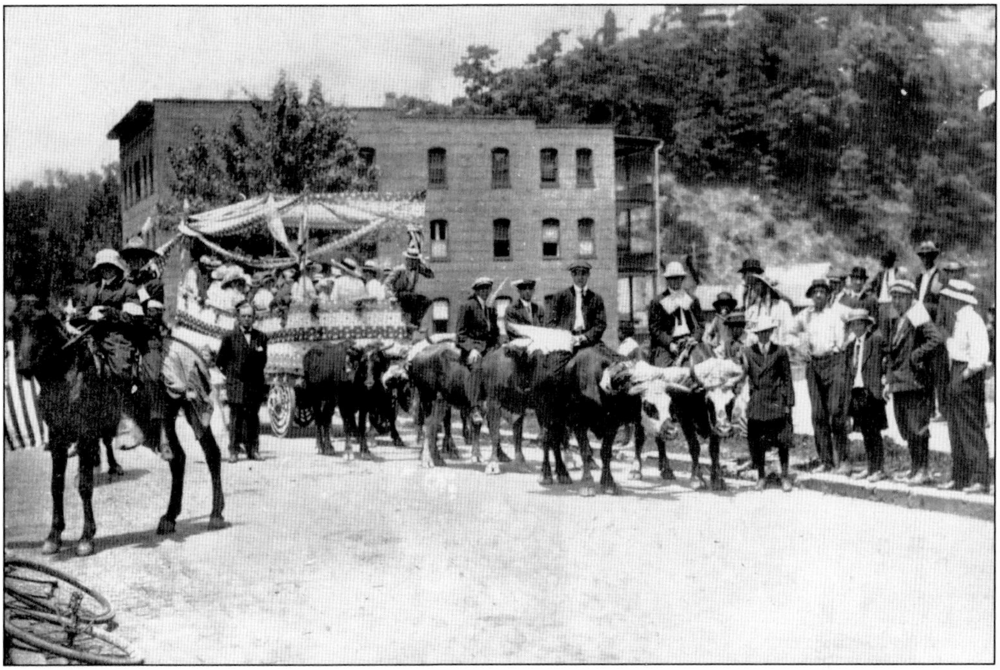

REBUILDING. A celebration takes place in front of new Pence Hotel, which was rebuilt one year after fire destroyed the original. (Courtesy of Frank Sexton.)

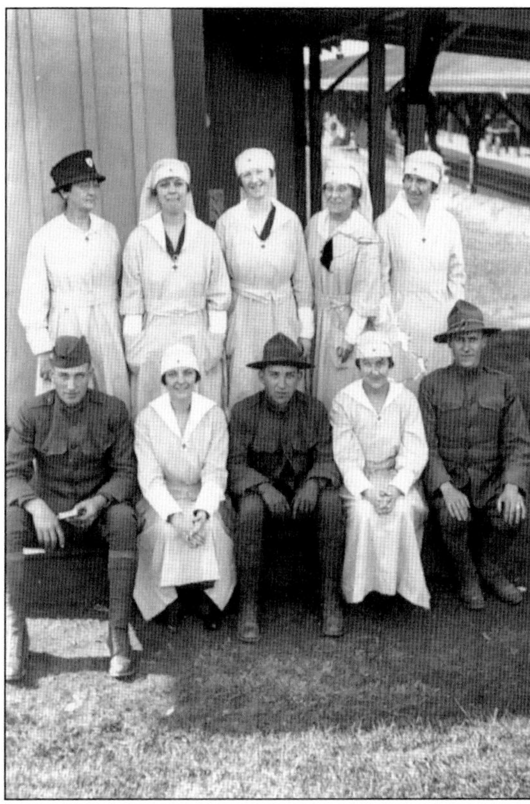

THOSE WHO SERVED. A great patriotic wave swept through Bramwell during World War I. Virginia Smith served with an army nurse unit. She is in the back row, second from left. (Courtesy of Eve Cooper Murphy.)

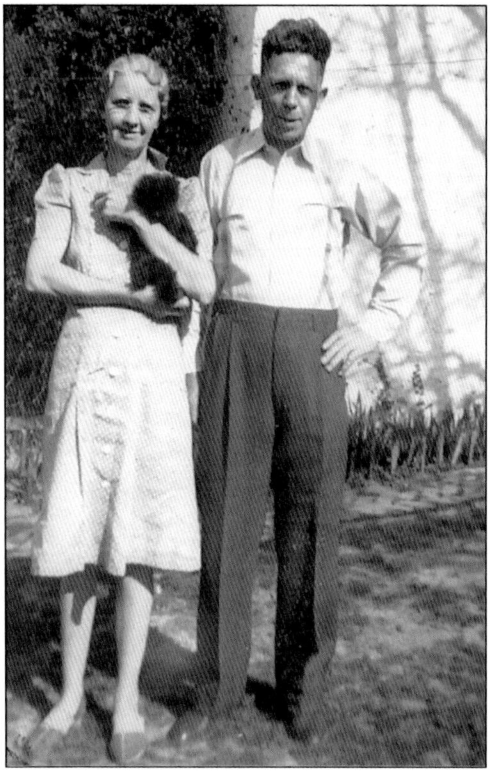

FAMILY. In the 1930s, Glenn Scott Sr. and his wife, Georgia Cowan Scott, watched all the hustle and bustle of the town from their family home on Bramwell Hill just above the downtown. (Courtesy of Glenn and Louise Scott family.)

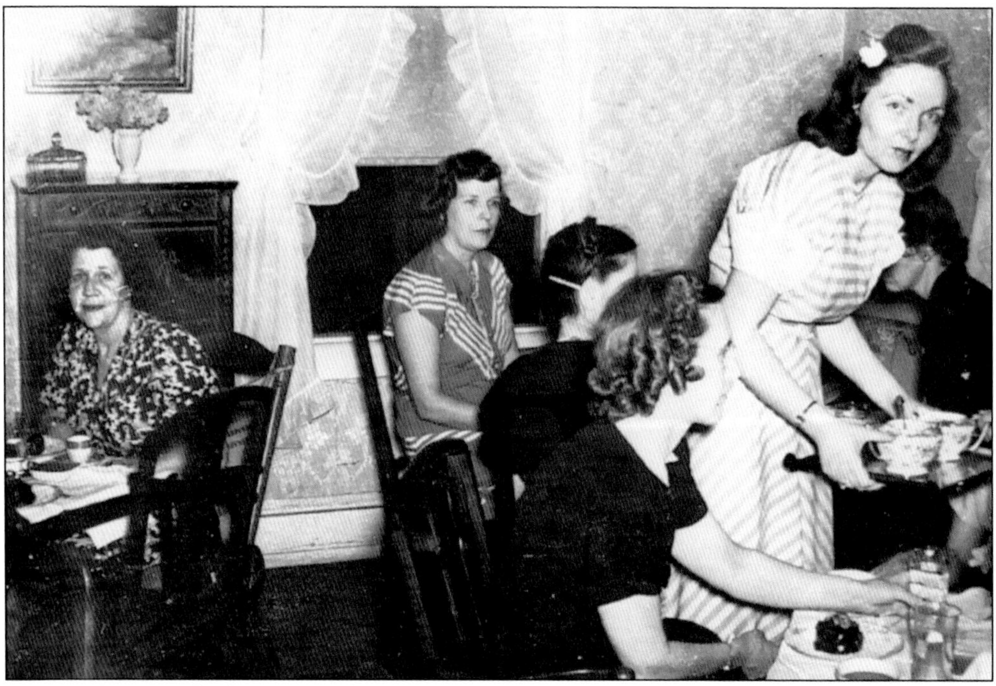

BRIDGE CLUB. A bridge party takes place in the 1950s in an apartment in the Pence Hotel building, later the Jameson apartment building. Serving tea is Nancy Vest Jones, and on left is Janie Clark Lyles. The others are unidentified. (Courtesy of Bill Jameson.)

New Business. Eleanor Booth Painter is in front of her parents' shop, the Bramwell Café, c. 1945. It was the place to stop for hot dogs with chili after a movie at the Bramwell Theatre just down the street. (Courtesy of Vickie Painter Rushbrook.)

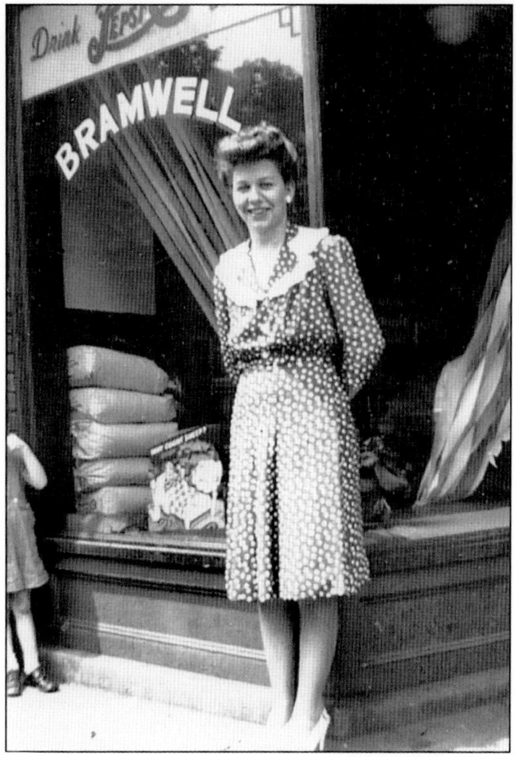

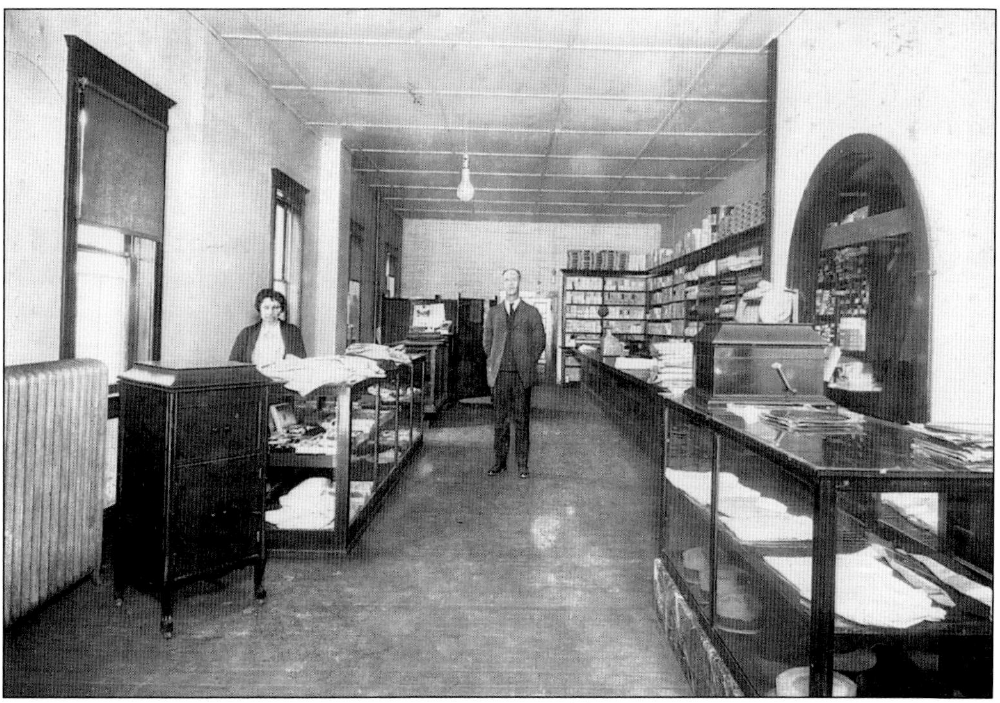

More Business. Mr. and Mrs. William Cowan operated their Main Street store in the mid-1920s. It was located on the first floor of the four-story Pence/Jameson/Scott building and sold dry-goods and more. (Courtesy of Glenn and Louise Scott family.)

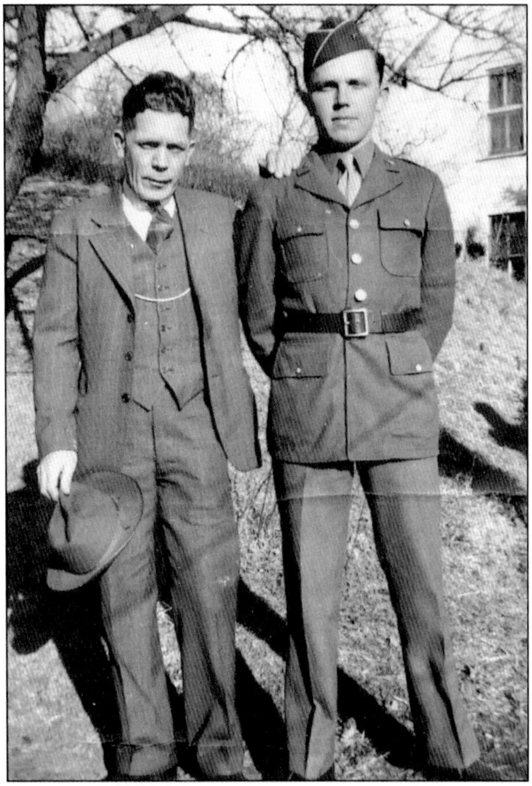

HOME FROM THE WAR. Glenn Scott Sr. and his son, Glenn Jr., are pictured at their home on Bramwell Hill. Glenn Jr. was home on leave from the army during World War II. The family home, built by Andrew Scott Sr., is in the background. (Courtesy of Glenn and Louise Scott family.)

PACK HOUSE. Buckeye Coal & Coke Co. built this Victorian structure shortly after 1900 for the general superintendent, J.C. Pack. (Courtesy of Bill Becker family.)

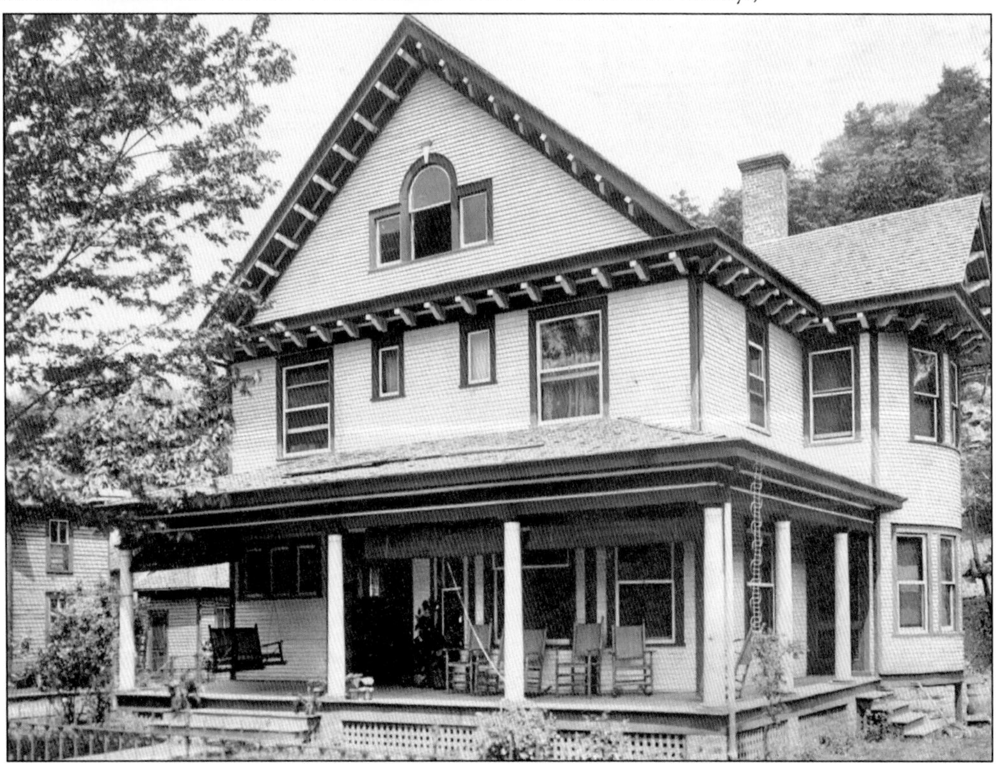

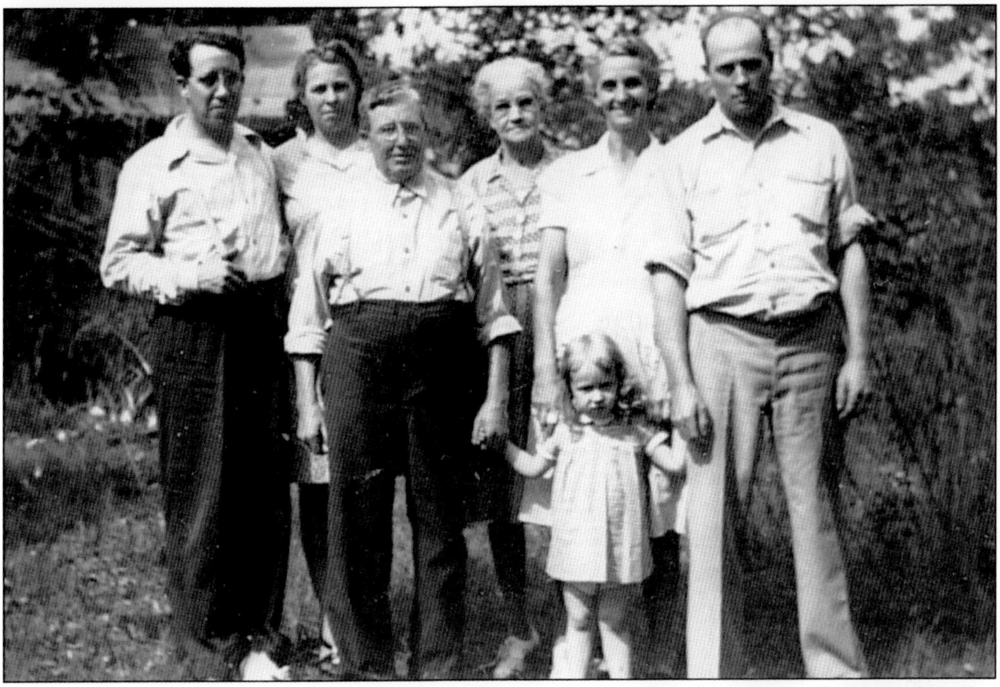

Water and Ice. In the early days, Thomas Painter operated the Bramwell Water Works, followed by his son, John, and later his grandsons, Richard and Emmett. Each had a blueprint in his head of every water line in town. They also operated an ice business. From left to right are Billy and Mabel Painter; Thomas Painter and his wife, Jennie Cowan Painter; and Helen and Johnny Painter, with their granddaughter, Brenda, in front. (Courtesy of Vickie Painter Rushbrook.)

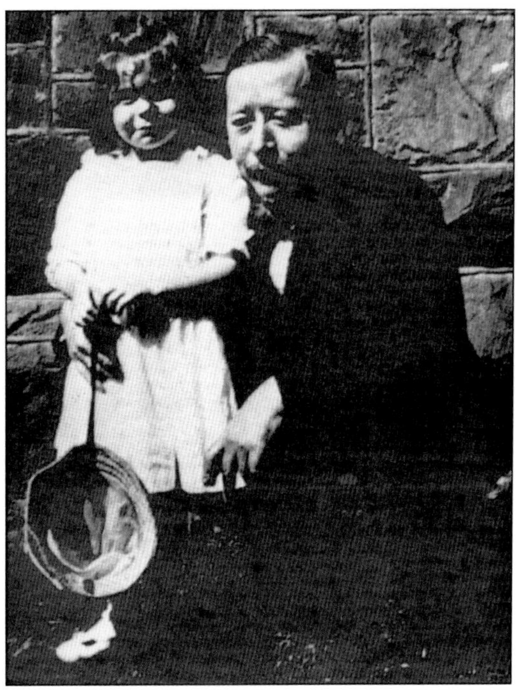

Perry. John B. Perry Sr. and his baby daughter, Helen, are pictured in front of the bluestone bank building. Perry came to Bramwell as the second employee of the bank. He and the last bank president, Isaac T. Mann, were from Greenbrier County.

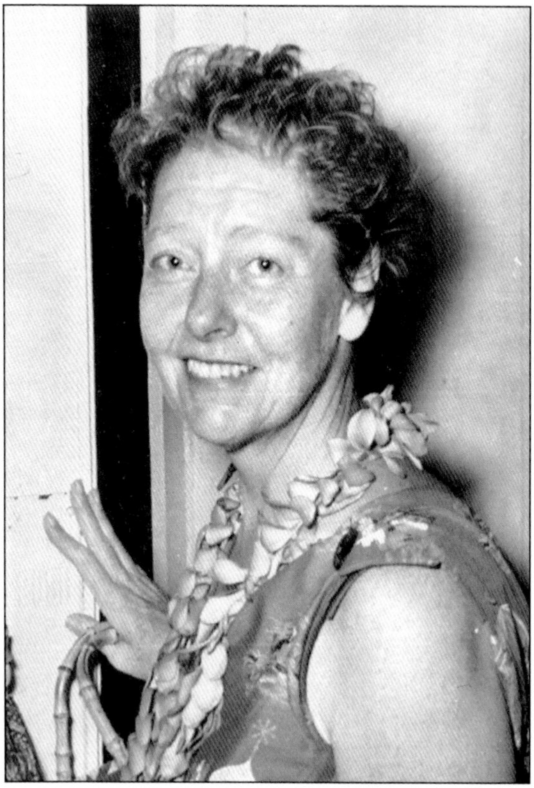

Banking. Caroline Perry was the daughter of John B. Perry Sr. He was the second employee to be hired by the Bank of Bramwell, as the assistant cashier. In 1916, John Perry was named cashier of the bank. He remained in that position until it closed August 15, 1933. The date of the photograph is unknown. (Courtesy of Kelly Murphy Eller and Kim Murphy.)

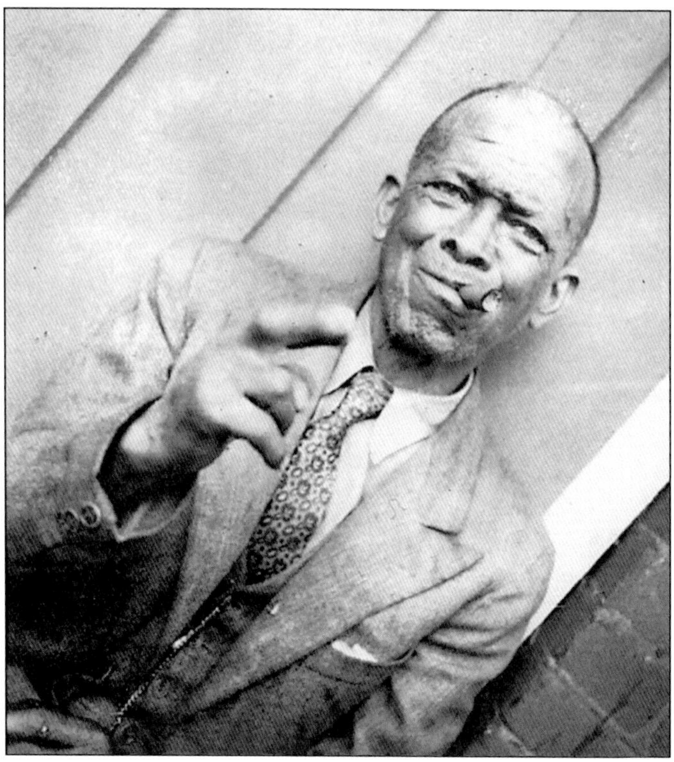

Gotcha! Pictured is the famous Henry Wade, who pushed a wheelbarrow full of cash down Main Street from the bank to the train station for payroll at the mines every payday. He was never robbed.

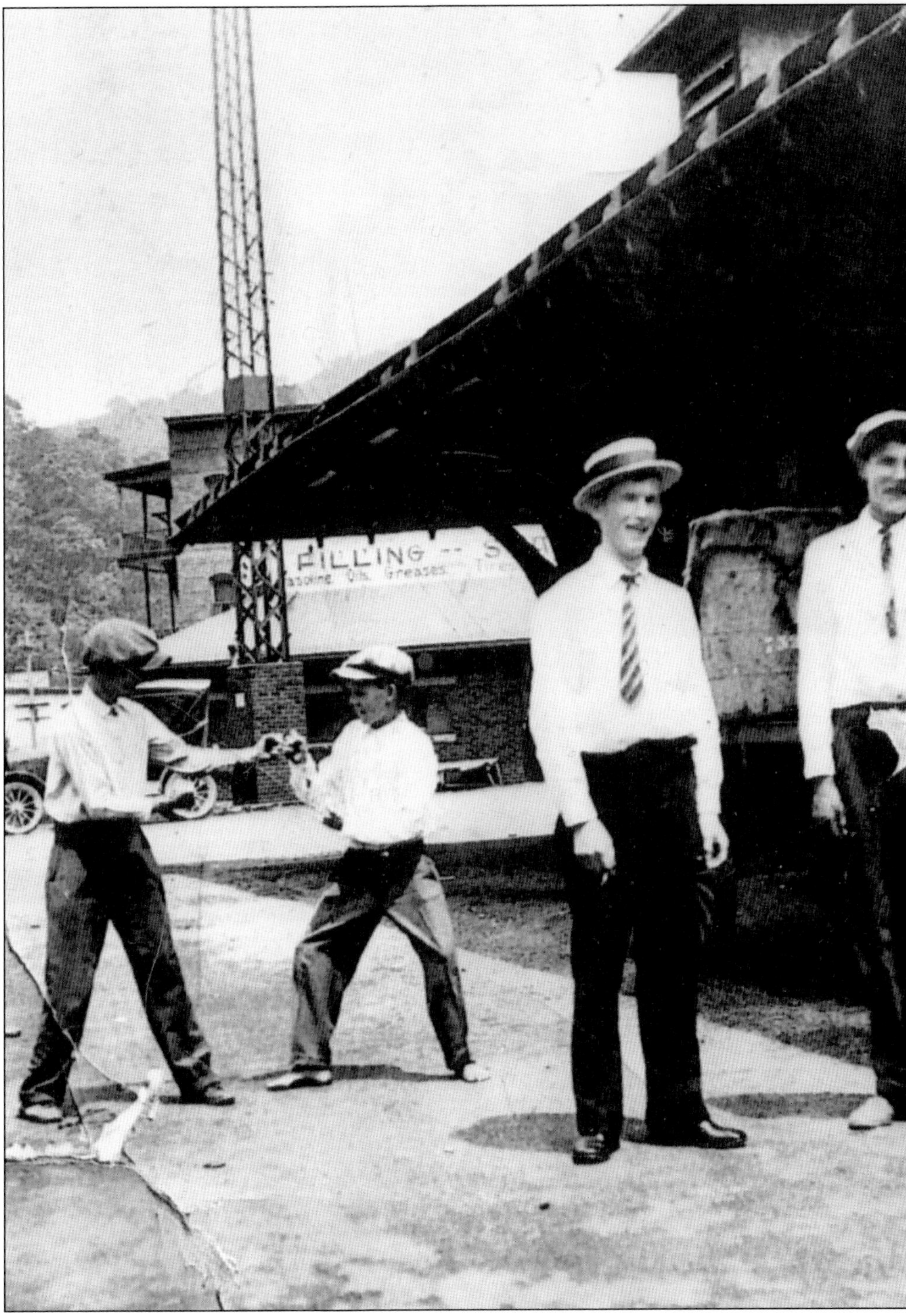

TELEGRAPH OPERATOR. Sam Harris (second from right) was the station clerk and telegraph operator at the Bramwell train station in the 1930s and 1940s. Here, he takes a break with friends beside the station. The Pence Hotel and Main Street Esso are in the background. (Courtesy of Edith Harris Butt and Elbert "Dizzy" Harris.)

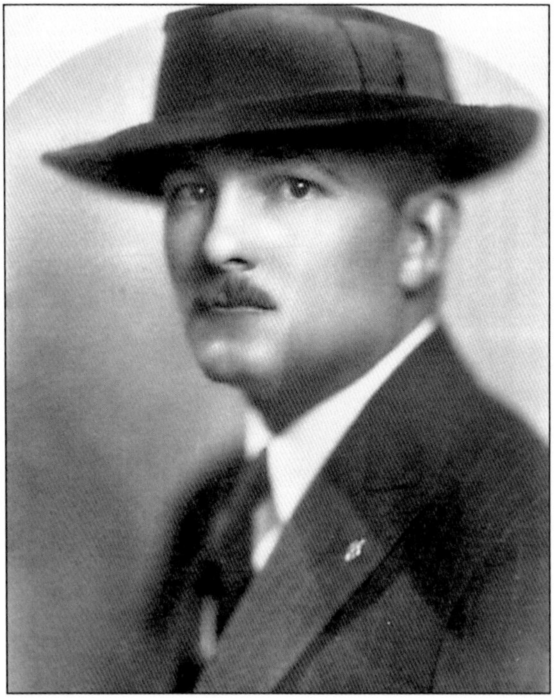

BUSINESSMAN. Edward Cooper Jr., a third-generation coal baron, also had many other business interests. One of them was owning and captaining his fishing boat, the *Pocahontas III*, at Pass-A-Grille, Florida. (Courtesy of Kelly Murphy Eller & Kim Murphy.)

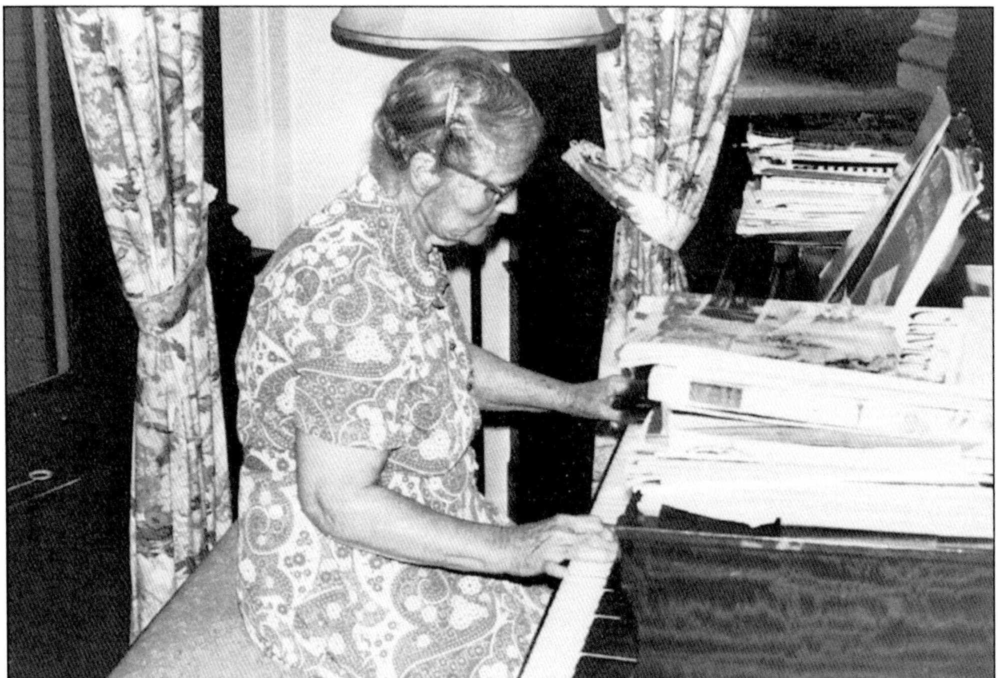

MUSIC, C. 1985. Mildred Mitchell was a student at Peabody Conservatory in Baltimore when she met Edward Cooper Jr. She was visiting the Pack family in Bramwell during Christmas break. "I met Eddie on that visit to Bramwell and he swept me off my feet," she reminisced 50 years later. After her graduation, they married and lived in the "Honeymoon Cottage" built just for them. (Courtesy of Kelly Murphy Eller and Kim Murphy.)

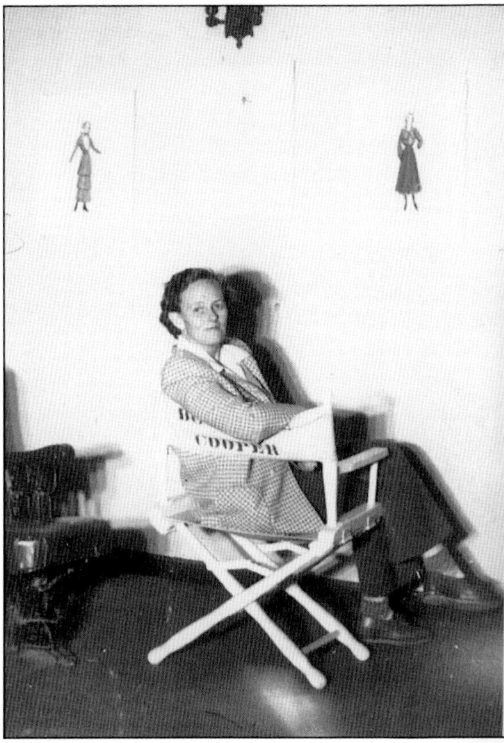

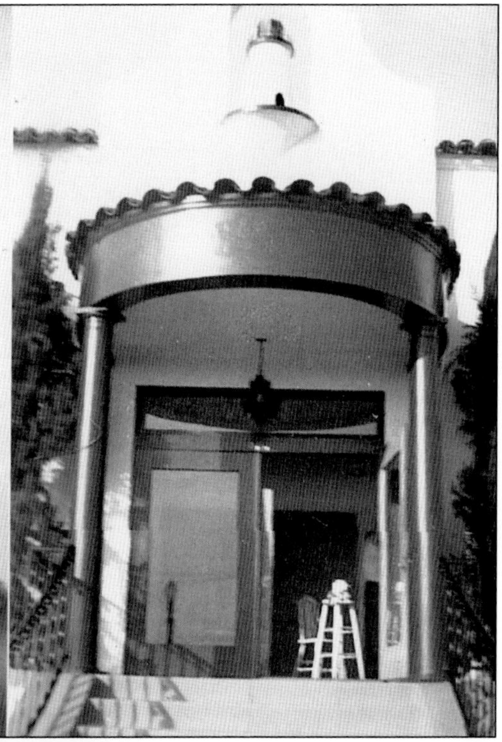

It's Hollywood. Douglass "Dougle" Cooper was the sister of Edward Jr. With acting in her blood, she moved west . Graduating from the University of Southern California as a theatre major, she established her own playhouse and trained aspiring actors. Her *Call Board* theatre in West Hollywood is pictured, along with the founder. Many of her students became major stars, including Rock Hudson. (Courtesy of Kelly Murphy Eller and Kim Murphy.)

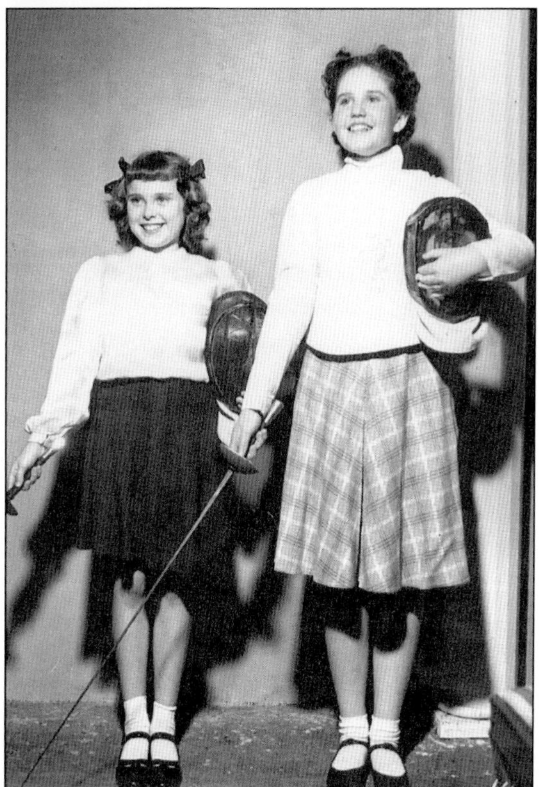

Curtain Going Up! Eve Cooper caught the acting bug when she went to Hollywood for an extended visit with her Aunt Dougle. She was about 12 when she appeared in a production at the *Call Board*. Eve is the actress on the right; the other girl is unidentified. (Courtesy of Kelly Murphy Eller and Kim Murphy.)

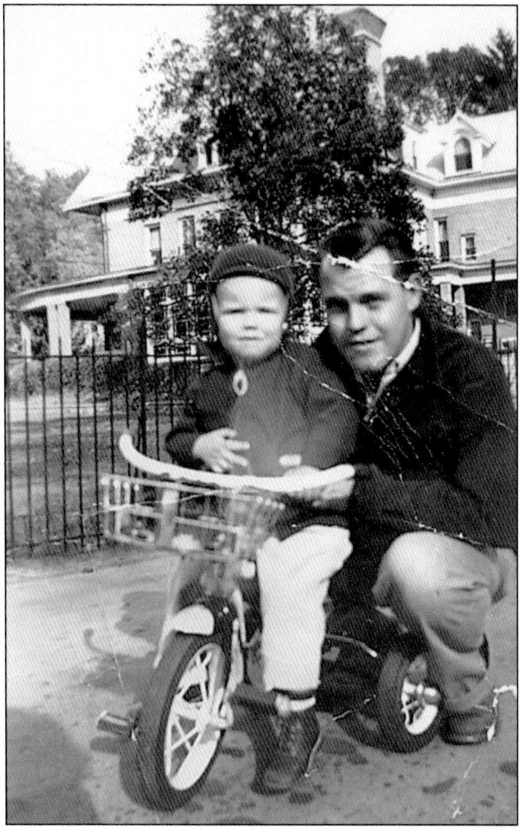

FATHER AND SON. Kim Murphy and his father, Harry Donnel "Donnie" Murphy, enjoy a tricycle outing behind their home, the Cooper mansion, in this c. 1954 photograph. (Courtesy of Kelly Murphy Eller and Kim Murphy.)

PLAYING A TUNE. Kelly was 16 and practicing the clarinet as her mother, Eve Murphy, plays piano to accompany her. There was always the sound of music coming out of the open doors of their house in the summer. (Courtesy of Kelly Murphy Eller and Kim Murphy.)

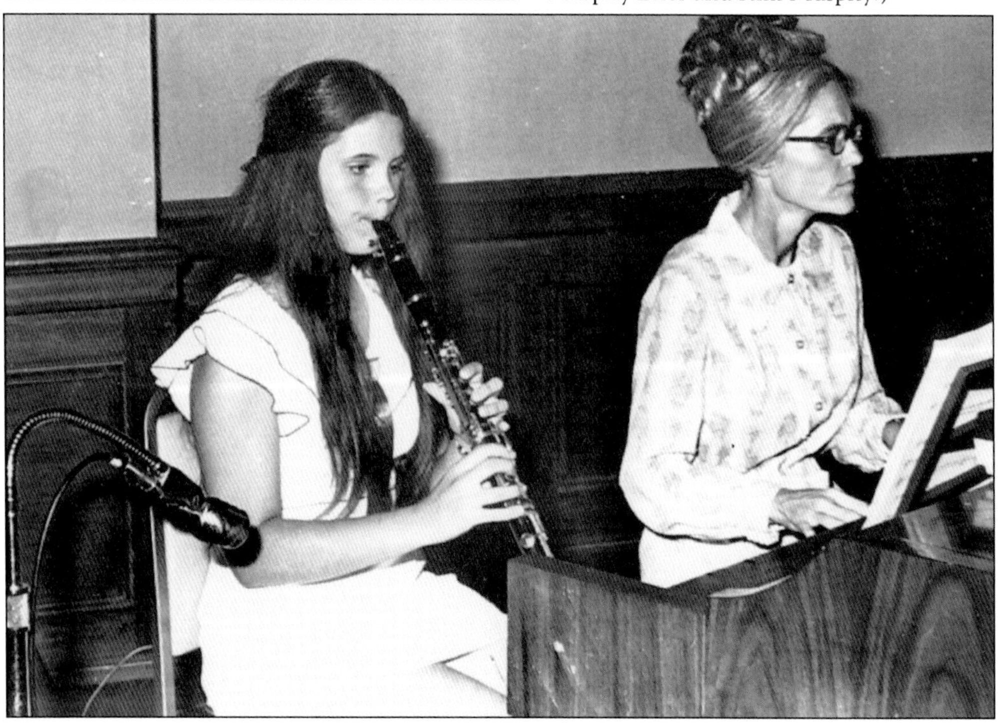

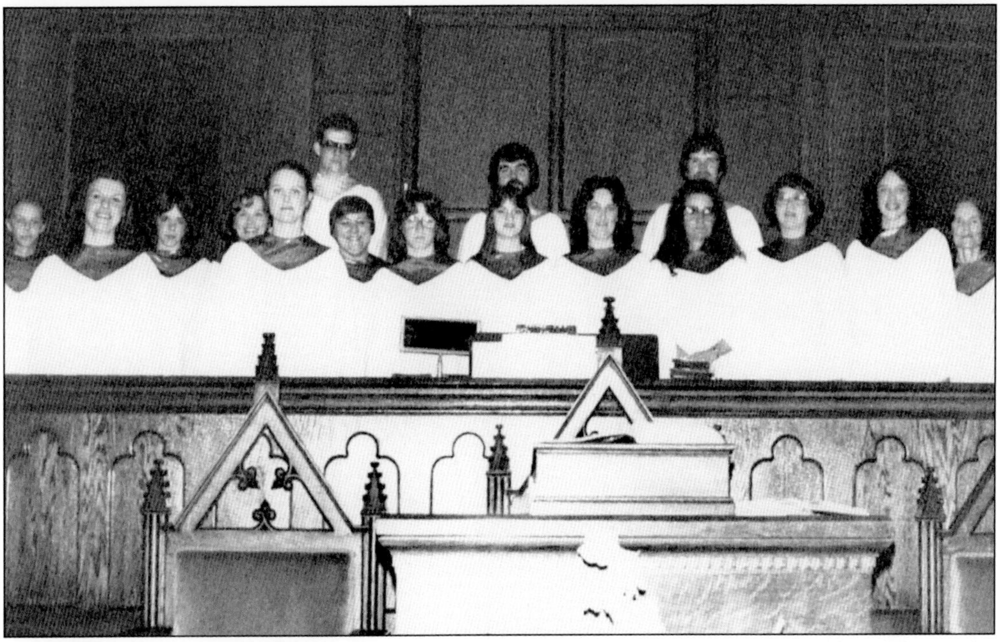

Choir Practice. Bramwell Presbyterian Church choir is pictured in the 1980s. From left to right are (front row) Michelle Baugh, Terri Meskinish, Dora Shrader, Kelly Eller, Betty Kirby, Carol Scott, Debbie Painter, Dawn Murphy, Casey Vance, Terry Murphy Reed, Selina Goins, and Eve Murphy; (back row) Cris Hill, Jeff Vance, Ken Kirby, and Kim Murphy. Eve Murphy was the organist for 35 years at the church. (Courtesy of Kelly Murphy Eller and Kim Murphy.)

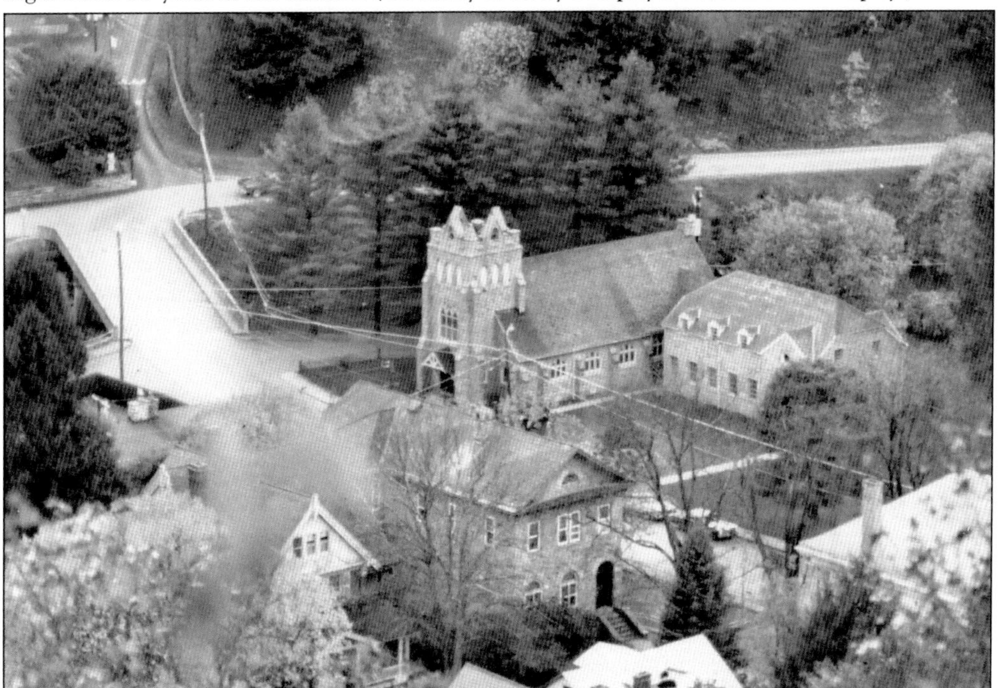

From Above. This overview shows the Presbyterian church with Sunday school ell built by Italian stonemasons in the 1930s. Also visible is the famous Bank of Bramwell.

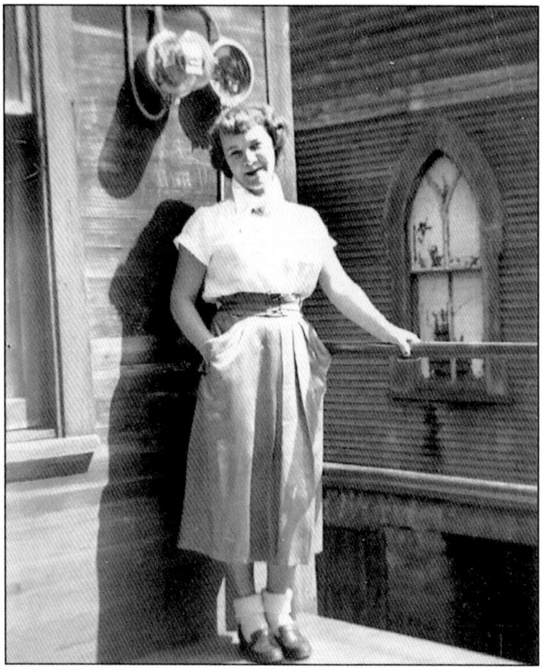

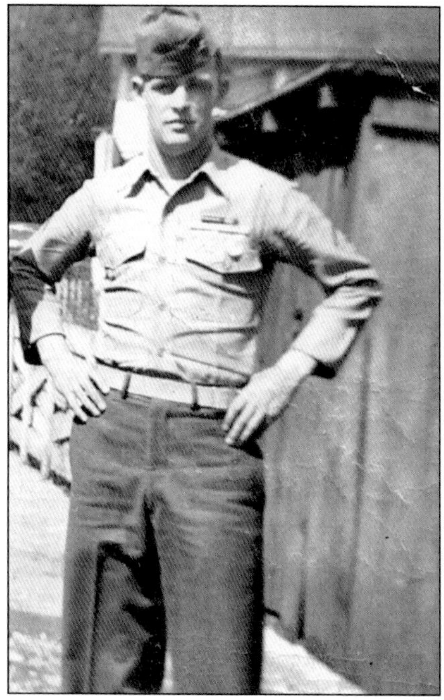

HOME ON LEAVE. It was 1955, and Shirley Walker Gibson was 18. She was on the porch of her apartment building located where the fire station now stands. Visible to her left is a church window from the original Presbyterian church. Her husband, Randy, stands in front of the apartment building near the Bramwell Hill Road. The buildings behind him were torn down when the road was widened and Route 20 became Route 120. (Courtesy of Shirley and Randy Gibson.)

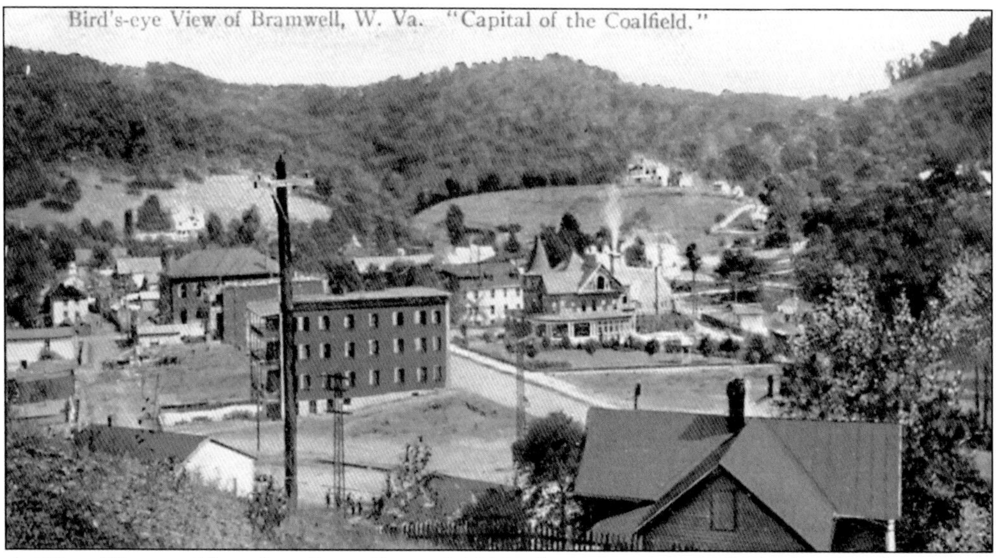

A NEW TOWN. After the Great Fire of 1910, there was a new look for the downtown. An ordinance was enacted that all new construction be as fireproof as possible. Gone were the frame buildings with the Victorian touch. In place of businesses on the south side of Main Street, the Cooper Mansion with a copper roof commanded the street. It was beginning to look "modern."

Three

Ellis Island Connection

Beneath thy sunny skies
O Wales, I long to roam,
And feel thy turf beneath my feet,
My Father's Native Home.
—May Llewellyn Jones, daughter of Jenkin Jones

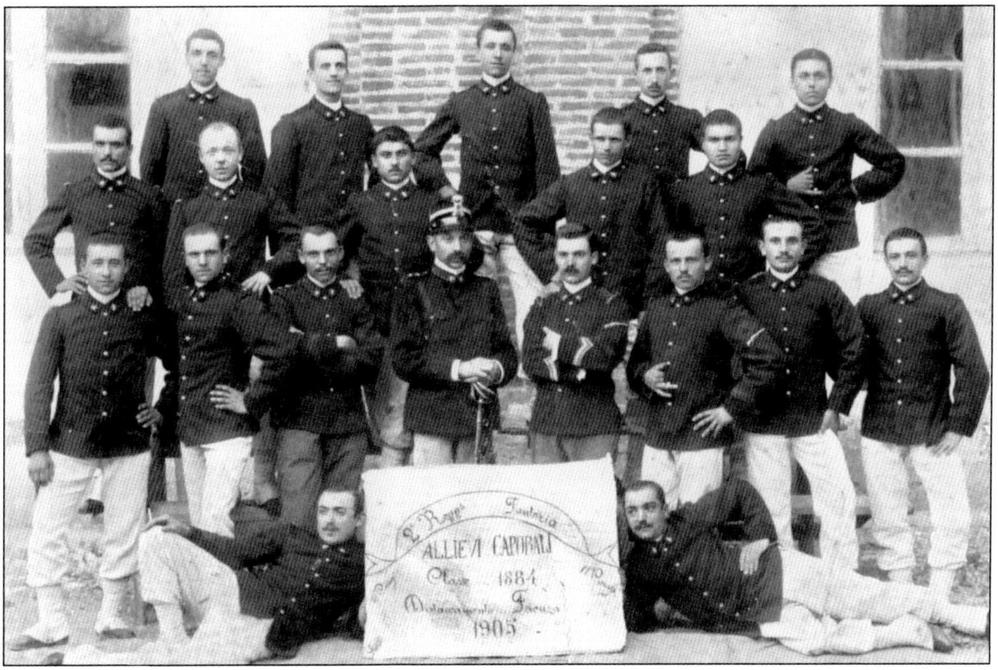

Piedicavallo Connection. Some of the finest stone masonry work to be found is in Bramwell and was crafted by Italians from northern Italy. Mauro Peraldo Guiellmin was in the Italian Army in this 1905 picture. He is on the right, on his side. He, his wife, son, and daughter arrived in Bramwell soon after the Great Fire of 1910. Reconstruction included all of the stone work. (Courtesy of Marianna and Bobby Stoker.)

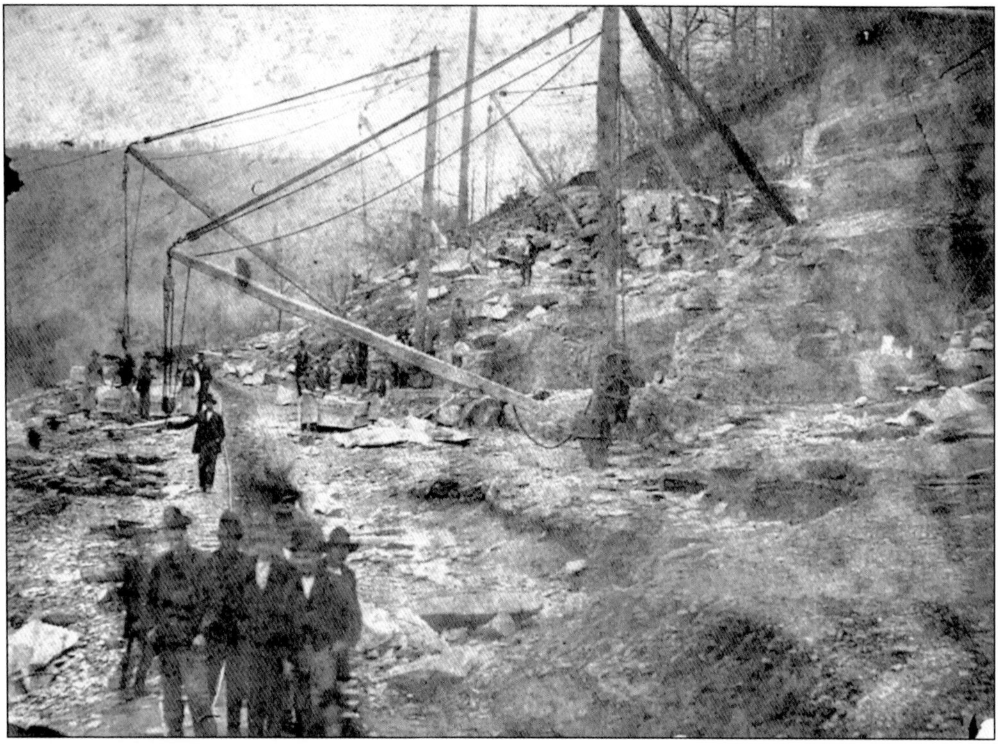

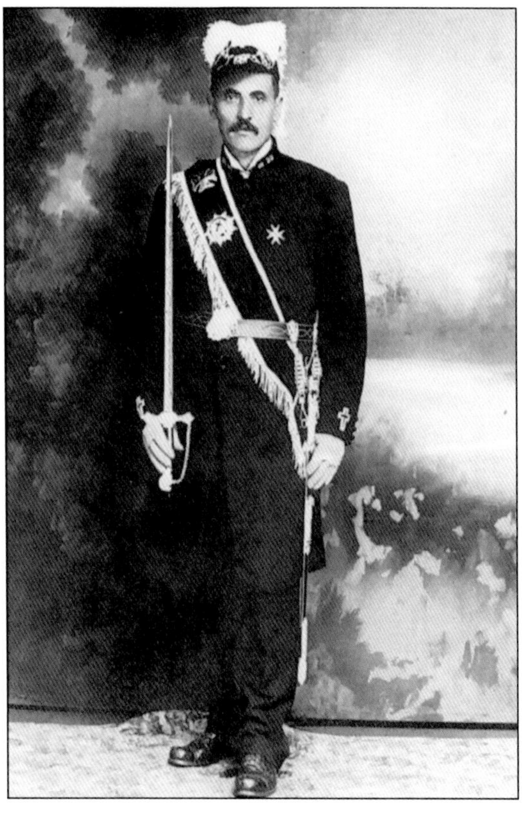

STONE QUARRY. On a mountaintop overlooking the downtown, stonemasons blasted away on the rocks, hand cut the stones, and moved them to building sites by mule-drawn wagons. Though work at the Thomas Quarry was the hardest manual labor, the works of art stand today for us to appreciate. (Courtesy of Eva Yon Hill.)

STONEMASON IS A MASON. This Shriners' photograph was taken about 1920. Mauro Peraldo Guiellmin was born in a small Italian village on the Swiss border. Although Italian was his native language, he was fluent in French and English. (Courtesy of Eva Yon Hill.)

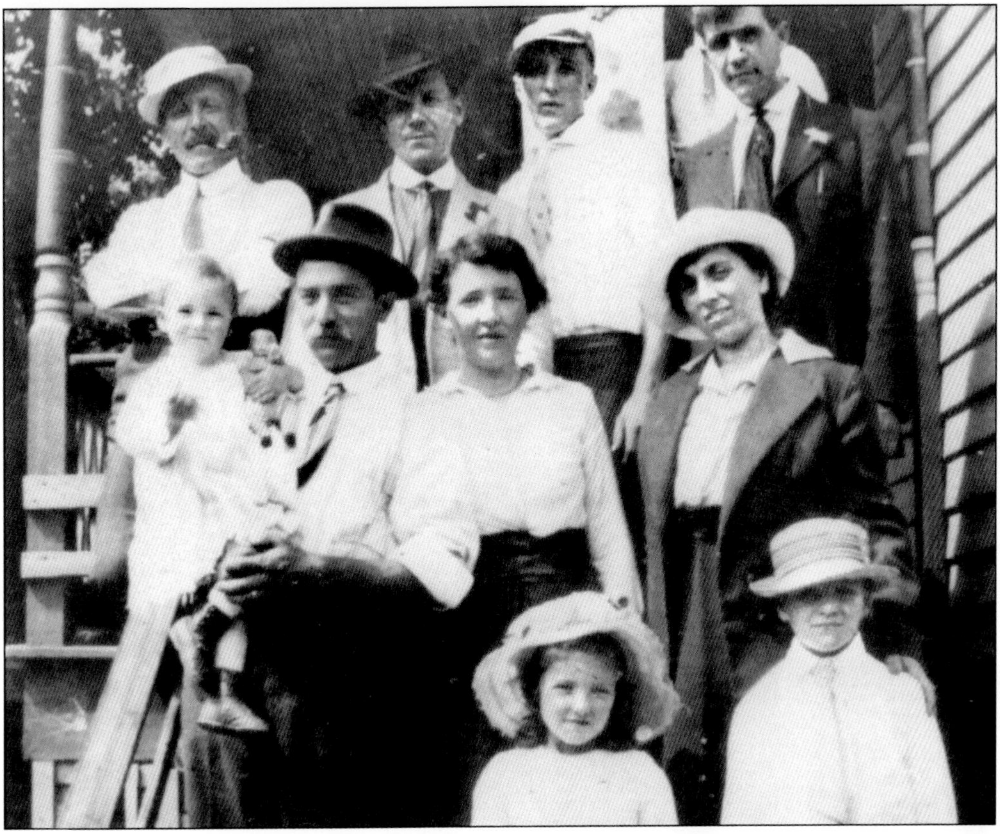

Peraldo & Gross. By 1916, Mauro Peraldo Guigliellmin's family added another daughter. He became Mauro Peraldo, and he owned a home on Renova Street. Pictured from left to right are (front row) his Italian-born children, Catharina and Leo; (middle row) Mauro, holding Bramwell-born baby, Dea; his wife, Maria; a sister, Isabella Gross; (back row) Albino Gross and his sons, Ennio, Londa, and Nino. The name Gross was changed from Janutolo. (Courtesy of Marianna and Bobby Stoker.)

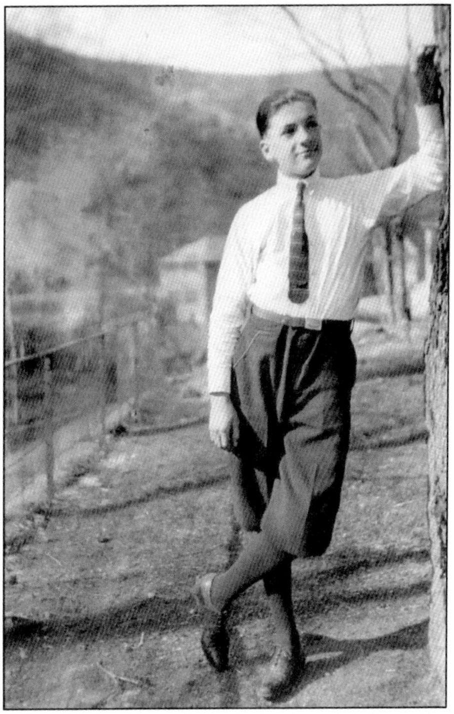

Not a Stonemason. Leo Carl Peraldo, although born to a stonemason, decided at an early age the work was not for him. His gift was violin, and his career became teaching and playing. He taught violin classes at the schools in Mercer and McDowell Counties and played with community orchestras. At the local silent picture shows, Leo with his violin and Leonard Pasley at the piano provided musical accompaniment. (Courtesy of Leo Peraldo and Camille Brunner.)

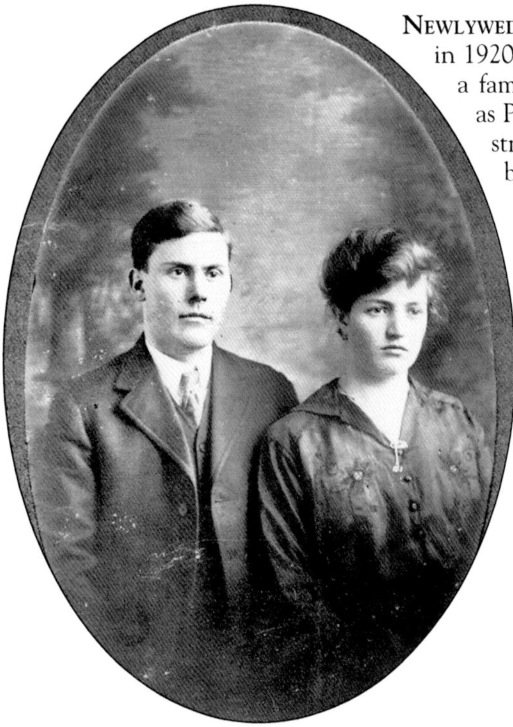

NEWLYWEDS FROM ITALY. Livio and Cristina Yon married in 1920, came to Bramwell, built a house, and raised a family. Livio's career was as a stonemason, just as Peraldo and Gross. He worked on many of the structures in town, including the house pictured below. (Courtesy of Eva Yon Hill.)

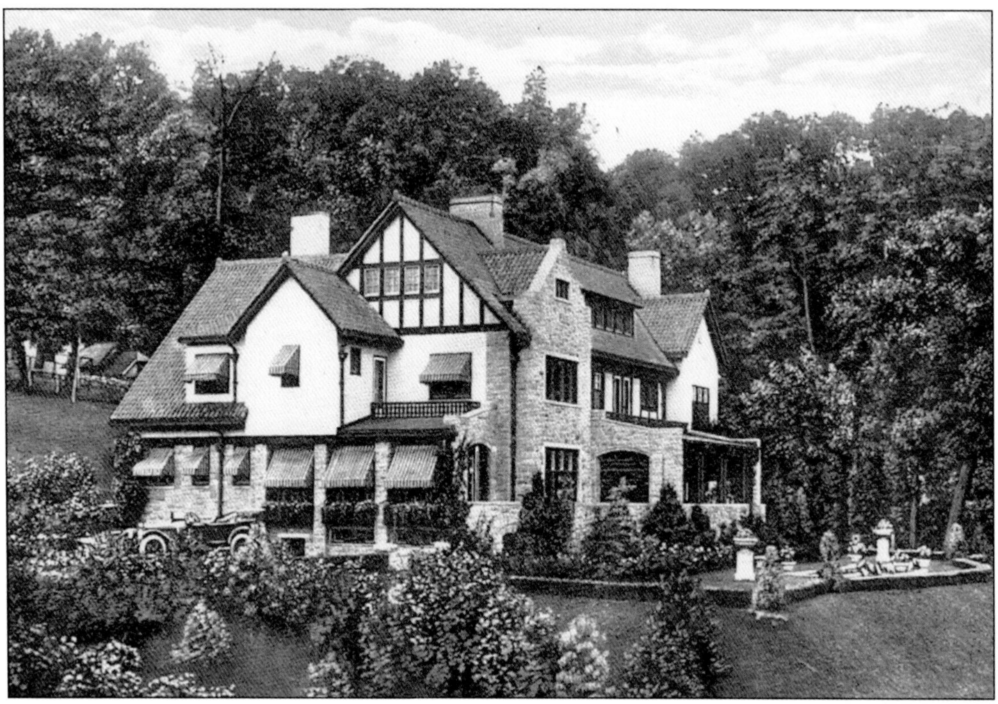

THOMAS HOUSE. This mansion on a knoll commands attention of all who pass. The construction started in 1909 and was fully underway when the Peraldo family sailed to this country. Mauro Peraldo, along with his relatives Yon and Gross, worked with the crew building the house until 1912 when it was finished.

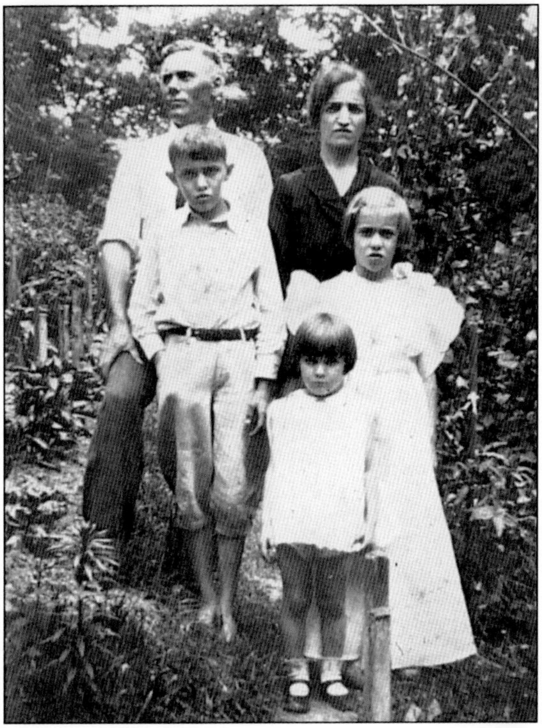

YON AND FAMILY. In the lush gardens of the Yons, Livio and Cristina stand with their Bramwell-born children, Harry Itlo, Eva, and young Alma in the front. The family photo was taken about 1934. (Courtesy of Eva Yon Hill.)

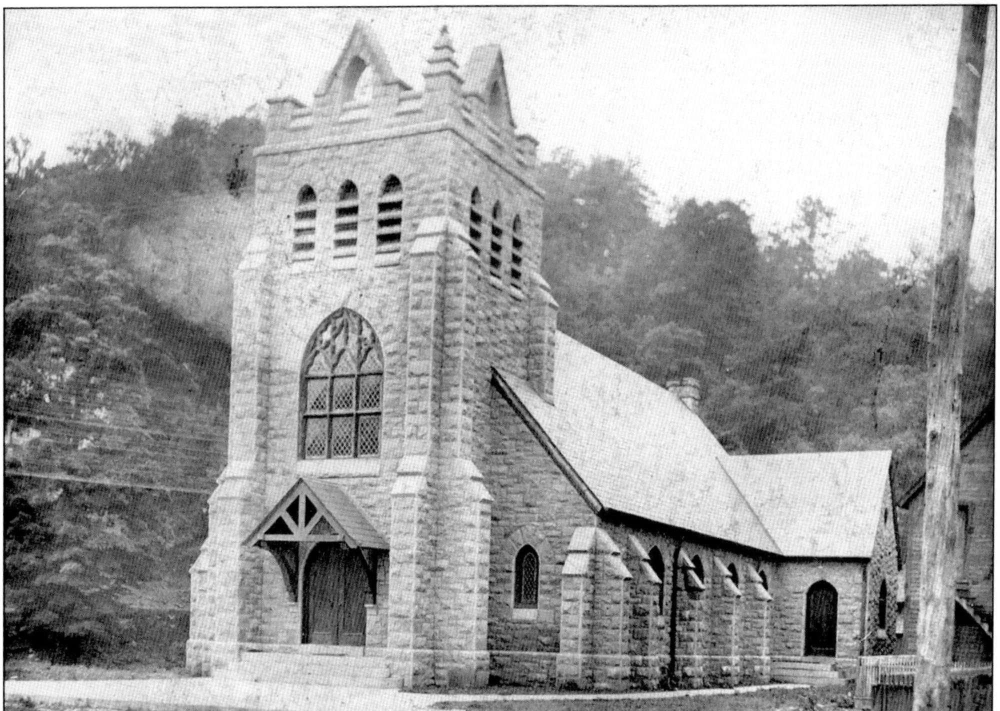

STONEMASONS' HANDIWORK. Bramwell Presbyterian Church, built in 1903, is an example of the artistry required by early-day stone cutters. Built of native bluestone found near the edge of Bluestone River, the church survived the Great Fire of 1910 and was enlarged in 1934.

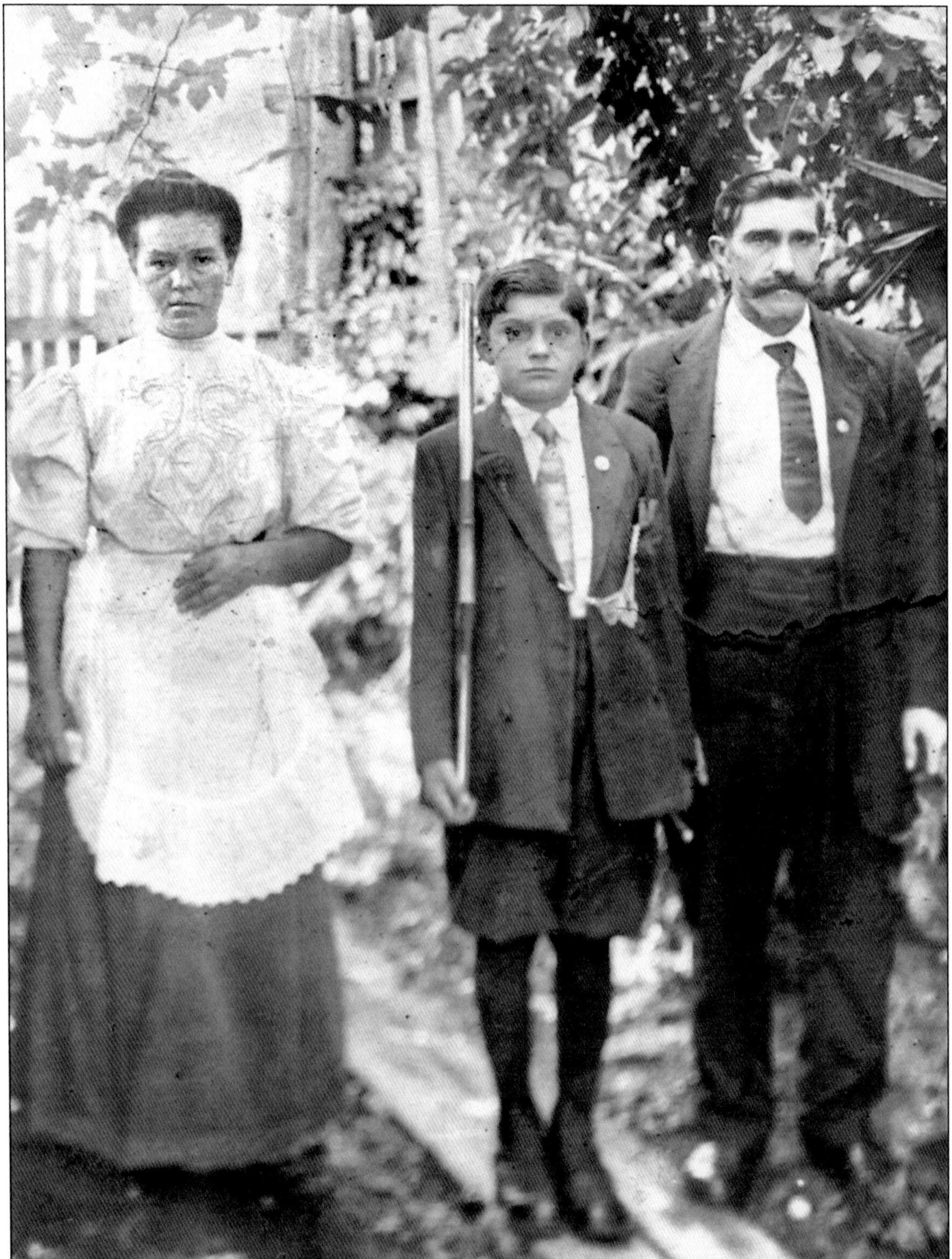

Coal Mining. Rich coal seams and plenty of work beckoned families from many nations. Anna Bodant and Andy Sabol married in Hungary. With their son, Joseph, they immigrated to Pennsylvania, where their last name was changed to Sabo. They moved south to Freeman, to work in the coal mines. They lived near other families who were from eastern European countries. (Courtesy of Sandy Collins and Bonnie Dawson.)

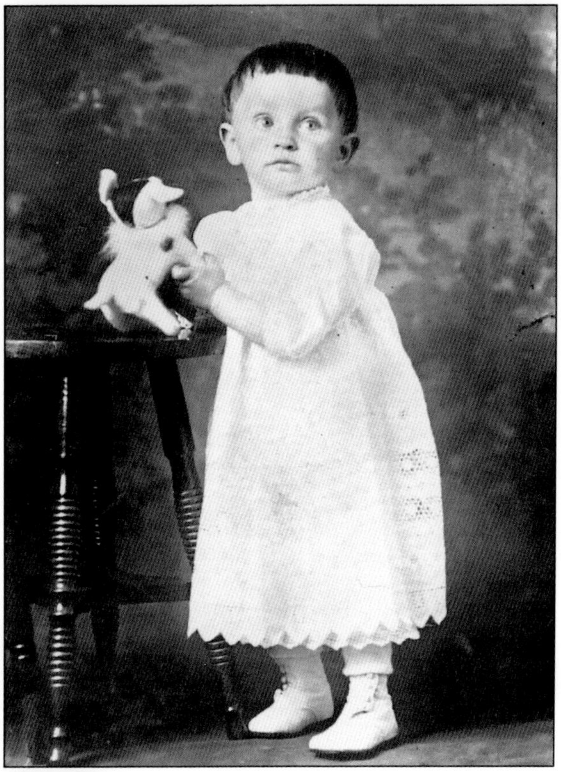

BORN IN AMERICA. James Jacob Sabo was born to Anna and Andy in 1916. He was about one year old when this picture was taken. He followed in the coal mining footsteps of his father. (Courtesy of Sandy Collins and Bonnie Dawson.)

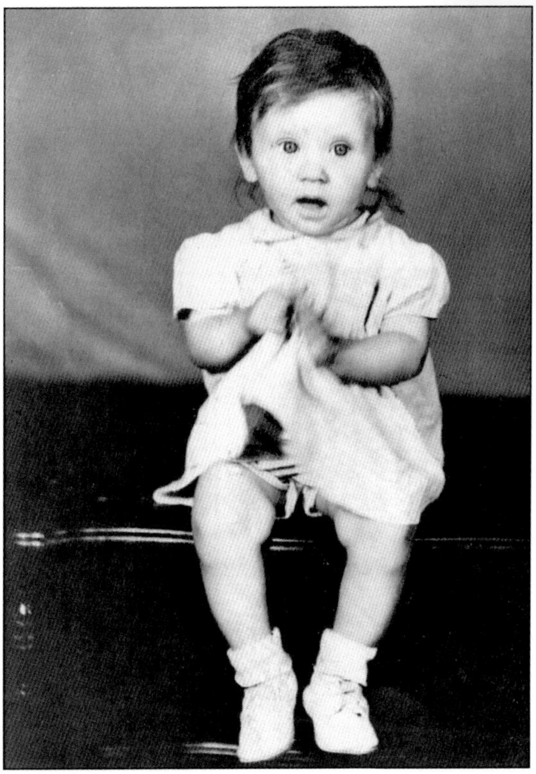

THIRD GENERATION. Bonnie Sabo Dawson, shown here in 1945, is a third-generation Sabo living in the same small community to which her grandparents immigrated during the Industrial Revolution. (Courtesy of Sandy Collins.)

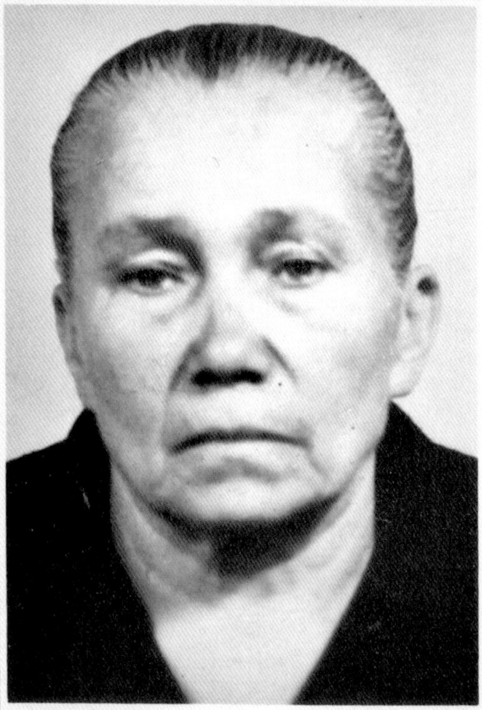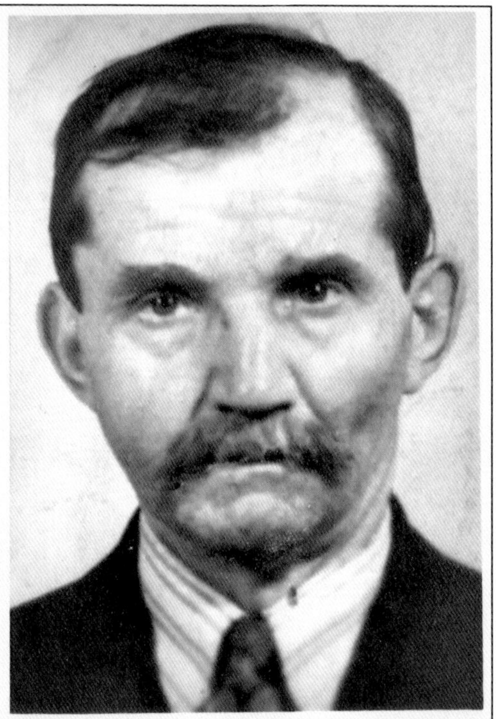

From the Old Country. Mike Fitzko Sr. and Anna Louise Fitzko immigrated to America in 1904. They lived in the coal mining area of Bramwell and raised seven children. (Courtesy of Margaret Carver.)

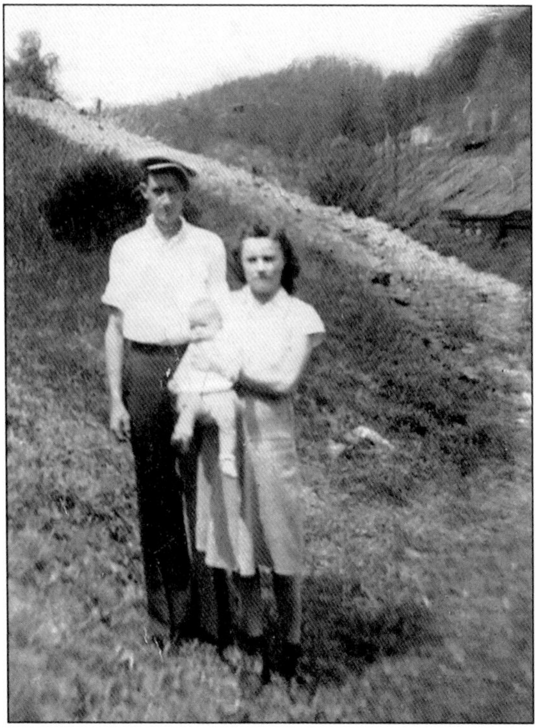

Buckeye Hollow. With four coal mining operations in and near Bramwell, there was plenty of work for all who came. Lee and Margaret Fitzo Carver with their baby daughter, Cynthia, stand on a knoll with the Buckeye machine shop roof visible behind them. The first mayor, John Hewitt, was a founding partner in Buckeye Coal & Coke Co. operations. (Courtesy of Margaret Fitzko Carver.)

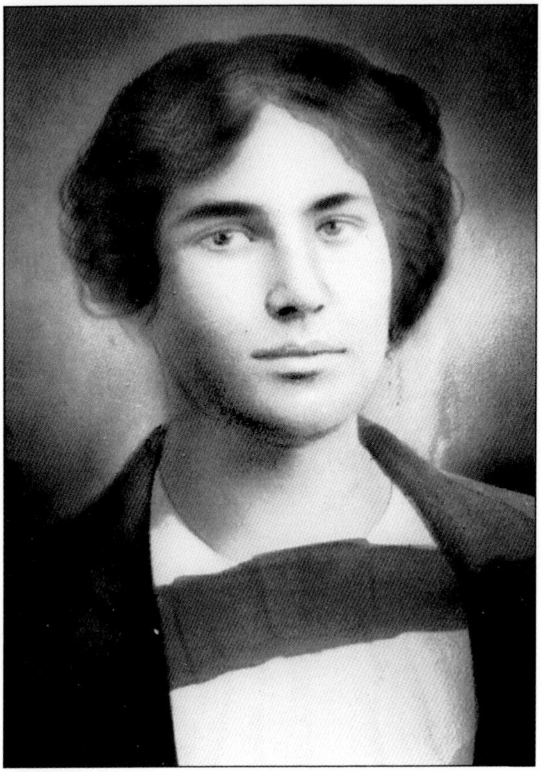

Austrian Beauty. Mary Lucas was born shortly after her parents emigrated from Czechoslovakia. She and Arthur Wright married and lived on top of Jones' Hill. When offered the opportunity to own a downtown mansion filled with oak woodwork, she refused it, saying she could "never live in such a dark place." One daughter was a stewardess for American Airlines, and their son was a NASA engineer. (Photo restoration by Ken Davidson.)

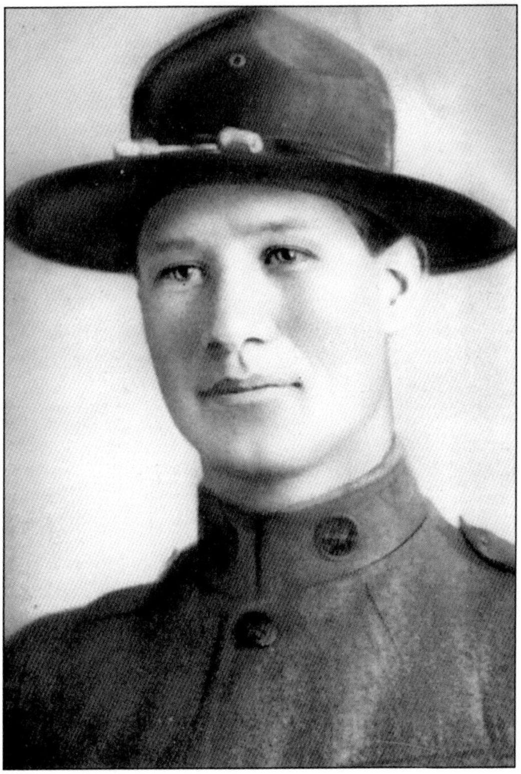

World War I Veteran. Arthur Wright was one of many who traveled north across the mountains North Carolina, where work was plentiful in the coalfields. A foreman for Caswell Creek Coal & Coke Co., his family lived in a larger company house. When the company ceased operation at Freeman, the houses were sold and the Wrights bought their house and property. (Photo restoration by Ken Davidson.)

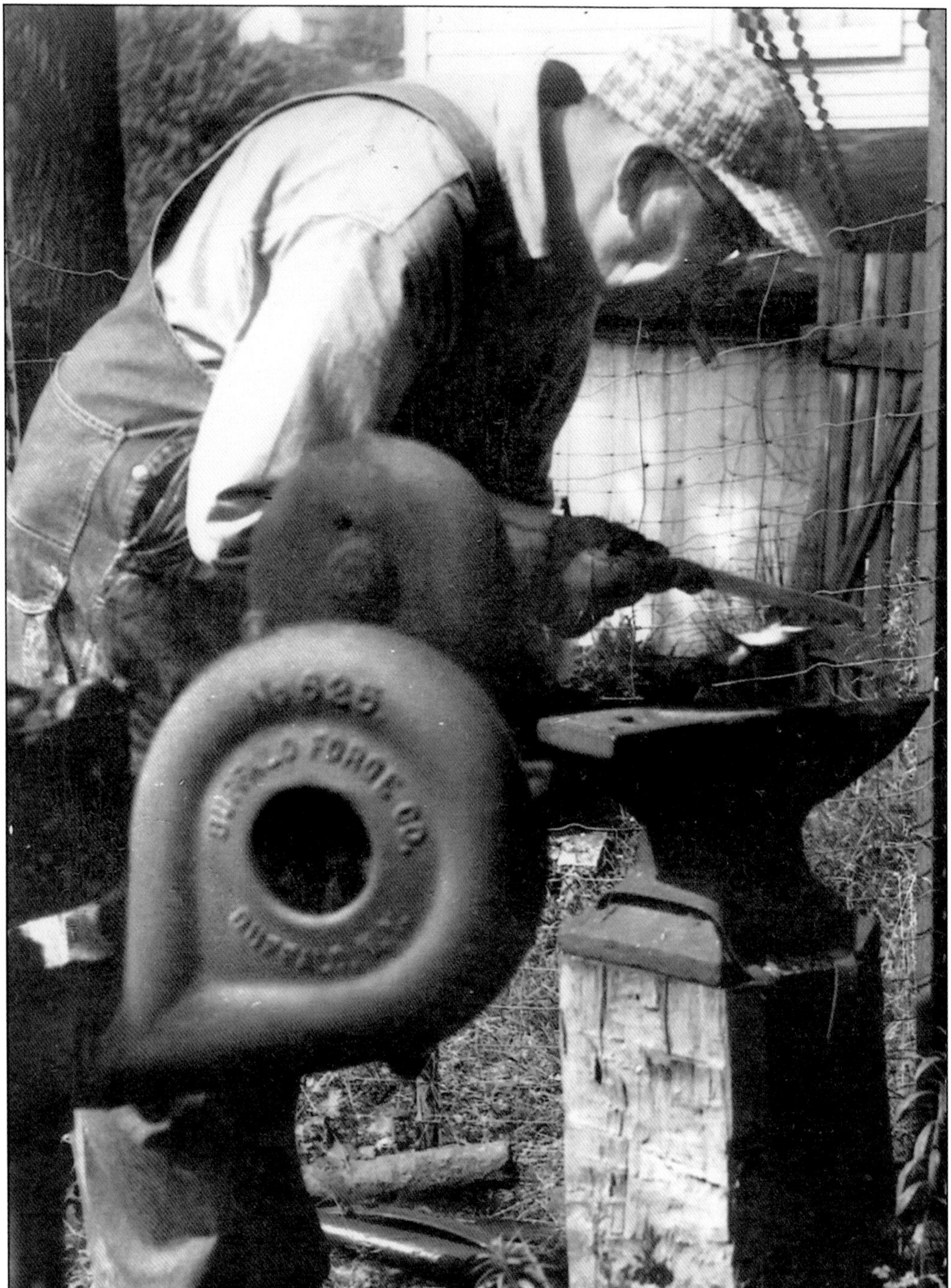

BLACKSMITH. George Palco was born in the Bramwell area in1897 to parents who emigrated from Czechoslovakia in the 1890s. He was a blacksmith for Caswell Creek Coal & Coke Co. and lived in one of its larger company houses. He had a blacksmith shop at work and his own at home where he did independent jobs. (Courtesy of Kathleen Palco Sexton.)

IN THE GARDEN. George Palco takes a Sunday break from his blacksmith job. He and his wife, Bertha Harman Palco, are standing by their grape arbor in this 1942 photo. They were parents of three children: Dorothy, Kathleen, and Charles Ray. (Courtesy of Kathleen Palco Sexton.)

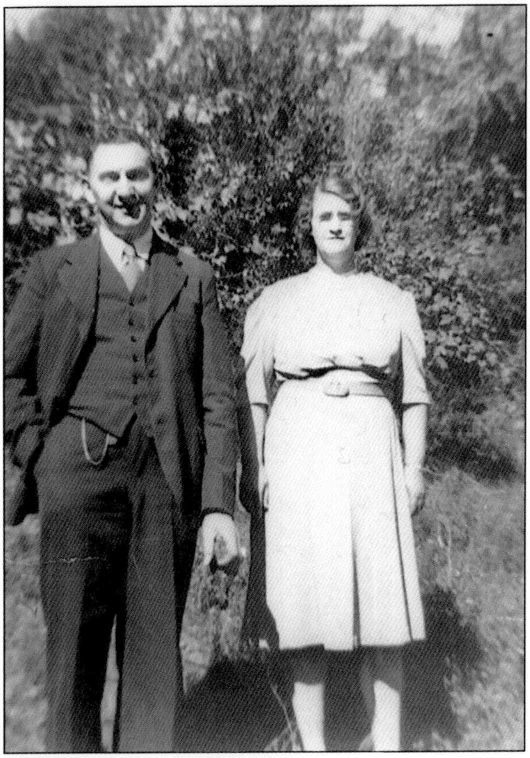

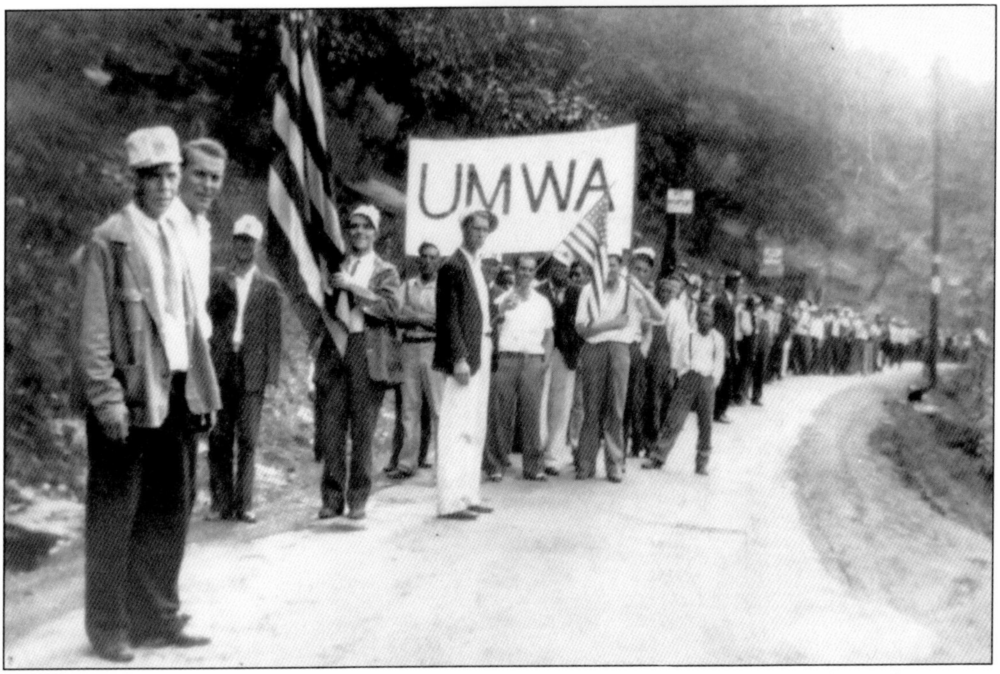

WALKING FOR THE UNION. Coal miners fought to start the United Mine Workers of America (UMWA) and worked to keep it active, even parading on April 1, John L. Lewis Day. The long parade was marching on Route 120 from Freeman/Simmons to Bramwell for a union rally. They stopped for the picture when they were almost to the town hall.

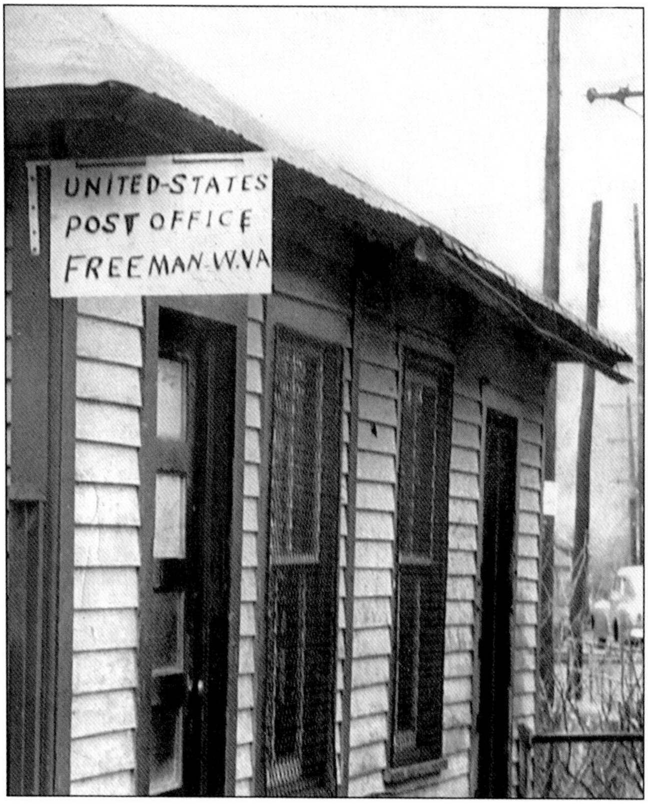

EARLY UNITED STATE POST OFFICE. The early Freeman post office was located in a small building beside the Buckeye Company Store and heated with a potbellied heating stove. The mail was shipped in by train to the Simmons Station across the Bluestone River. John Blanton was postmaster longer than any other.

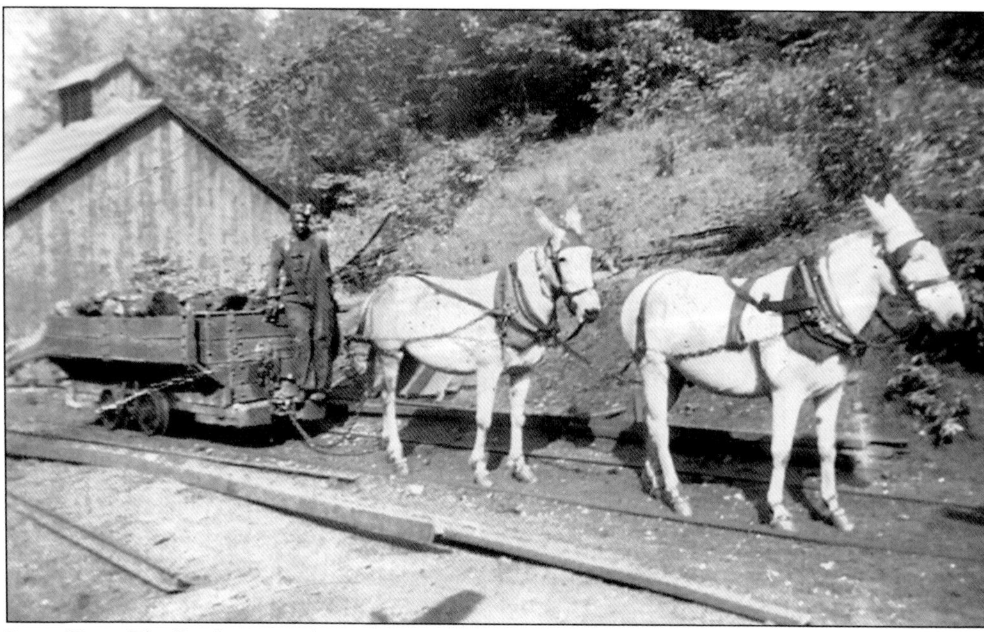

LAST TRIP. The Buckeye Coal & Coke Co.'s first mine opened in 1886 with John Hewitt as one of the first coal operators. The last mine car was pulled out of the Number 3 seam by mining mules in September of 1939. (Courtesy Katharine Hewitt Barringer.)

Four

FREEMAN, SIMMONS, AND SPICERTOWN

May the thoughts of long ago
Cause your hearts with warmth to glow,
And as life you travel through,
May God's blessing follow you.

—Dr. J. C. Newbold

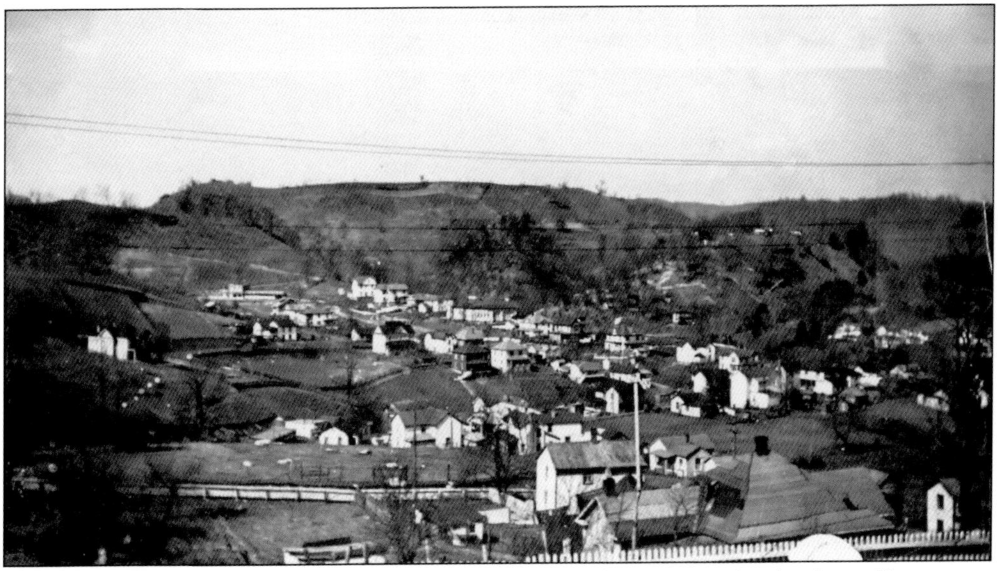

VIEW OF SPICERTOWN AND SCHOOLHOUSE HILL. The Spicer family from Tennessee, built their first house of logs, and named their acreage "Spicertown." Their children had a dairy farm in the area where the photographer was standing for this photograph. It overlooks Booth Hill, Rameytown, Freeman, and Simmons. By the second generation, Spicertown became the popular place to live. The distant mountain is Bramwell Hill. (Courtesy of Mary Helen Painter Cornett.)

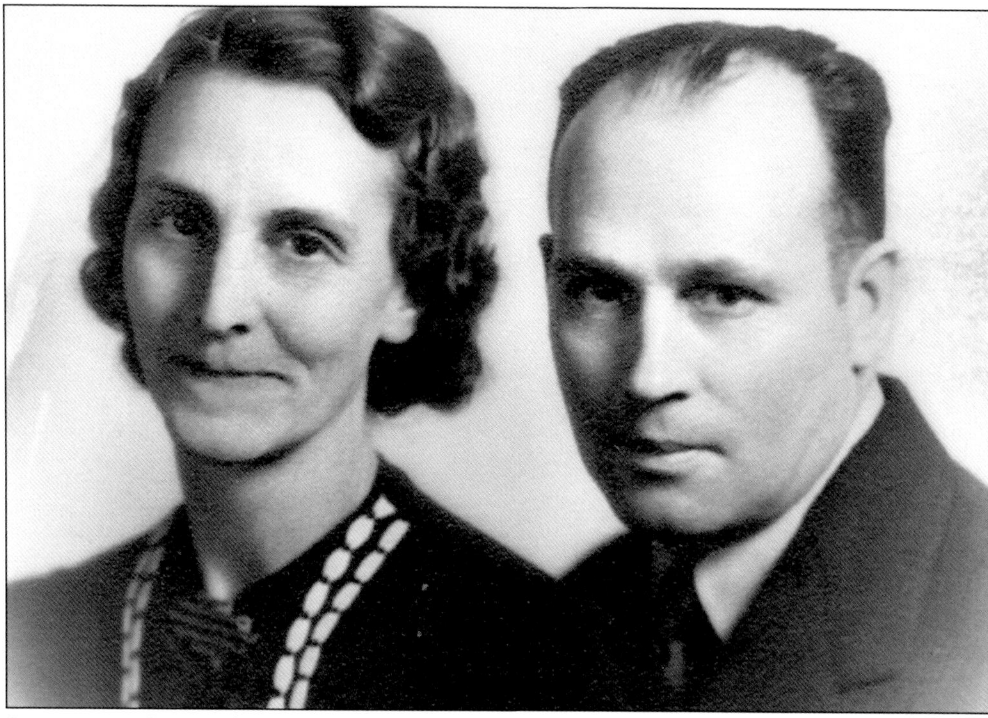

SPICERTOWN GIRL. When only 14 years old, Helen Shupe, a Spicer granddaughter, and Johnny Painter, a Bramwell boy, eloped. Her brothers were ready to go after him but decided they did not want to make their baby sister a widow. Helen and Johnny lived "happily ever after" and celebrated their 50th wedding anniversary. (Courtesy of Vickie Painter Rushbrook.)

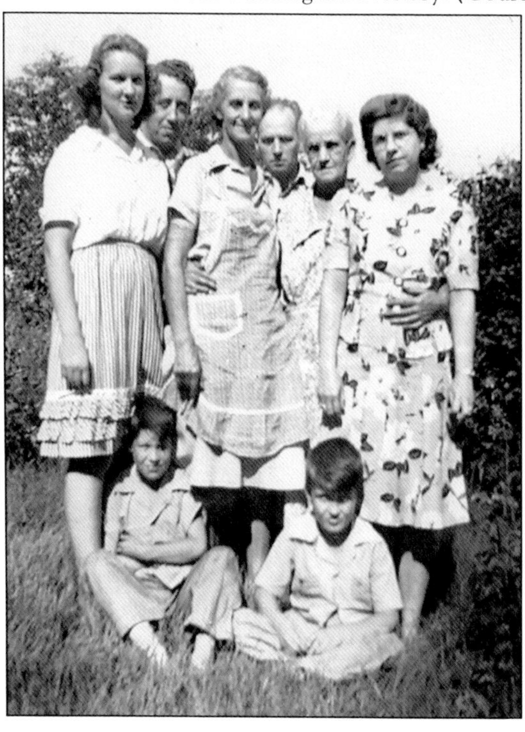

THREE GENERATIONS. Indeed, the Shupe-Painter marriage lasted, with five children plus grandchildren and more. From left to right are (seated) Thomas and Kenneth Maxey; (standing) Mary Helen Painter; Billy Painter; Helen and Johnny Painter; his mother, Jennie Cowan Painter; and his sister, Juanita Painter Maxey. (Courtesy of Vickie Painter Rushbrook.)

Bowen. Harry Bowen sits in his Booth-Bowen Coal Company office at Freeman, c. 1900. The son of Jonathan Bowen, he was one of several millionaires in his family. Legend is that the Bowen and Spicer families chose opposite sides of the Bluestone River to settle. Bowen's side had the coal; Spicer had a dairy farm and musical talents. Even today, Spicer descendants say, "Wonder how life would have turned out for us if our ancestor had chosen the other side of the river?"

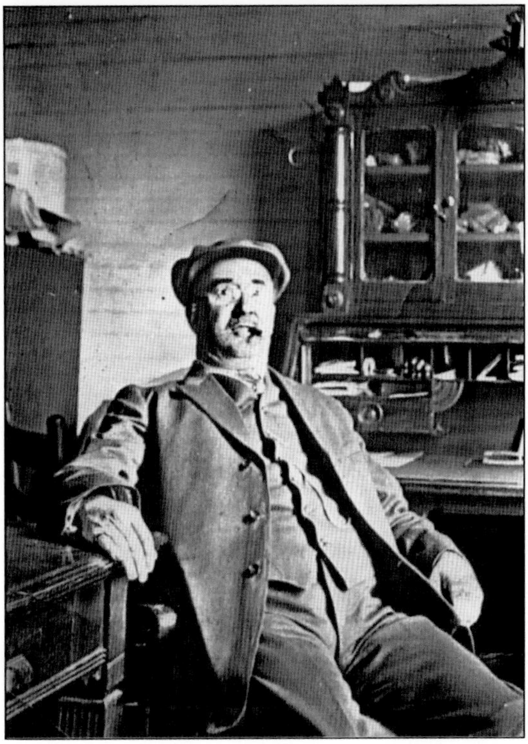

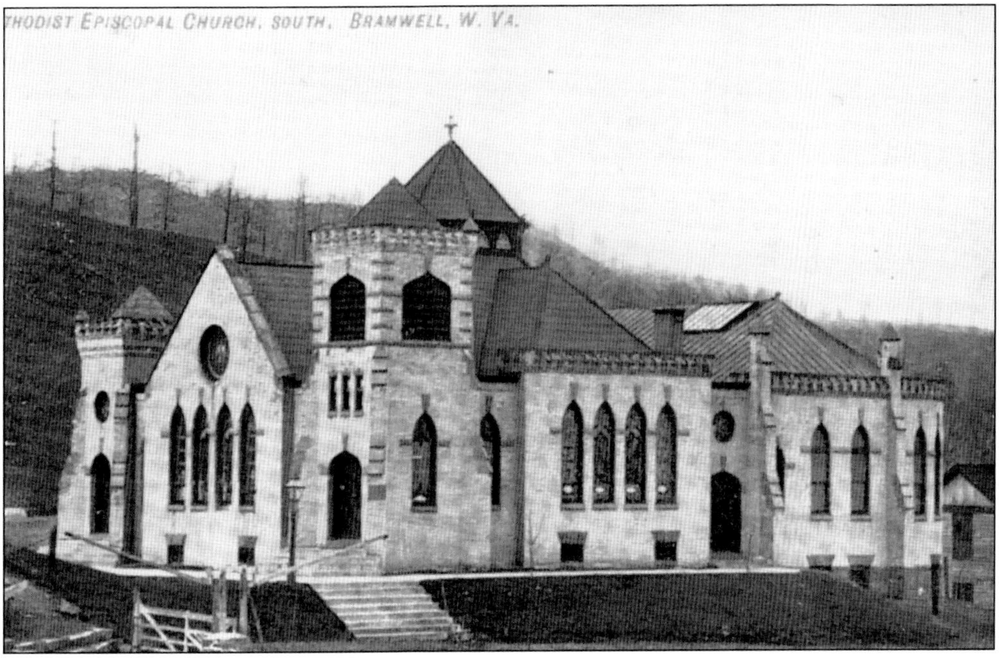

Methodist Church. The Queen Anne church commands attention from its perch on a knoll above Simmons/Freeman. Harry Bowen spearheaded the effort to have it constructed in 1905. Stories are that after Isaac T. Mann had the stone Presbyterian church built in 1903, Bowen wanted to outdo him. The oak interior and stained-glass windows seemed to fulfill Bowen's wishes. It became the Elizabeth Bowen Jones Memorial Methodist Church.

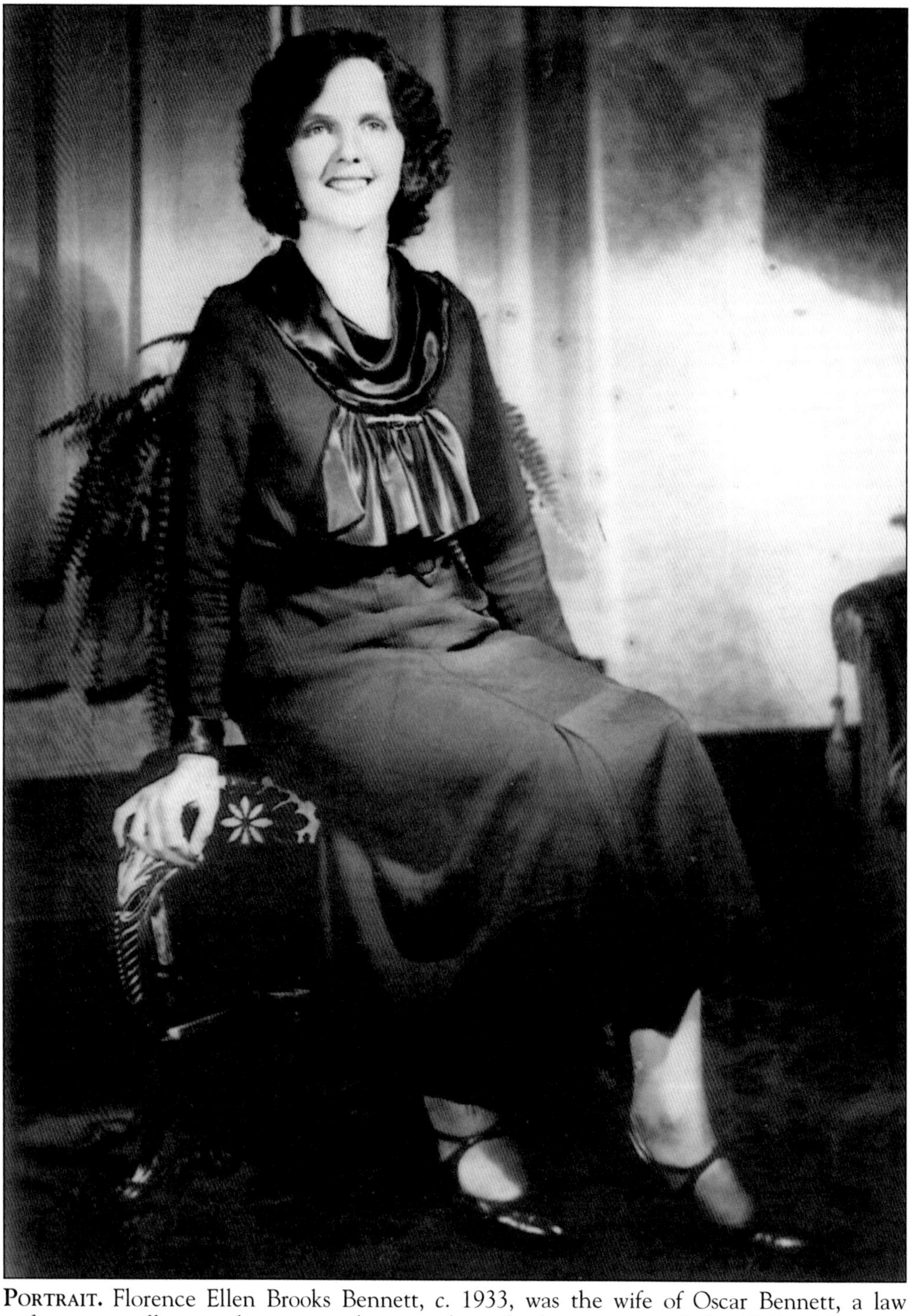

PORTRAIT. Florence Ellen Brooks Bennett, *c.* 1933, was the wife of Oscar Bennett, a law enforcement officer in the town and county from the late teens until the 1940's. He was a Baldwin-Felts detective and a survivor of the 1920 Matewan Massacre. The Bennett home was built on a stone cliff and looked across Spice Creek to Spicertown. (Courtesy of Betty Ann Hamilton and Jeannie Monte.)

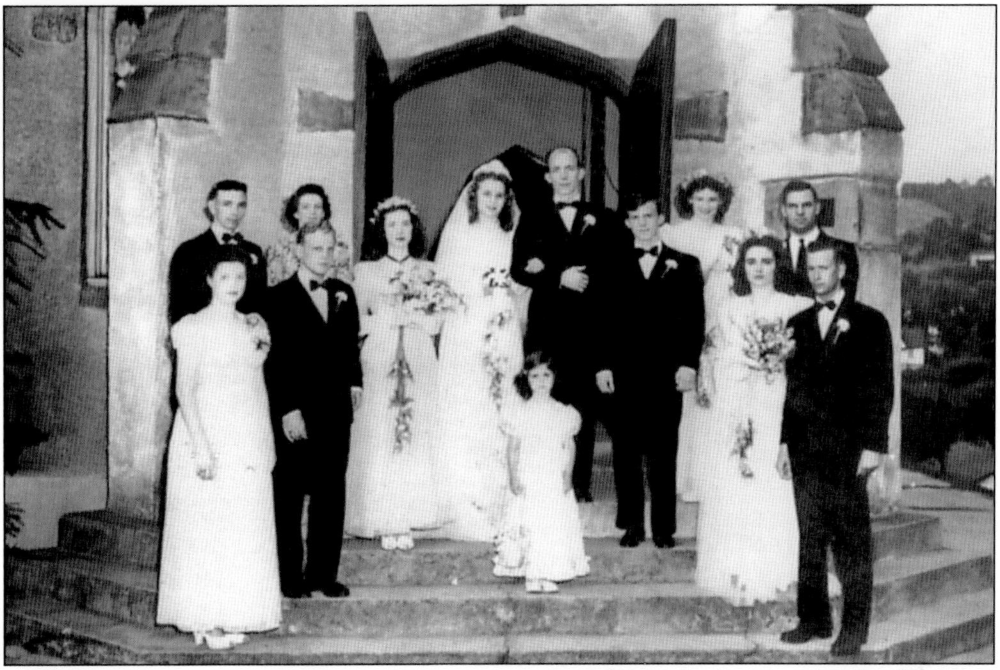

JUNE BRIDE. On June 15, 1946, a popular couple weds at the Methodist church. The flower girl in front is Ruth Gail Bennett. From left to right behind her are (front row) Dorothy Walker, Harry "Buddy" Bennett, maid of honor Imogene Garnett, bride Betty Ann Bennett, groom Romie Hamilton, best man Robert Hamilton, Margie Miles, and Raymond Corbin; (back row) Ray Haynes, organist Sadie Tabor Shupe, Lee Hamilton, and Reverend Pascal. The groom was a teacher and coach at Bramwell High School. (Courtesy of Betty Ann Hamilton and Lenora Jean Bennett.)

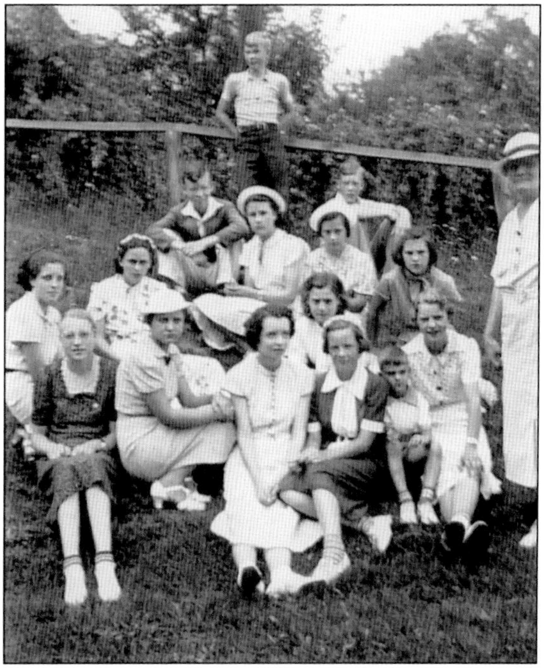

SUNDAY SCHOOL. Pictured are Mrs. Robert (Beulah) Hill's Sunday school class in 1935. She is standing at the right, and the others are unidentified. The picture was taken beside the Elizabeth Jones Memorial Methodist Church. (Courtesy of Lava Yost Staton.)

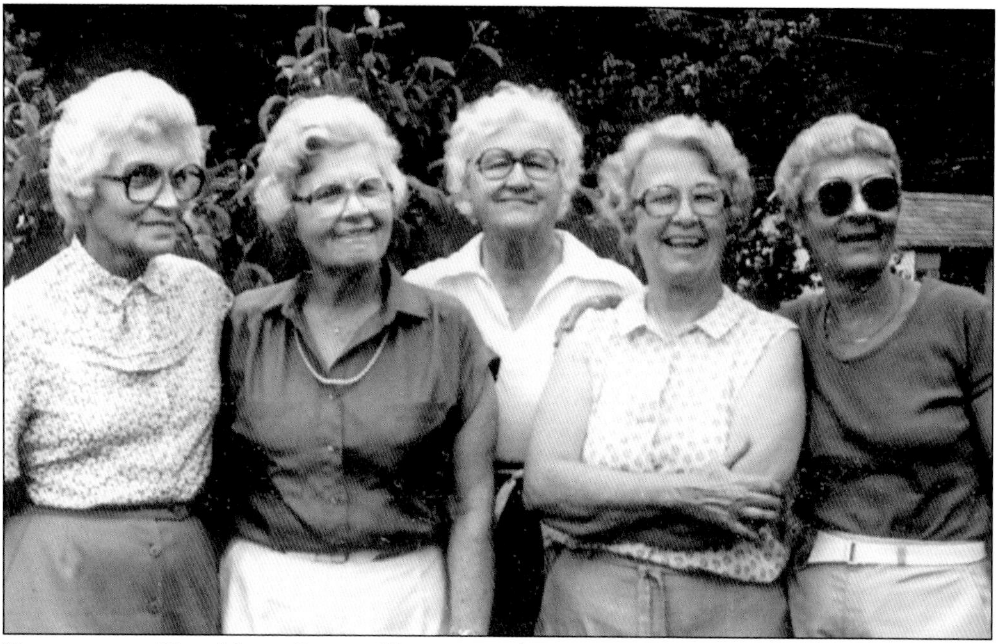

DESCENDANTS. To celebrate Bramwell's centennial year in 1988, Doris Belcher Hall (left) joined the "Hill Sisters," great-granddaughters of Col. Greene Belcher, an original settler of Bramwell Hill following the Civil War. They are, from left to right, Lillian Pierce, Marie Tabor, Dorothy Edmunds, and Lois Dudash. Lil, Dot, and Marie were pillars of the Methodist church. All four of the sisters were excellent cooks, but Marie was known far and wide for her yeast rolls. (Courtesy of Dr. Wilson Tabor.)

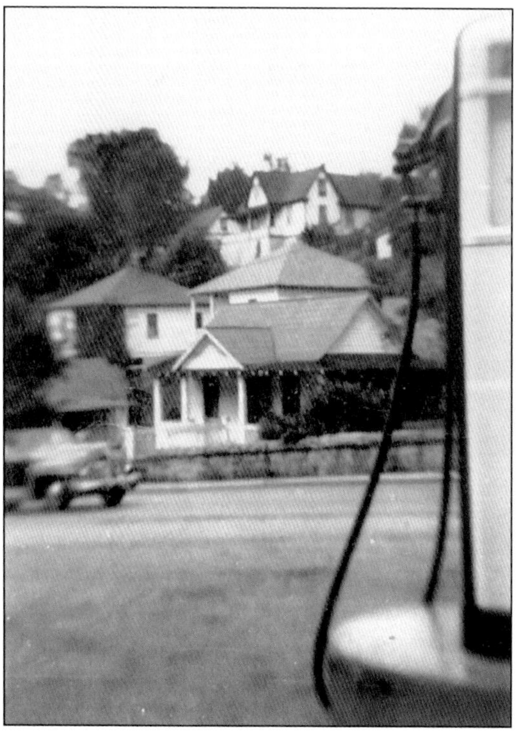

THE HILL. Booth Hill was located on the Spicertown side of Route 52. During the days when coal mining was a booming industry, very few areas of land were vacant. In this snapshot taken from Gibson's Esso Station, the largest house visible was built by the Blanton family in 1896. None of these houses exist today. (Courtesy of Lenore Jean Bennett.)

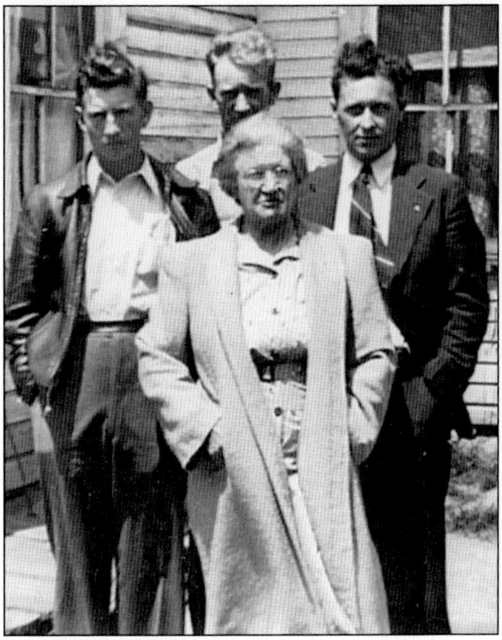

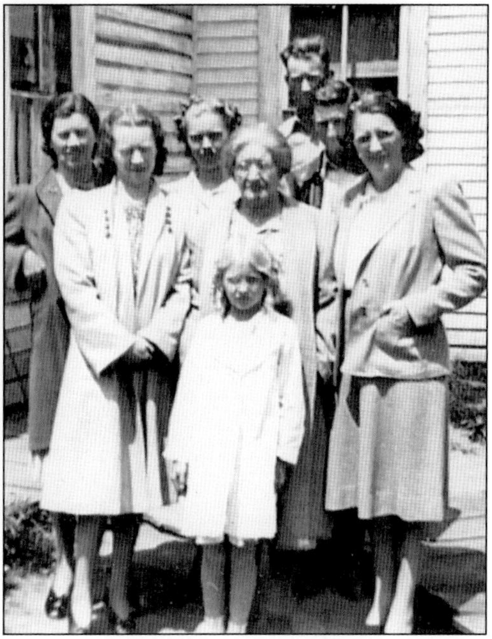

DUNAGAN. Jennie Dunagan moved from Bramwell Hill to Booth Hill in the 1940s. Her family gathered at the homeplace on the mountain for photographs in 1938. In the left image she is with, from left to right, her sons, Charles and Emory, and her son-in-law, Arnold Brown. In the photograph on the right, from left to right, are (first row) the baby, Josephine; (second row) Edna, Jennie (mother), and Irene; (third row) Elizabeth, Vieda, and Charles; (fourth row) Emory. (Courtesy of Josephine Carver.)

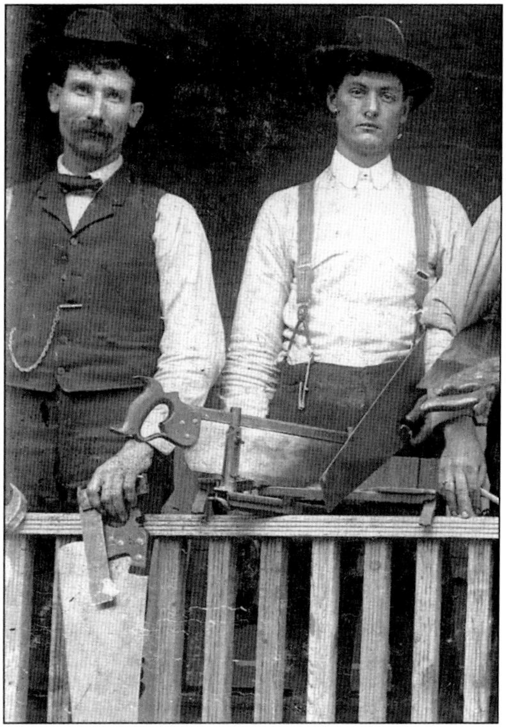

CLARK. J. Lee Clark and son Ivan were building contractors and entrepreneurs. Their work was seen in several counties and two states. Ivan owned Clark's Store at Spicertown. Taking advantage of any investment opportunity, he erected the first pre-fab houses after World War II. Knowing there would be a great influx of workers when a railroad tunnel was started at Coopers in 1947, he built a dozen houses almost overnight. (Courtesy of John Butt.)

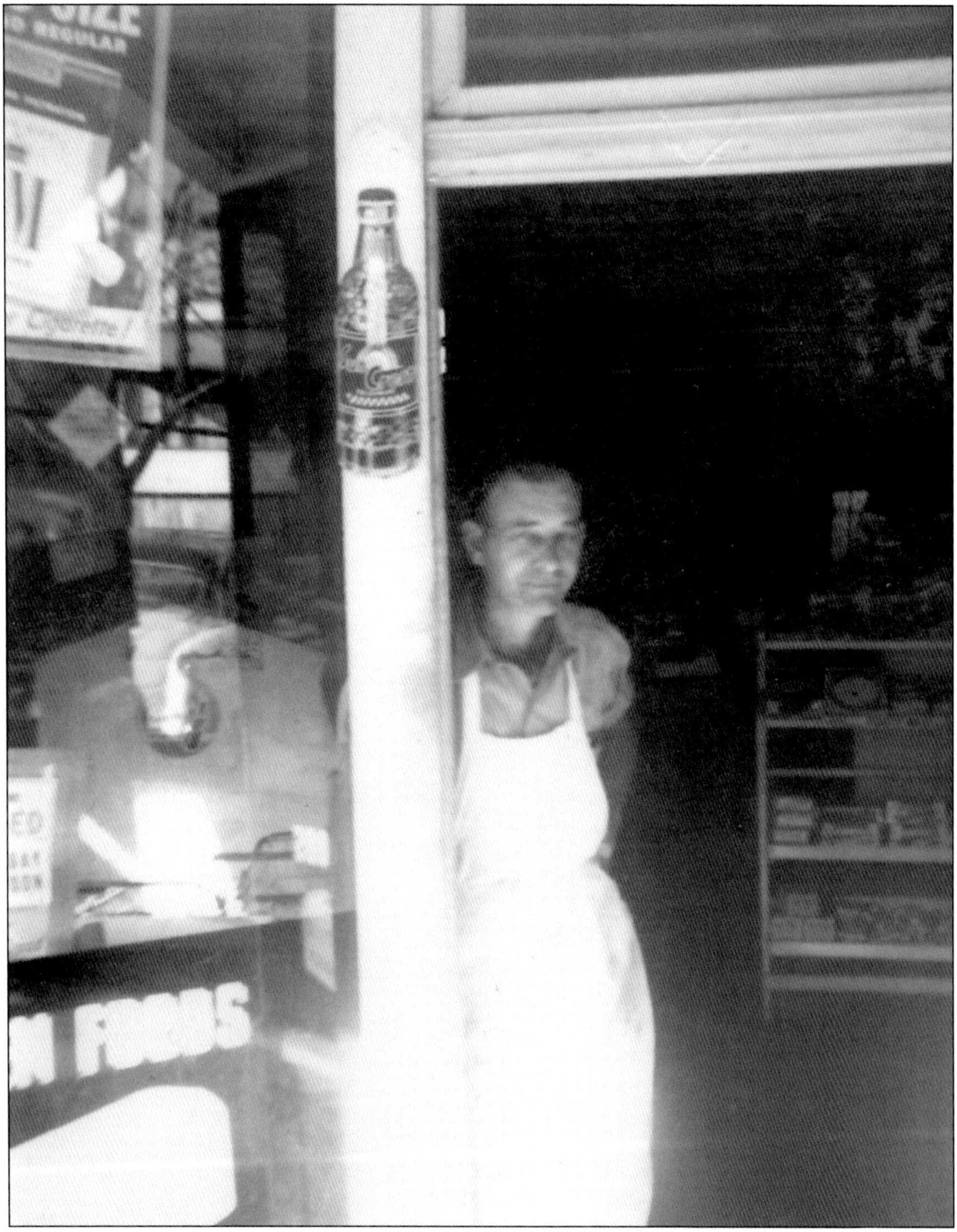

Jot 'Em Down. Sexton's Store was opened by Douglas J. Sexton and predated World War II. One side housed groceries and the other dry goods. Doug's one-stop shopping and convenience store rolled into one was unique and carried everything without competing with the four coal company stores of Bramwell, Freeman, and Coopers. The day the war ended, Doug brought out fireworks and Roman candles, which he had been saving. Children who had never seen fireworks watched all evening as the August sky was lit, as much in awe of them as they were that the war had ended. Later, Doug's nephew, Reginald Sexton, who worked as an engineer during the war, and moved back home. Here, he stands at the door of Sexton's Store in this 1955 photo made by James "Buzzy" Dawson.

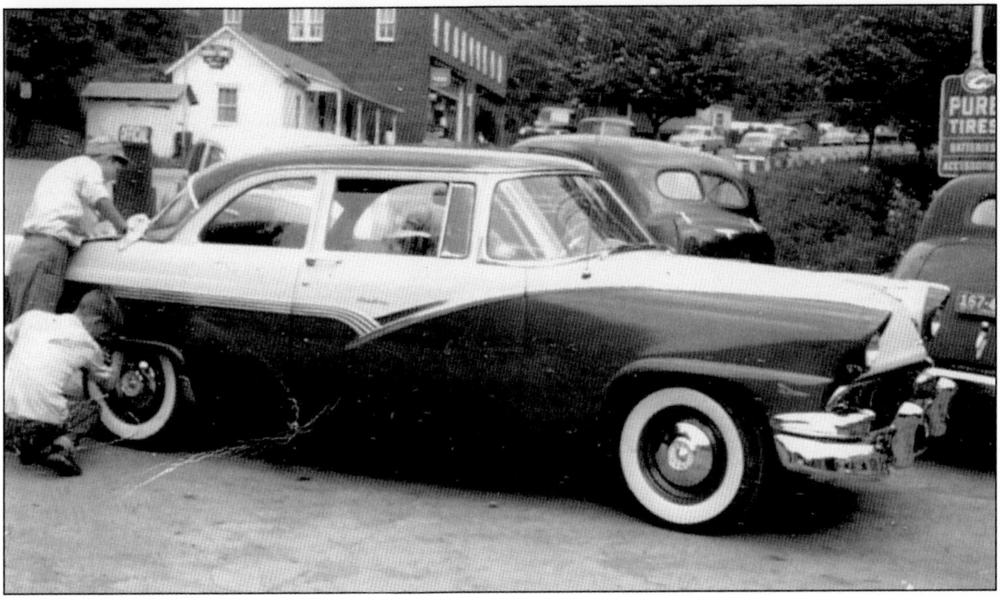

GLEAMING CHROME. The new 1956 Ford Fairlane is being polished at the Pure Oil Service Station located on a busy Route 52 in Freeman. Sexton's Store is the brick building in the background.

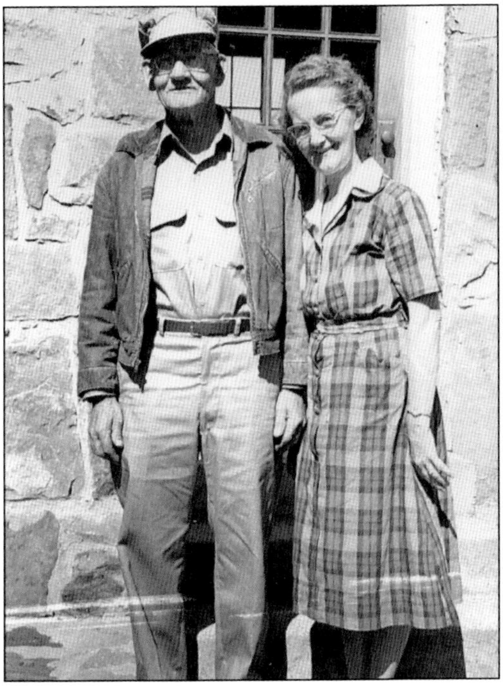

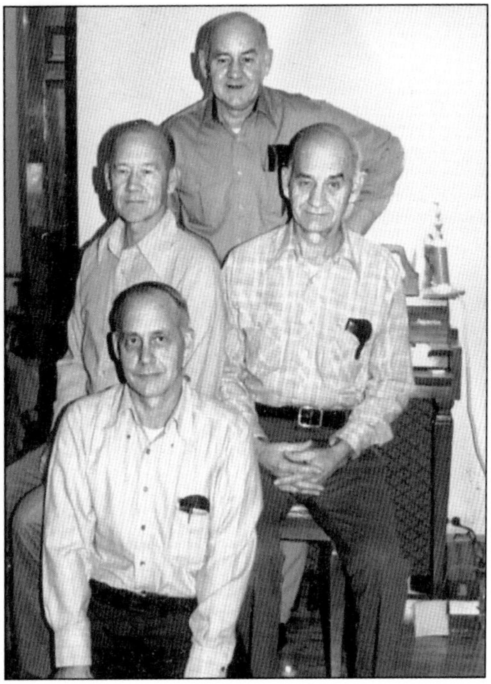

SEXTON. Mason "Mate" and Bertha Harman Sexton are pictured with their boys. Sexton was a businessman, and his wife was active in the Democratic party. In the right photograph are, from left to right, (front row) Harman; (middle row) Ray and Reginald; (back row) Frank. Each has been successful in his field; Reginald M. Sexton was an engineer on the Manhattan Project in Oak Ridge, Tennessee, from the late 1930s through World War II. (Courtesy of Harman "Corky" Sexton.)

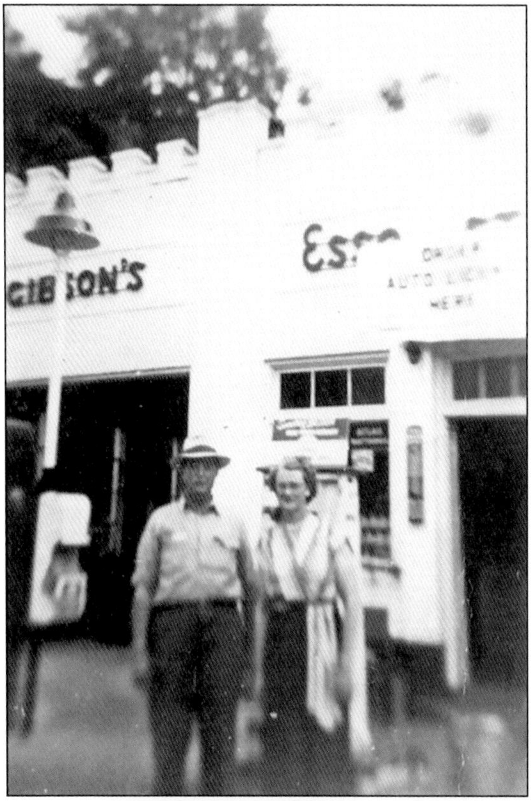

FULL SERVICE STATION. Fletcher and Eva Gibson owned and operated Gibson's Esso Station across Route 52 from Sexton's Store. They pumped the gas, fixed the flats, and employed many teenagers so they could earn "show fare." This photo was made *c.* 1948. (Courtesy of Lenore Jean Bennett.)

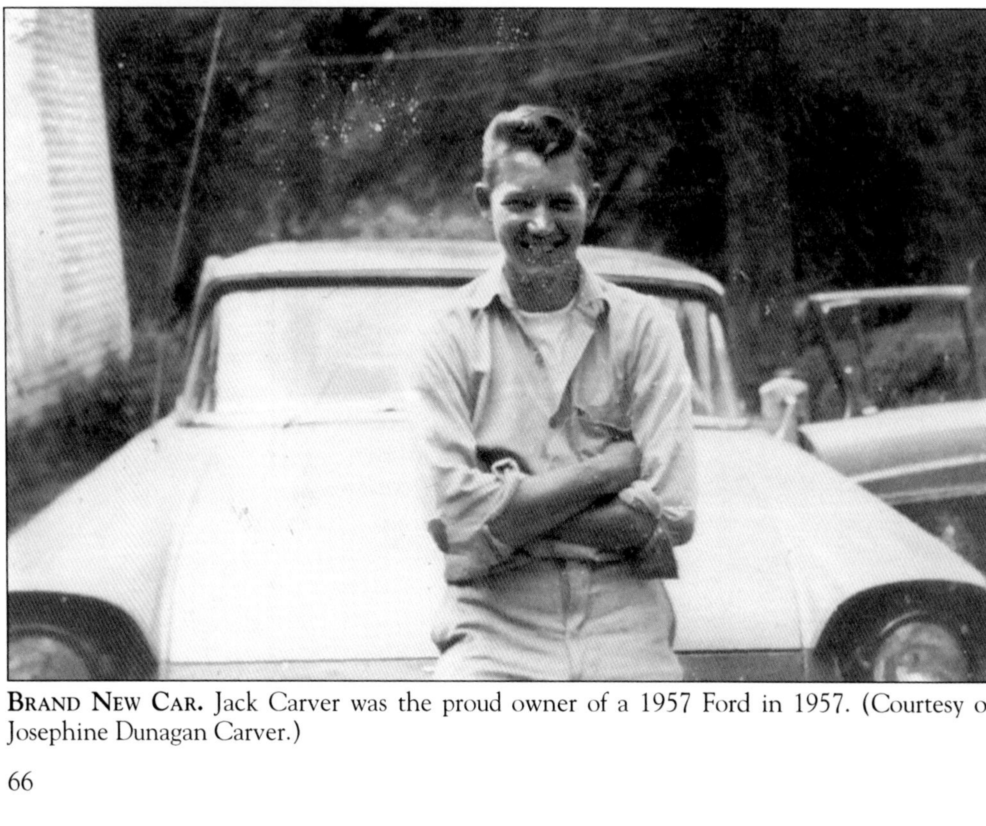

BRAND NEW CAR. Jack Carver was the proud owner of a 1957 Ford in 1957. (Courtesy of Josephine Dunagan Carver.)

JUST RESTING. Buddy Miles, Fletcher Gibson, and Harry Bennett take a break down at the Esso gas station. Bennett went by two different nicknames, "Beef" and "Buddy." (Courtesy of Lenore Jean Bennett.)

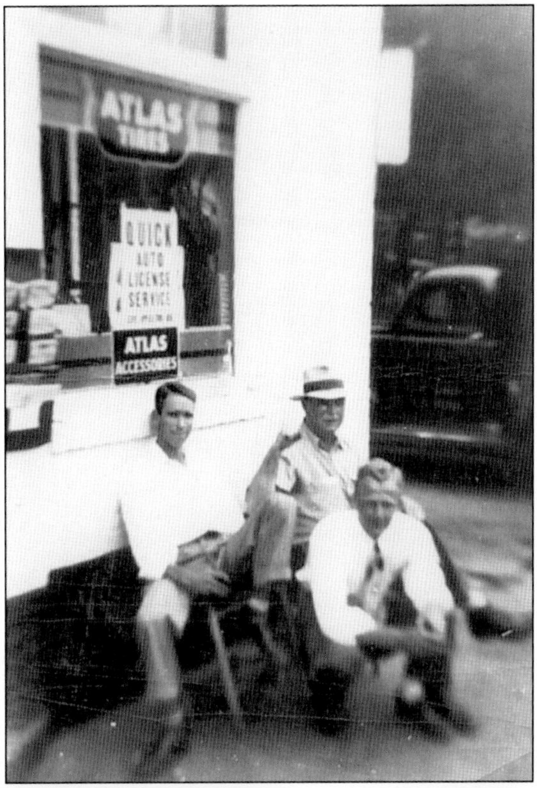

WOMEN OF THE CHURCH. On Easter Sunday, March 21, 1965, the senior women of the Methodist church were honored for their years of service. They were all early residents of Bramwell and longtime members of Woman's Society of Christian Service (WSCS). From left to right are (front row) Della Yost, Louise D. Thacker, Mae Bennett, Beulah Hill, Jenny Dunagan, and Ann Jones; (back row) Effie Maxey, Pearl Queen, Cora Lee Scott, Bess Haynes, Effie Kelly, Effie Miles, and Hattie Kelly. (Courtesy of *Bluefield Daily Telegraph*.)

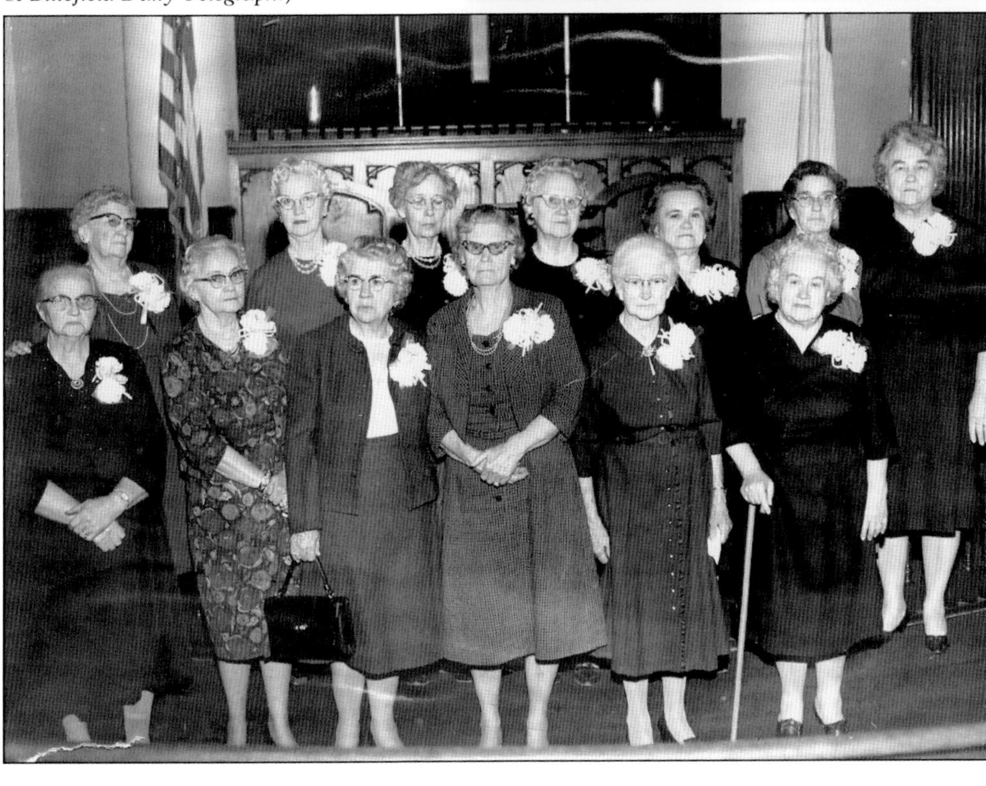

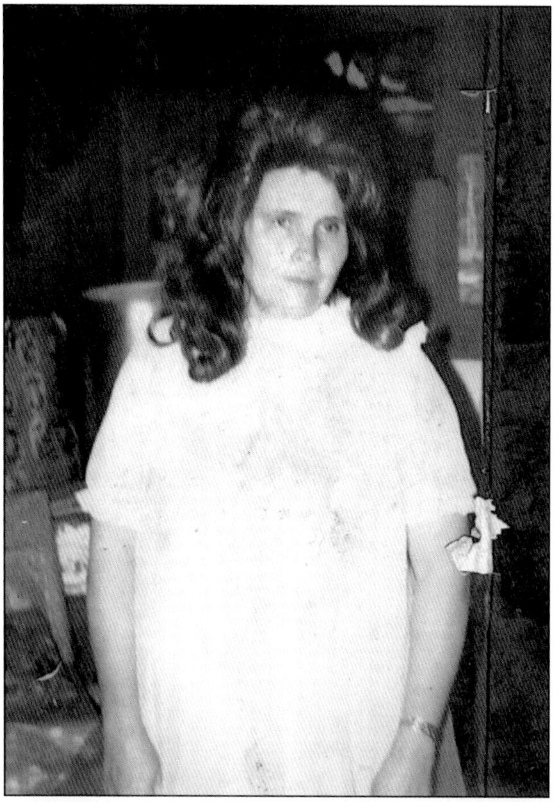

LAMBERT. Ruth Lambert Lewis was the daughter of "Granny" Lambert, who had a dairy on top of the mountain above Spicertown. All of her children worked with her. Granny was a petite woman who always wore a sunbonnet and apron when she delivered milk all over Bramwell. Ruth and her husband, Harry, bought the original Spicer homeplace where she resides. (Courtesy of Debbie Lewis.)

LEWIS. The Lewis family also lived on the mountain above Spicertown. The brothers are William, Harry, and John Lewis. Harry and Ruth Lambert married and lived near the dairy for many years. They later purchased the oldest house in Spicertown, the original Spicer homeplace. (Courtesy of Debbie Lewis.)

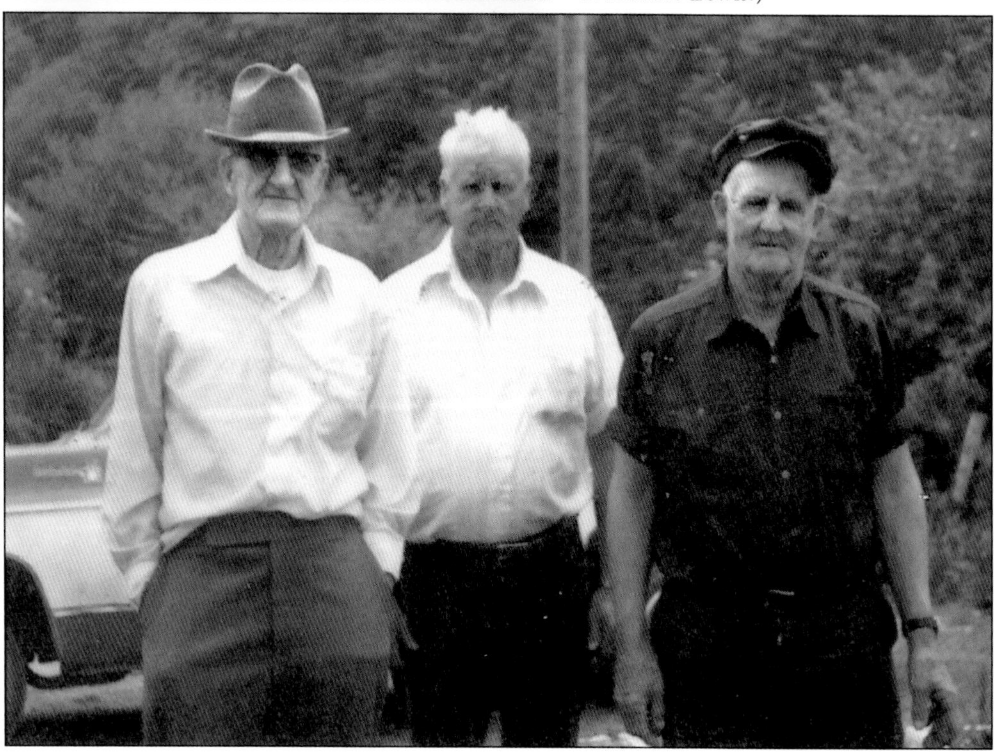

YOST DAIRY. One of the independent businesses in the Bramwell area was the Yost Dairy, down the river. Thurman Yost stands in front of the dairy building *c.* 1939. (Courtesy of Lava Yost Staton.)

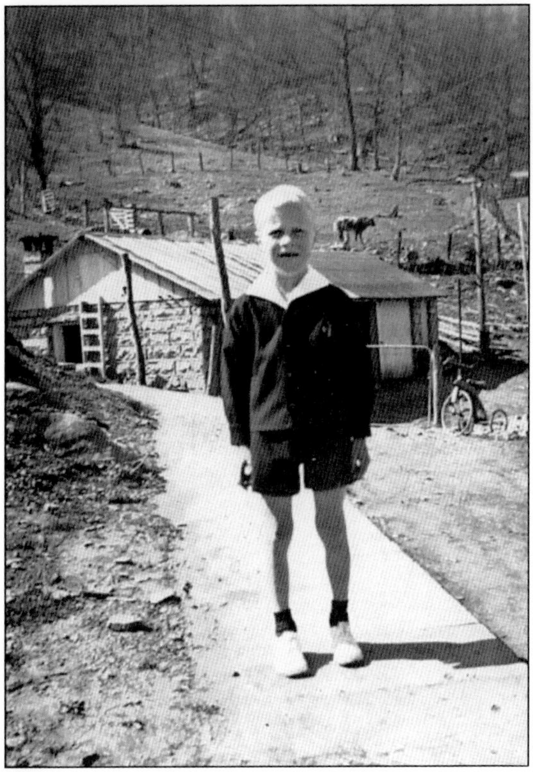

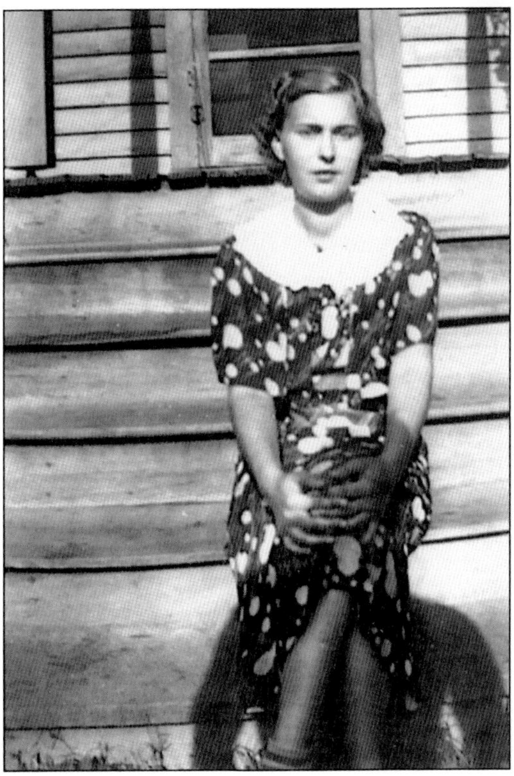

HALL. Jessie Walker Hall is pictured *c.* 1926. Jessie's grandmother built, rebuilt, and operated the Pence Hotel on Main Street in Bramwell. Jessie sits on steps of their Buckeye Coal Company house at Simmons/Freeman. (Courtesy of Jeannine Hall Smith.)

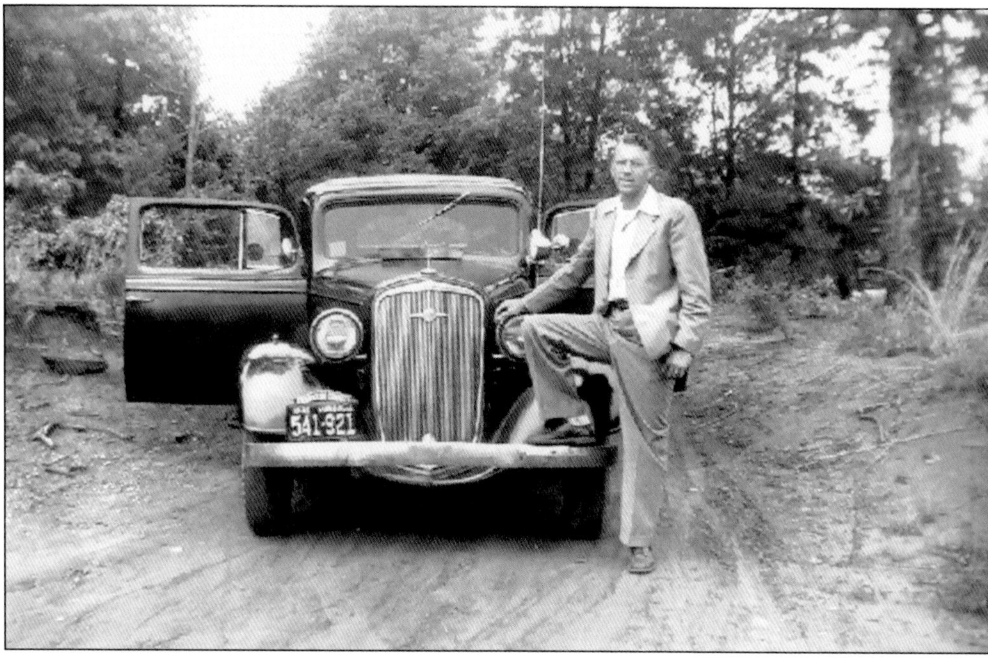

Near Freeman. Donald Jones, who grew up at Simmons/Freeman, was the proud owner of a new car in the mid-1930s. (Courtesy of Steve Goins.)

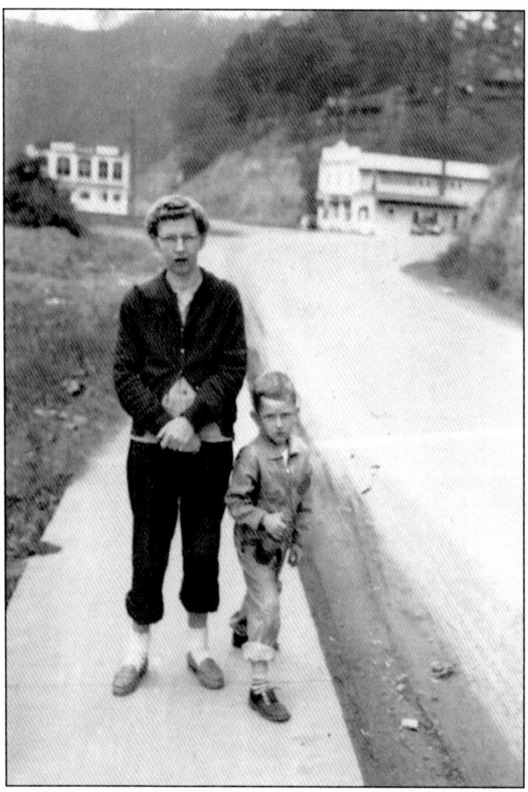

Company Stores, c. 1954. The Caswell Creek Coal & Coke Co. Store and the Booth-Bowen Coal & Coke Co. Store, located at Freeman, are visible in the background. The store on the left was torn down many years ago, while the store on the right has been altered. Both were built when the companies started in business. In the foreground are Grace Hall and Ricky Smith. (Courtesy of Jeannine Hall Smith.)

Buckeye Hollow. Flora Griffith Walker and her baby daughter Daisy are pictured at their homeplace up Buckeye Hollow about 1949. Flora and her husband, Walter "Sawmill" Walker, were the parents of eight children. (Courtesy of Daisy Walker.)

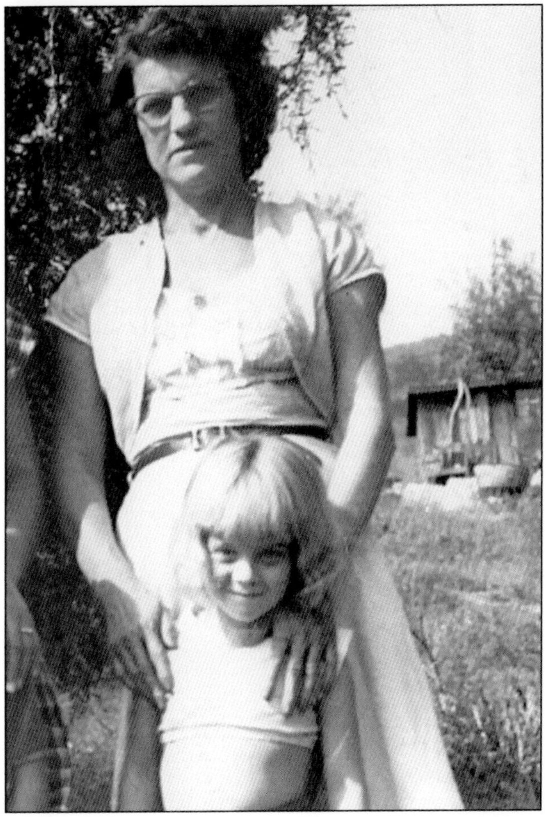

Pinnacle Heights. Looking over this scenic view of land below Pinnacle Rock is the location where Henry H. Tabor first settled. He was instrumental in the organization of the Methodist church. The first church service in the area was held in Tabor's sawmill shed. From there developed the church building we see the Elizabeth Bowen Jones Memorial Methodist Church on page 59.

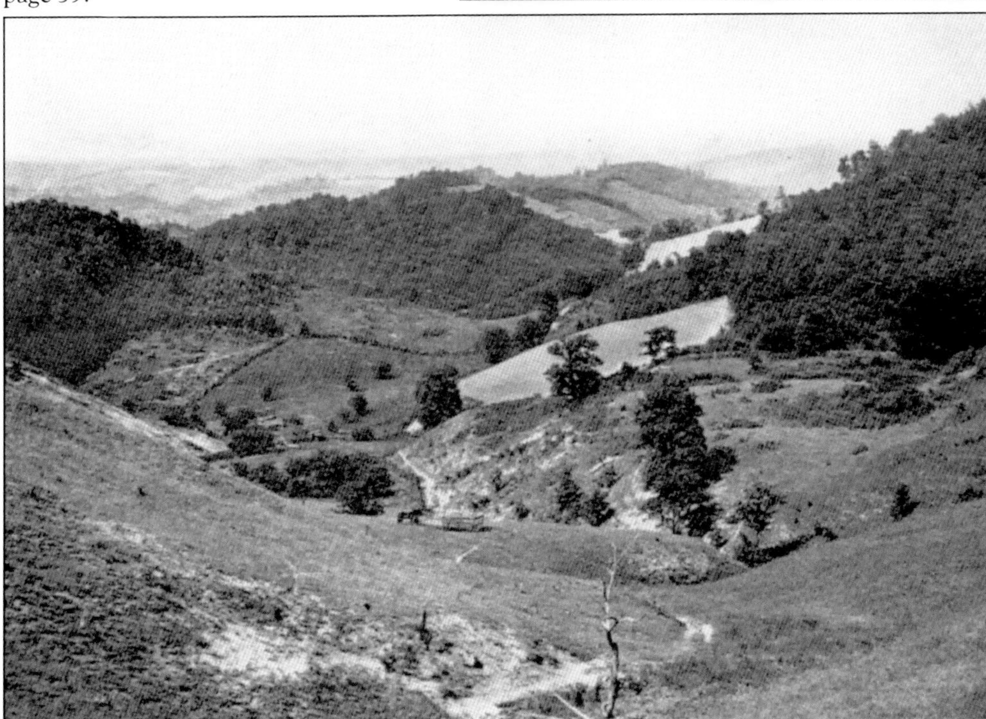

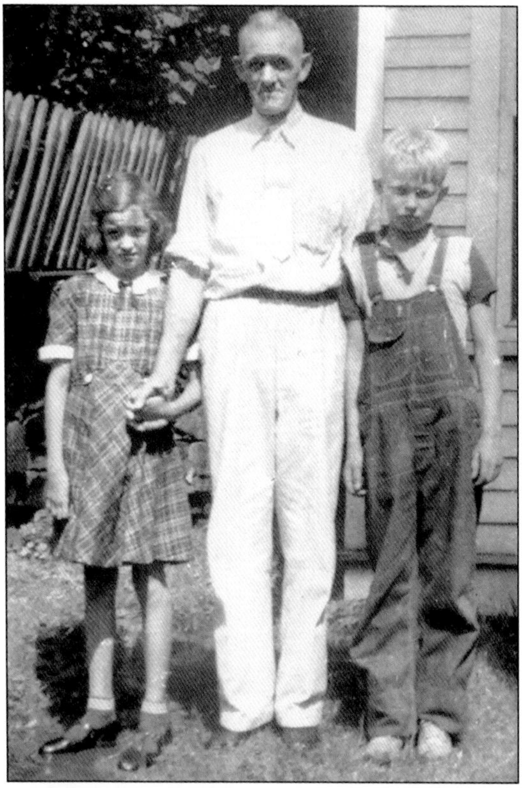

Descendants of Tabor. Samuel Walton Tabor was the grandson of Henry H. Tabor. With him in this photograph from 1938 are his eldest grandchild, Peggy Tabor, and his youngest son, Donald. (Courtesy of Dr. Wilson Tabor.)

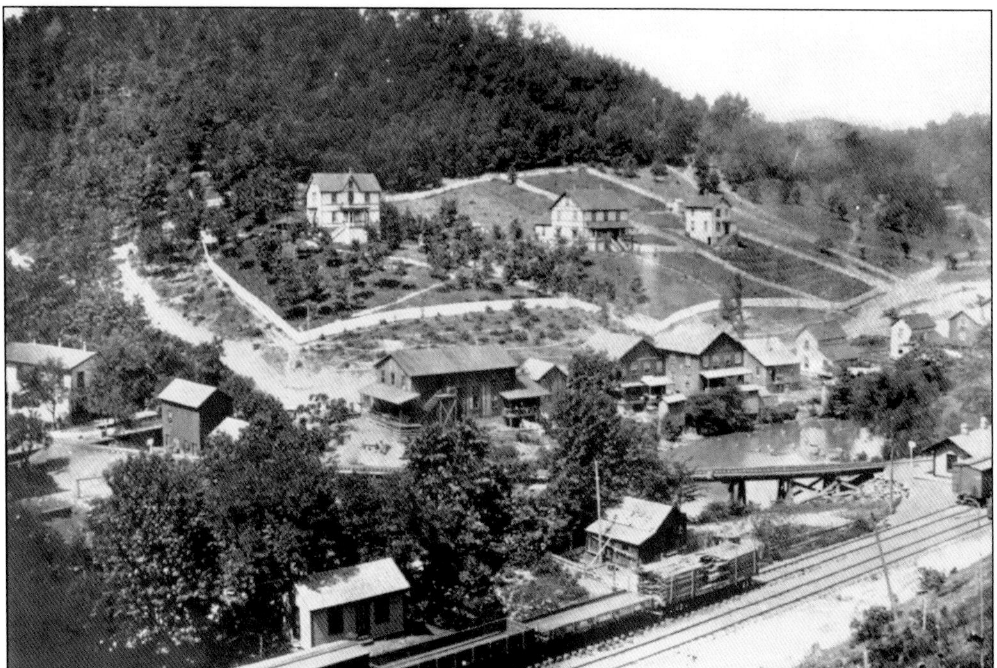

Freeman. This is a bird's-eye view of Freeman as it looked in 1890. The Simmons train station is in the foreground to the right. (Courtesy of Frank Sexton.)

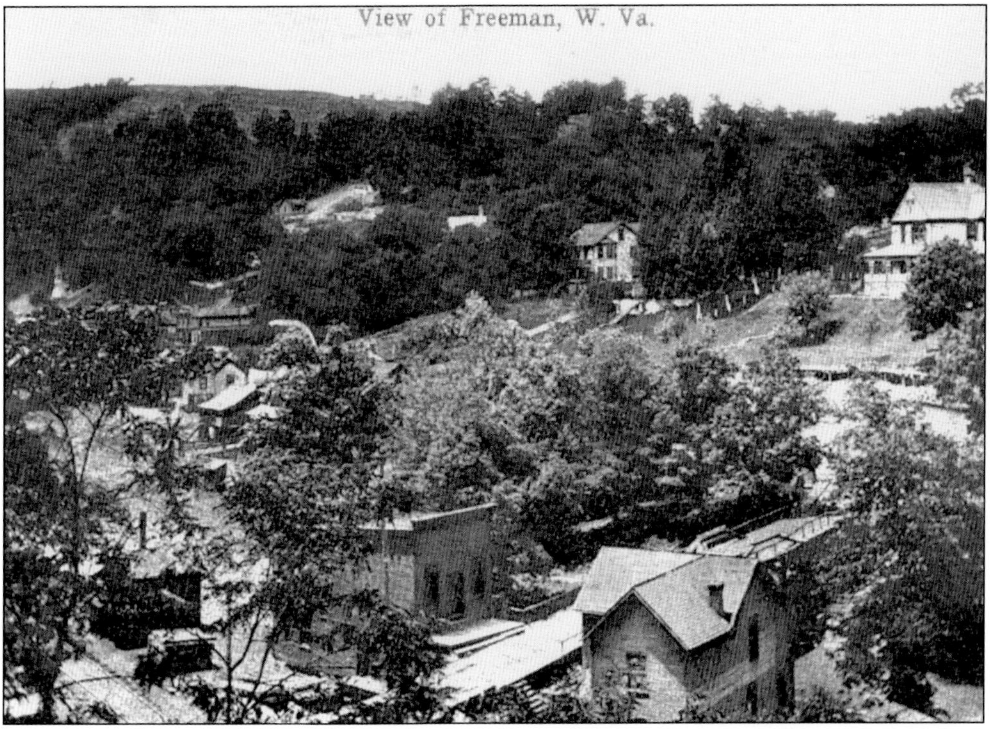

ANOTHER VIEW OF FREEMAN. This later view shows a different angle of Freeman, one taken from Booth Hill. The houses on the distant hill are Caswell Creek Coal Company houses. They are on Jones' Hill, named after Welsh-born Jenkin Jones. The photograph was made *c.* 1915.

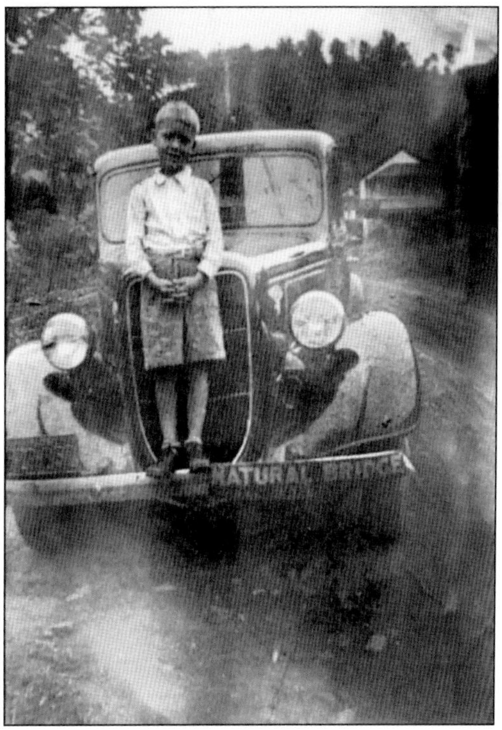

SMILE. In the background of this 1936 snapshot, the Dillard house is visible. Harman Sexton is the boy on the bumper of the 1934 Ford. (Courtesy of Harman "Corky" Sexton.)

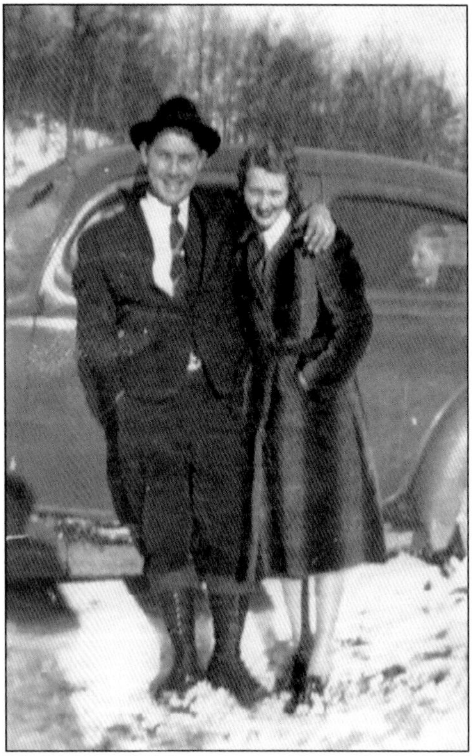

Freeman Residents. Mack and Blanche Bange had chains on their tires in this *c.* 1940 photograph. Their son, Charles, is in the back seat. (Courtesy of Joan Bange Buchanan.)

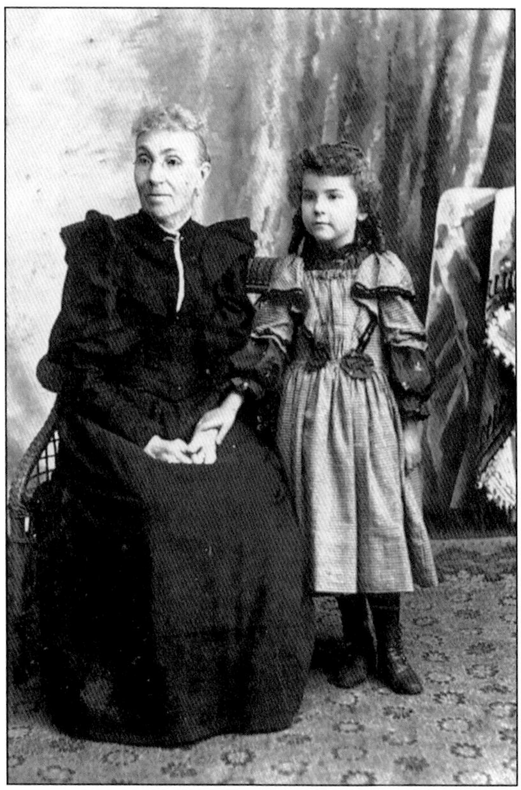

Grandmother Freeman. Pictured are Isabella Freeman and her granddaughter, *c.* 1895. "Belle" was the matriarch of a family destined to succeed in coal mining; she and her third husband, John Freeman; a son-in-law; two sons; and two grandsons were millionaires in Bramwell's heyday. Belle's son Wes was the most colorful member of this fascinating family. The community was officially named Freeman when a post office was established in the area.

The Visit. Sandra Martin, a young neighbor, pays a dress-up visit to Mrs. C.W. "Wes" Freeman in her mansion in "uptown" Bramwell *c.* 1956. (Courtesy of Sandra Martin Beggs.)

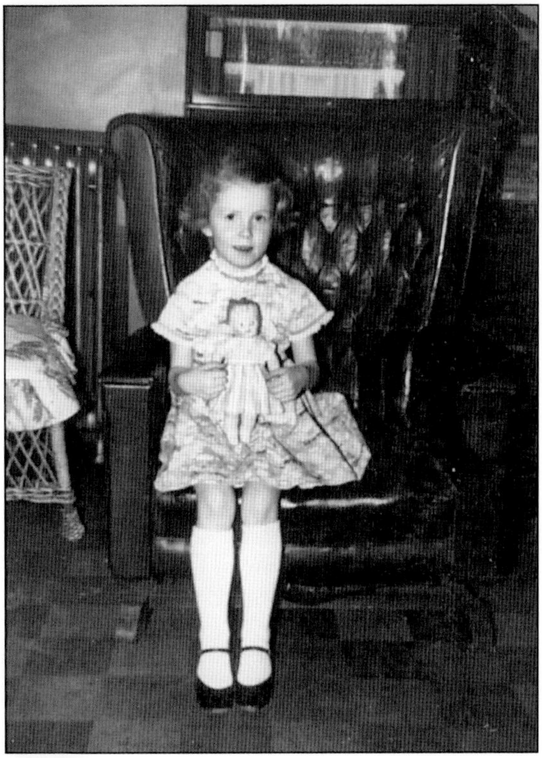

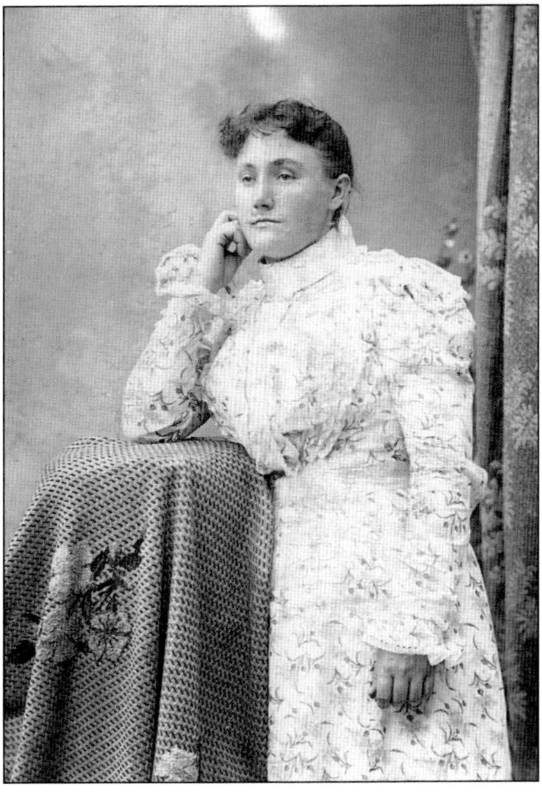

Pianos for Sale. Mrs. W.W. Hamilton and her husband moved to Bramwell in the 1890s to open a piano business. They sold player pianos and advertised "reasonable terms and satisfaction guaranteed." The photograph was made *c.* 1895.

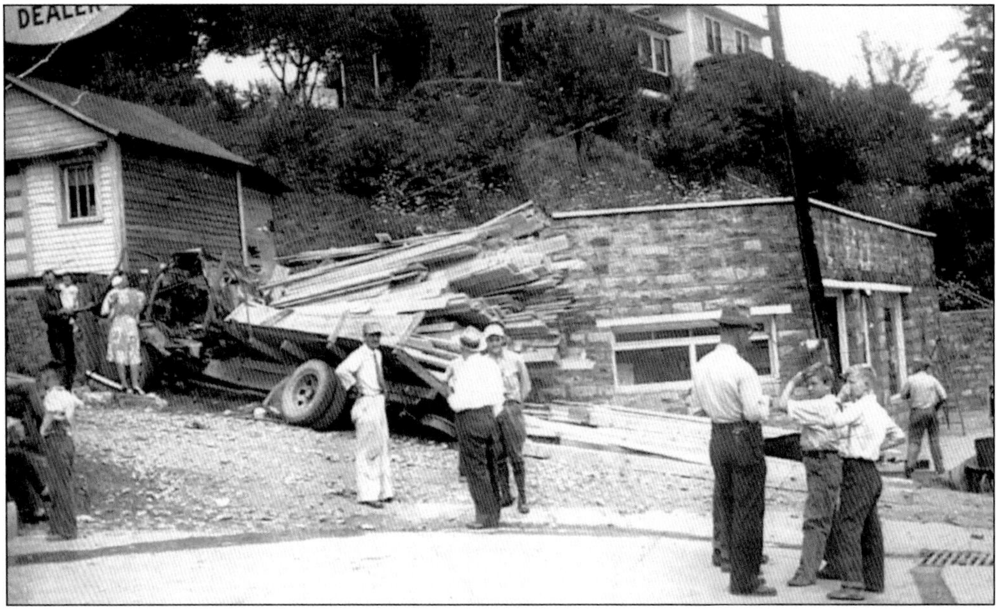

The Sugar Bowl. The stone soda shop the Sugar Bowl was the favorite hangout for teenagers in the early 1940s. All of the school children were "walkers" if they lived as near as two miles from the school. This shop was a good halfway stop for those who lived in Simmons or Spicertown and up Pinnacle way. At least one student would have a nickel for the jukebox. The wreck shown above occurred in 1941 and ended with two fatalities. (Courtesy of Vickie Painter Rushbrook.)

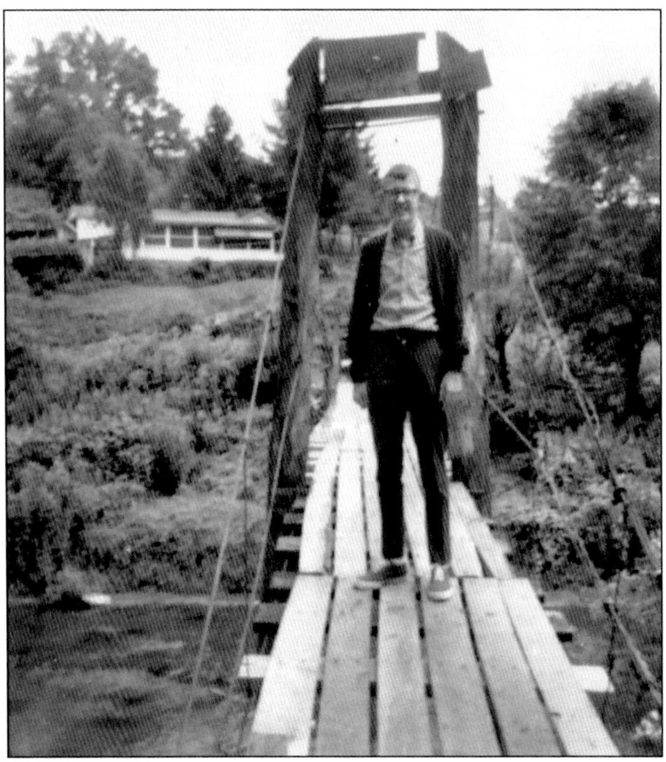

Swinging Bridge. The Bluestone River flows through the community. There were several ways to cross it, and an early one was by the swinging bridge. The bridge spanned the river just past the Baptist church. George Palco's grandson, Mark Wildermuth, tried out the bridge. (Courtesy of Kathleen Palco Sexton.)

Five

Black History

Let me learn now where Beauty is;
My day is spent too far toward night
To wander aimlessly and miss her place;
To grope, eyes shut, and fingers touching space.
—from "Questing" by Anne Spencer

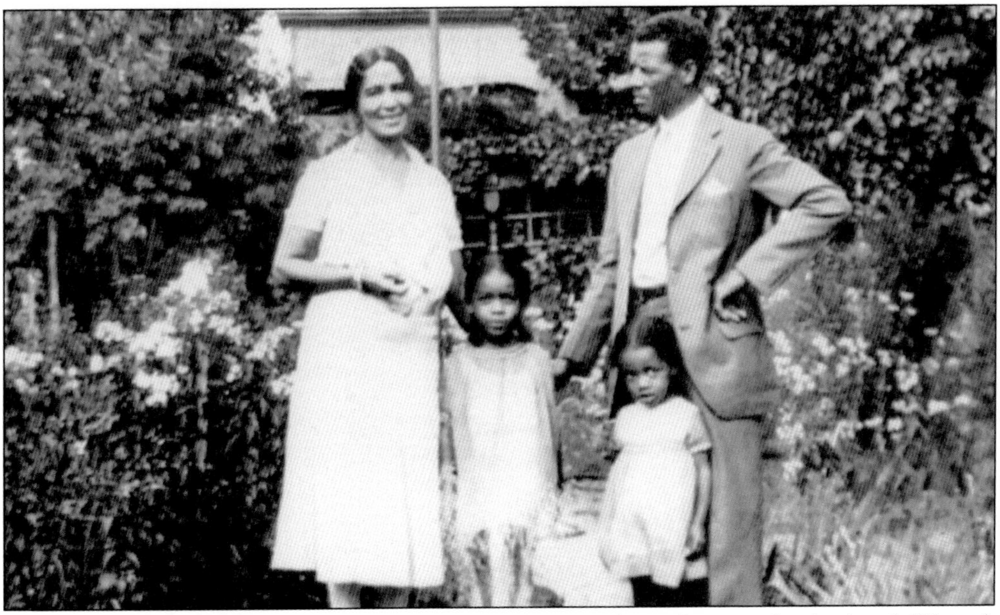

Harlem Renaissance Poet Anne Spencer and Family. Anne Spencer, her husband, Edward; and two grandchildren are shown in her famous garden at their home in Lynchburg, Virgina. Born in Virginia in 1882, Annie Bethel Bannister and her mother, Sarah Louise Scales Bannister, came to Bramwell around 1885 and lived with the family of Sarah's cousin, William Turner Dixie, one of two Negro barbers in town. Anne attended the Virginia Theological Seminary and College in Lynchburg from 1893 until her graduation in 1899. She and Edward were married in Bramwell in 1901 and lived the rest of their lives in Lynchburg, where Anne and her poetry were "discovered" by James Weldon Johnson. Her home was a gathering place for activists and artists including W.E.B. Dubois, Thurgood Marshall, Paul Robeson, and Langston Hughes. (Courtesy of Anne Spencer House and Garden.)

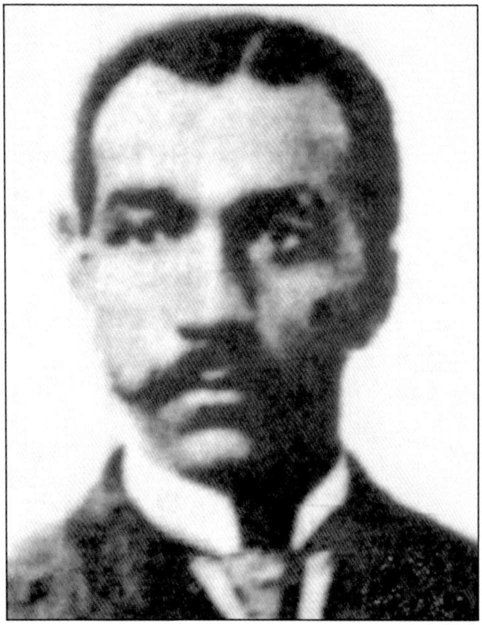

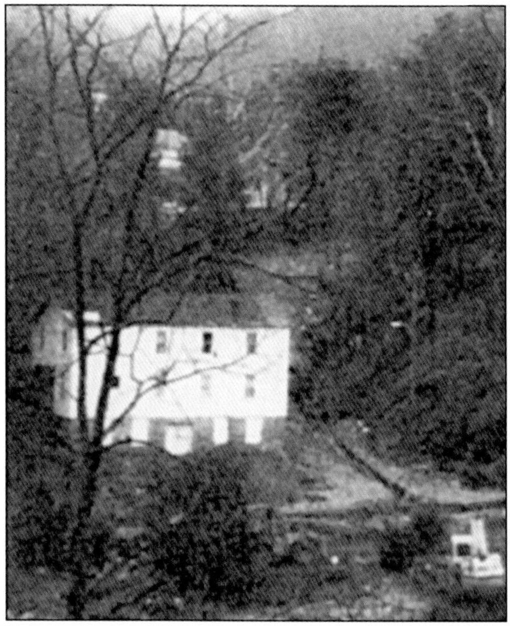

Dr. William Alexander Holley and King Hiram Lodge. Dr. Holley established his practice in Bramwell after receiving a medical degree from Howard University in 1892. He organized the King Hiram Lodge in Bramwell, was granted authority to organize the Royal Craft Grand Lodge, and became the first grant master in and for the State of West Virginia. The King Hiram Lodge, located in Freeman, celebrated its centennial anniversary in 1993.

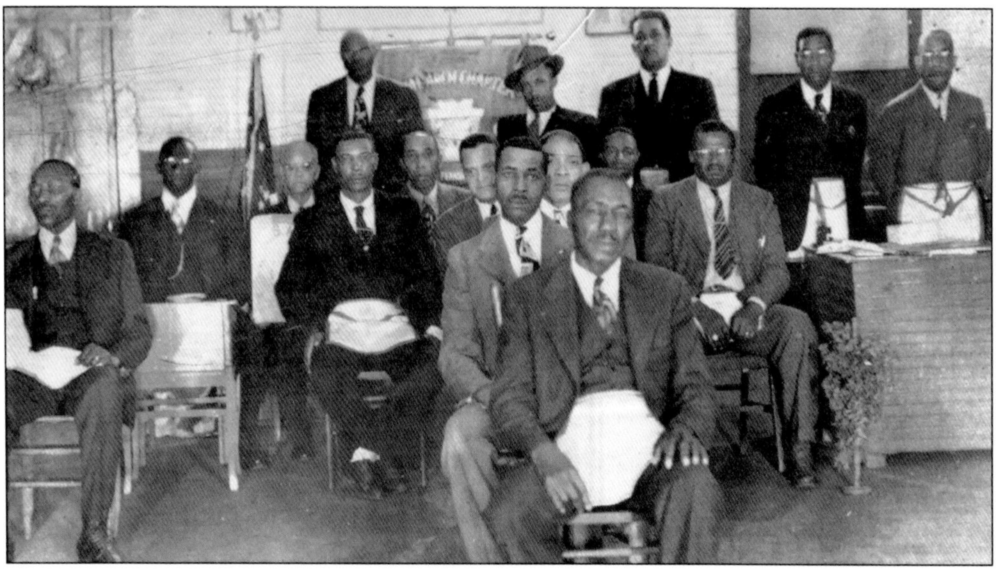

Bramwell Royal Lodge. The officers of chapter #6 are shown in this c. 1943 photograph. Three veils, front to back, are Jerry Williams, James Murrell and Harry Leonard Washington. Seated, from left to right, are Chaplain Martin Phipps, Treasurer Daniel Jackson, F.N. Robinson, Captain of the Host Charlie Robinson, Outside Guard Willie Wilkins, Thomas Hall, Inside Guard George Campbell, and Jerry Jackson. Standing, from left to right, are King Charlie Price, High Priest Ansley Carter, Scribe Lindsey Williams, Recorder Dave Vernon, and Financial Secretary Joseph T. Cook. (Courtesy of King Hiram Lodge collection.)

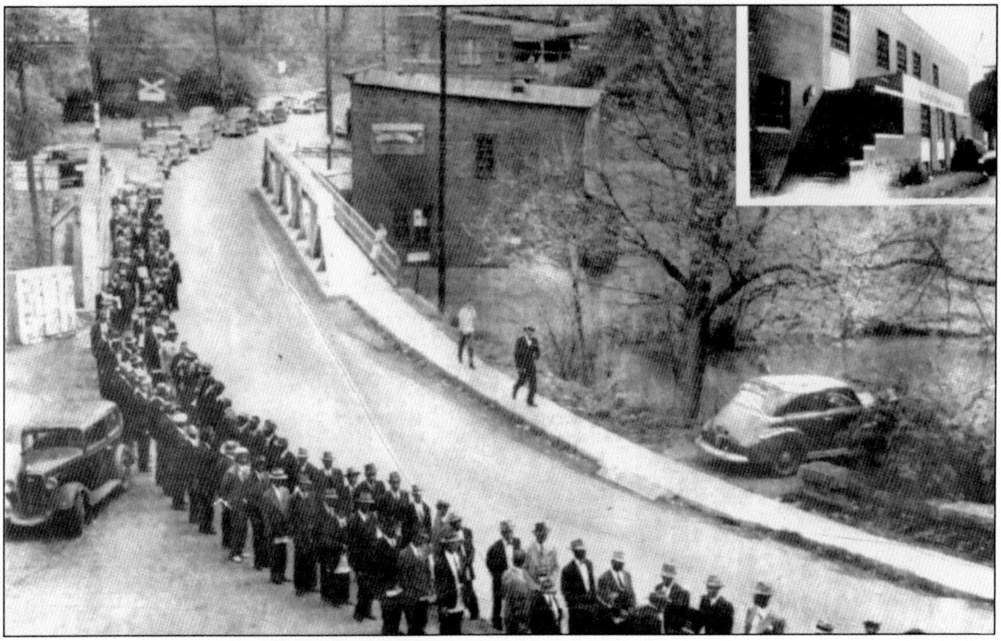

King Hiram Lodge Parade. The purpose of this early spring parade in 1948 from the lodge hall in Freeman to Bluestone High School (inset) was to dedicate and lay the cornerstone of the new school. King Hiram Lodge had 170 active members at that time. (Courtesy of King Hiram Lodge collection.)

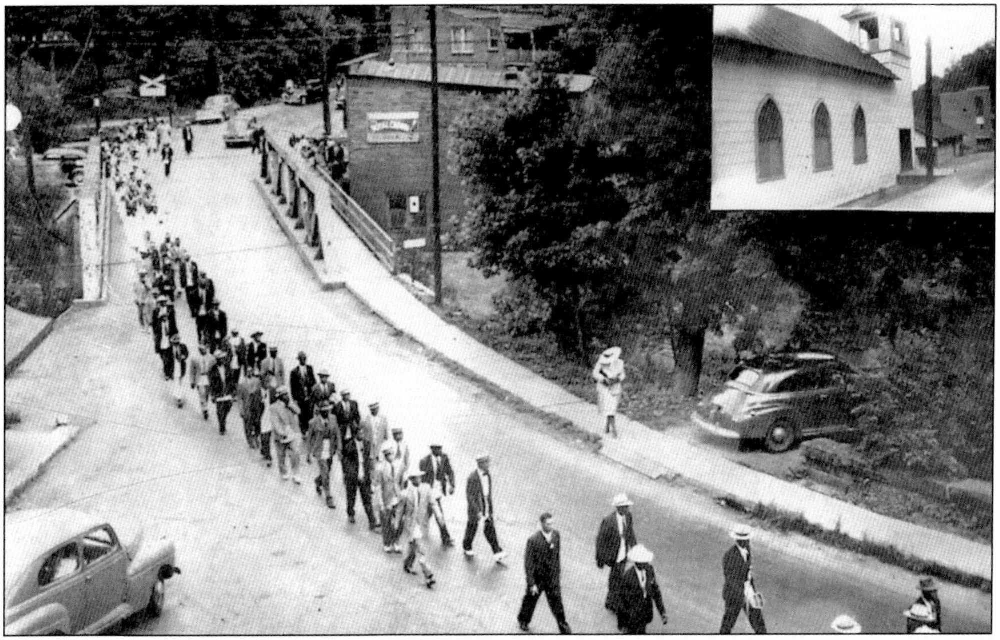

St. John's Day Parade. King Hiram Lodge members march in June 1948 from the lodge hall to Bluestone Baptist Church (inset), located beside Bluestone High School. On the sidewalk is Leona Ferrell Carter taking a picture of her husband, Lawrence, who has turned to face the camera. At the front of the parade in a white suit is marshall Leonard Washington. (Courtesy of King Hiram Lodge collection.)

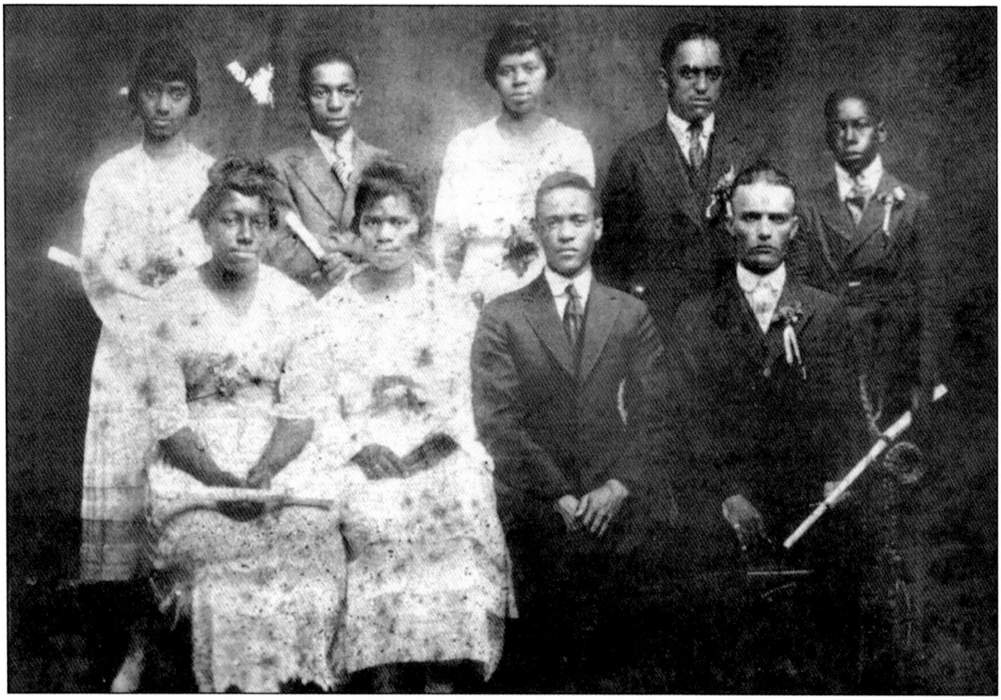

BLUESTONE SCHOOL CLASS OF 1920. From left to right are (seated) Zelma Glenn, Hattie Holley, Principal E.A. Bolling Jr., and Charles Rutherford; (standing) Elzada Tanzemore, Gregory ?, Evon McClanahan, and Freddie Philpott. Edward Anderson Bolling Jr., from Greenbrier County, West Virginia, was the first principal of Bluestone School.

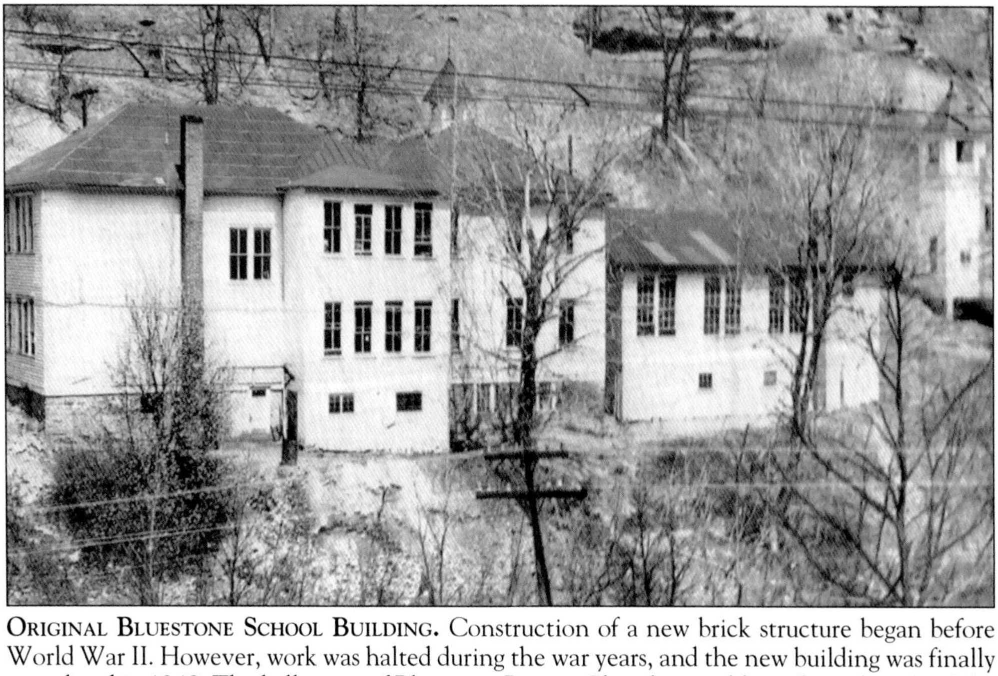

ORIGINAL BLUESTONE SCHOOL BUILDING. Construction of a new brick structure began before World War II. However, work was halted during the war years, and the new building was finally completed in 1948. The bell tower of Bluestone Baptist Church is visible at the right side of the photograph. (Courtesy of Bramwell-Bluestone High School Alumni Association.)

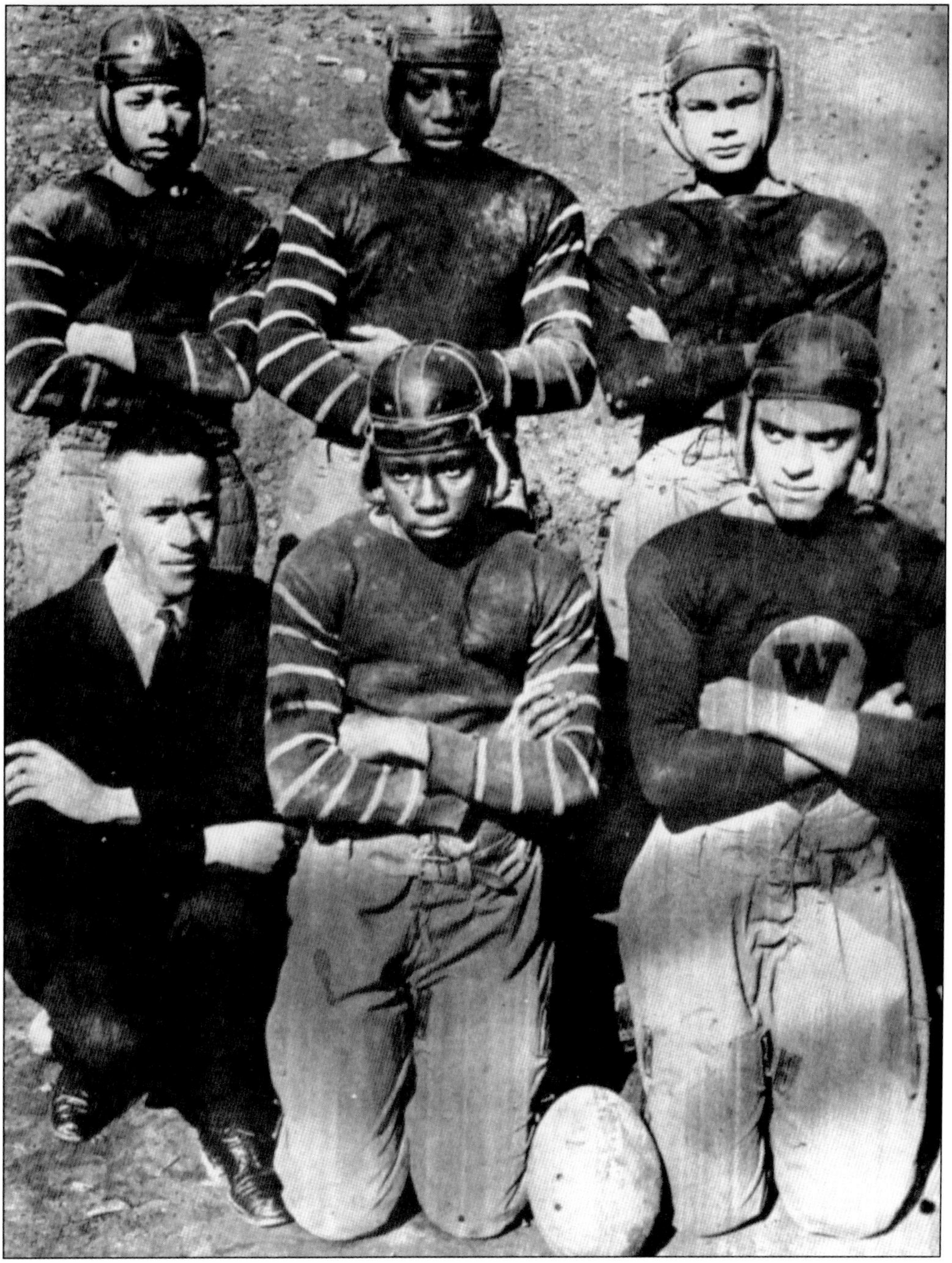

Early Football Players. In this photograph, unidentified team members are wearing leather helmets, customary equipment in the early days of the sport. Principal E.A. Bolling Jr. kneels in a suit. (Courtesy of Bramwell-Bluestone High School Alumni Association.)

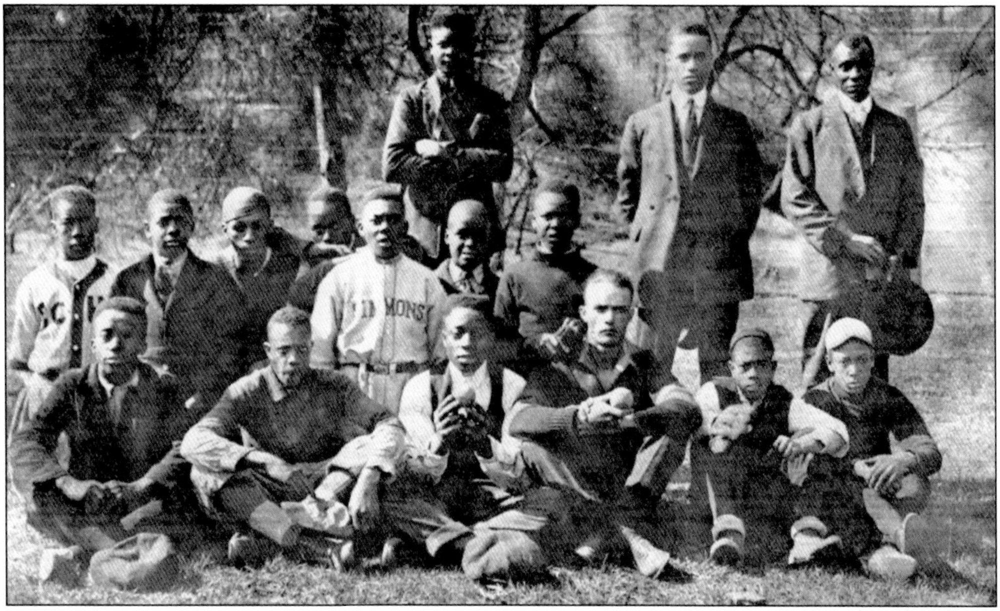

BASEBALL TEAM. Unidentified team members join Principal E.A. Bolling Jr. (standing second from right). "Simmons" is visible on the center uniformed player. Simmons Creek was the first name given to the section of town also known as Freeman. (Courtesy of Bramwell-Bluestone High School Alumni Association.)

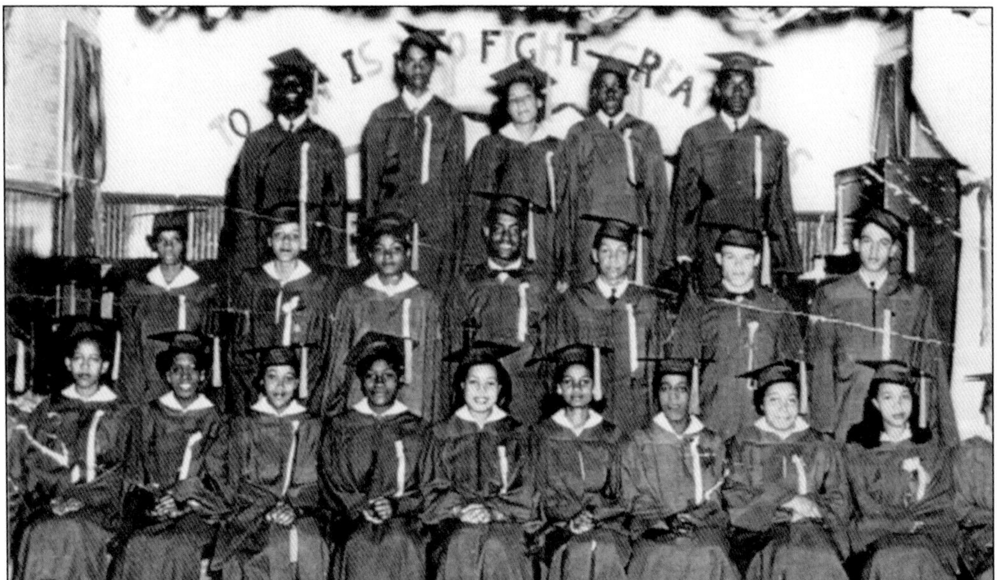

CLASS OF 1944. This smiling group of Bluestone High School graduates includes Edris Henry, who returned to Bluestone as a teacher after graduating from Bluefield State College. From left to right are (front row) Jacqueline Owens, Gladys Palmer, Mildred King, Edris Henry, Synepha Smith, Irene Avery, Thelma Palmer, Hester Coger, and Virginia Carter; (middle row) Alease Hamlit, Aymerlis Haden, Bertha Horton, Walter Lawson, Hopie Davis, Roosevelt Turner; and unidentified person; (back row) Edward Abercrombie, Stafford Wells, Mildred Hairston, Nelson Ferguson, and David Clark. (Courtesy of Edris Henry Miller.)

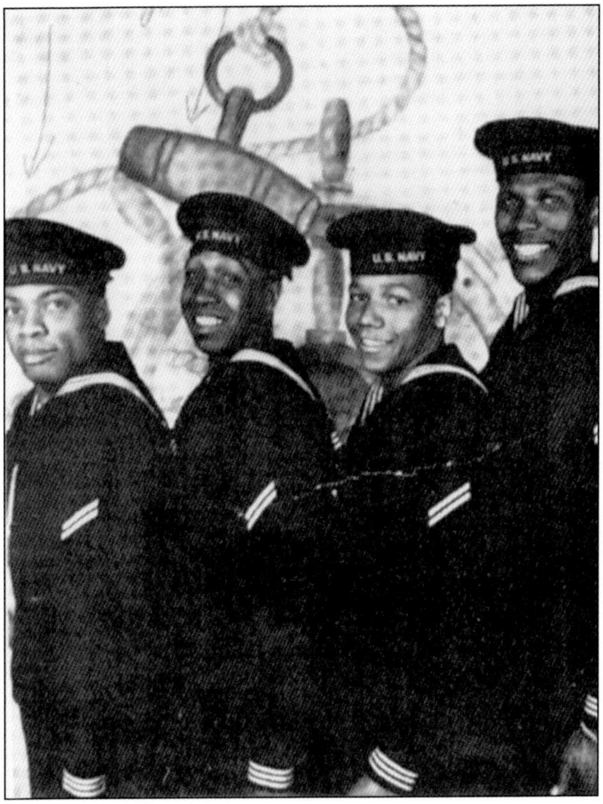

From Bluestone High School to the U.S. Navy. From left to right are sailors Connie Haley, Thomas Wilson Jr., Bobby Washington, and an unidentified person. (Courtesy of Bramwell-Bluestone High School Alumni Association.)

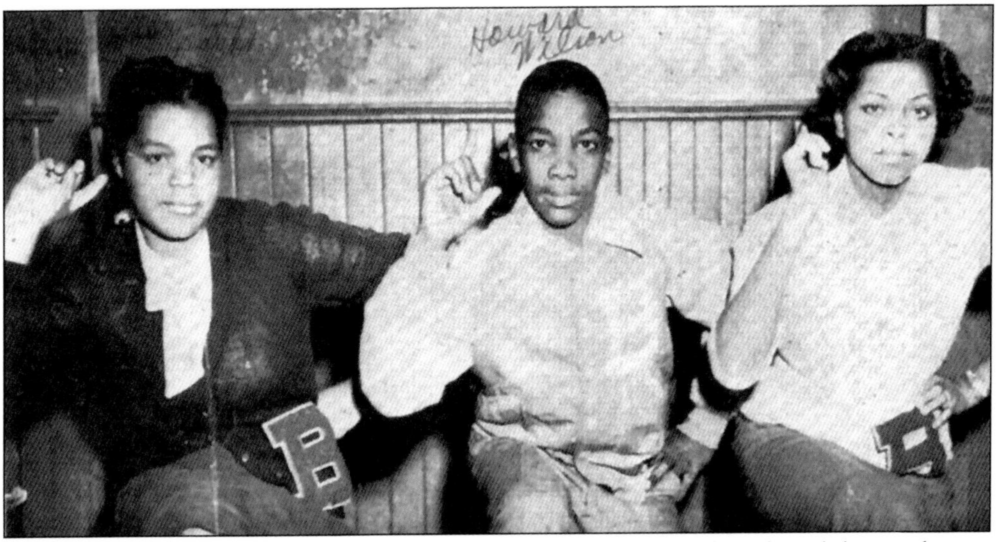

Green Hornet Cheerleaders. Bluestone High School cheerleaders, from left to right, are Dorothy Davis, Howard Wilson, and Madeline Green. (Courtesy of Bramwell-Bluestone High School Alumni Association.)

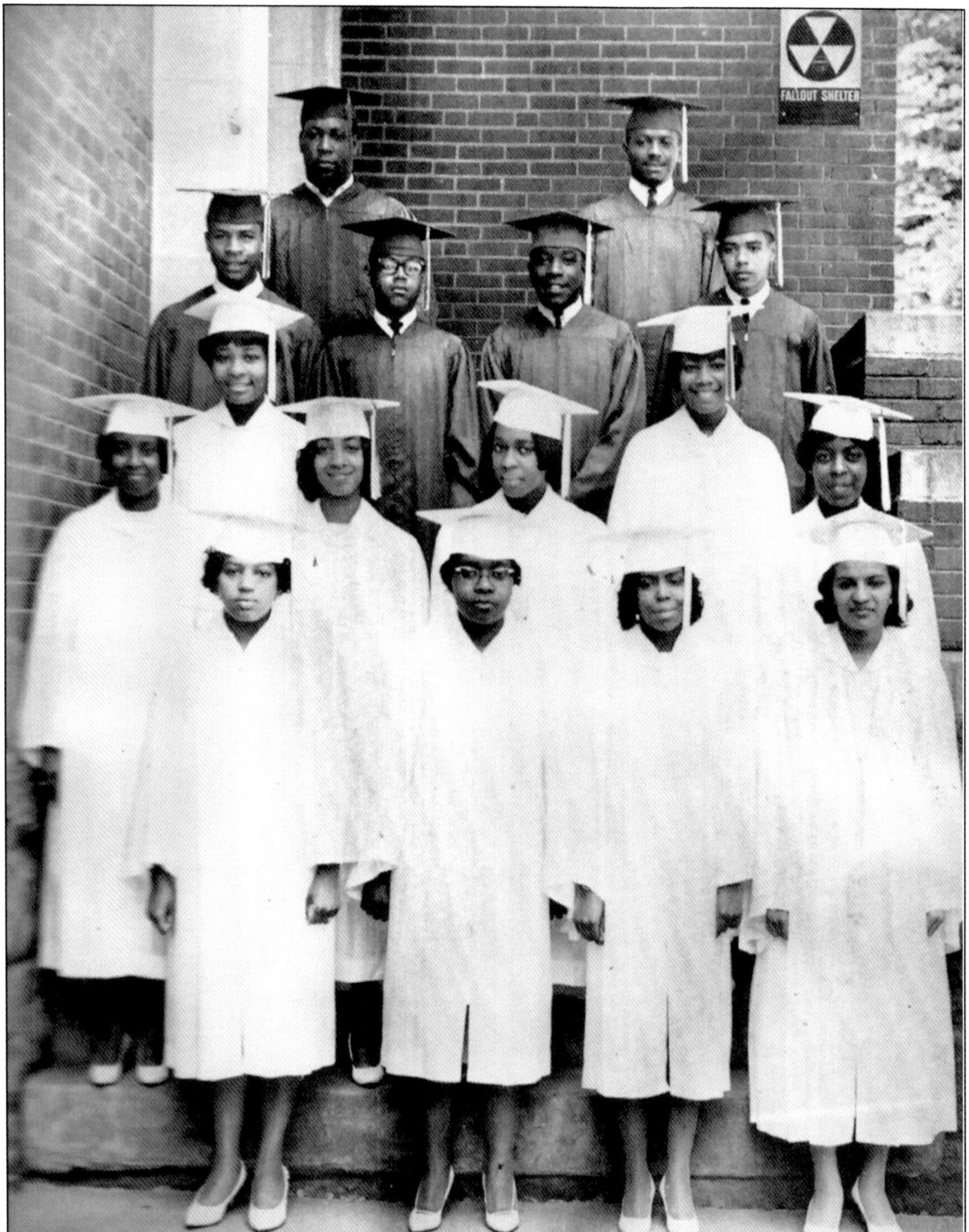

CLASS OF **1964.** The last graduating class of Bluestone High School is pictured on the steps of the school. From left to right are (first row) Lendola Stores, ? Pannell, Margie McDaniel, and Consuella Kinnermore; (second row) Dorothy West, Ernestine Wade, unidentified, Bernice Ward, unidentified, and Mattie Chapman; (third row) Morris Smith, unidentified, Willie Rogers, and Richard "Tippy" Davis; and (fourth row) "Pappy" Martin and Isaac Graves. (Courtesy of Bramwell-Bluestone High School Alumni Association.)

CALIFORNIA BOUND. Zelma Glenn graduated from Bluestone School in 1920. She later went to Hollywood to work for Douglass Cooper at her home. At her *Call Board Theatre* in West Hollywood, Zelma appeared in one of Miss Cooper's plays. She met and married her husband, Jules Darby, and together they made a home in California. (Courtesy of Kelly Murphy Eller and Kim Murphy.)

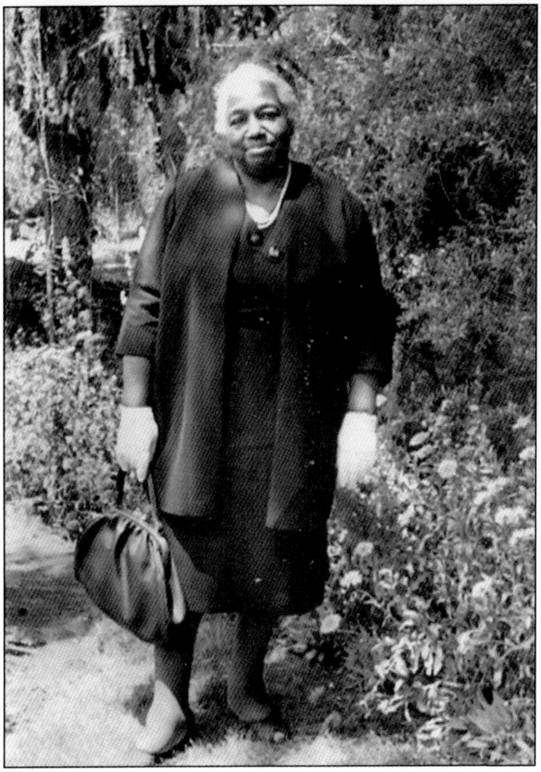

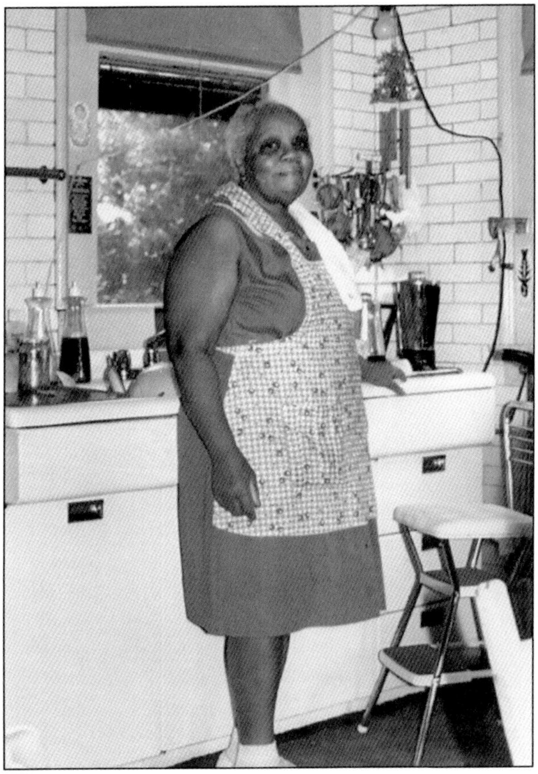

CHURCH PIANIST. Rixie Glenn, a Bluestone High School graduate, was the pianist for many years for the Bluestone Baptist Church. She is pictured here in the kitchen of the Cooper mansion on Main Street. (Courtesy of Kelly Murphy Eller and Kim Murphy.)

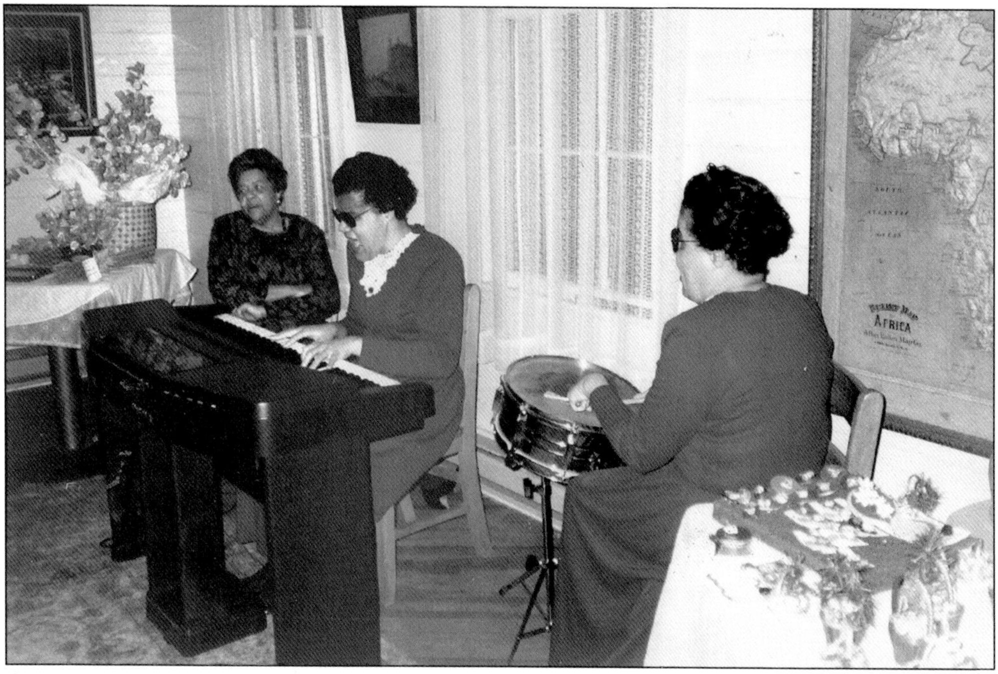

GIFTED MUSICIANS. The Davis twins, Sylvia and Sheilah, shown here with their mother Lillian Davis, have generously shared their gift of music and love of life since they attended school in Romney. They have played and sung around the two-state region. Mother and daughters were choir members of Jones Chapel Church. (Courtesy of Joan C. Browning.)

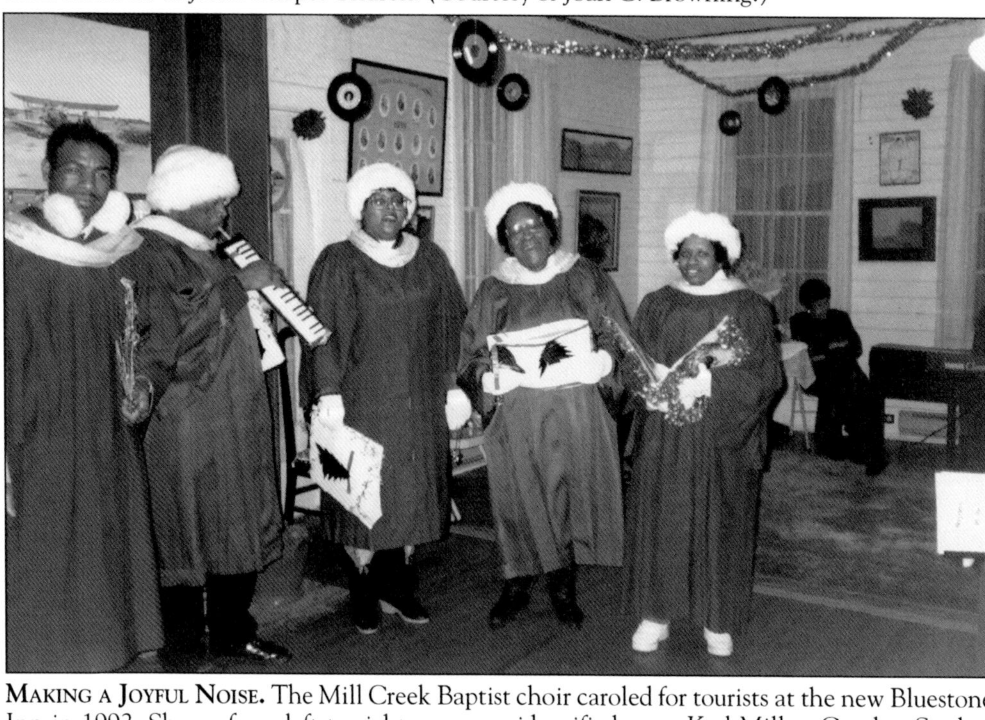

MAKING A JOYFUL NOISE. The Mill Creek Baptist choir caroled for tourists at the new Bluestone Inn in 1992. Shown from left to right are an unidentified man, Karl Miller, Carolyn Starkey Cosby, Edris Miller, and Karen Miller. (Courtesy of Joan C. Browning.)

Six

Coopers and Shinbrier

O sapphire is the sea
I look upon so blue,
O turquoise are the hills
My childhood days once knew.

—Eve Cooper Murphy

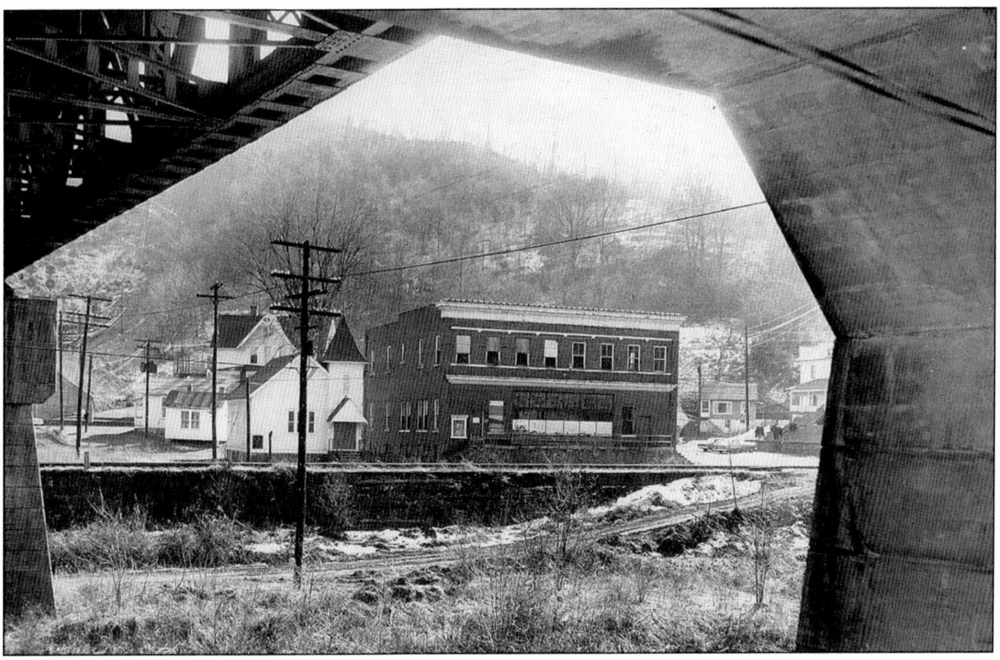

Welcome to Coopers. Founded in 1884 by John Cooper and Associates, Mill Creek Mining Company built houses, churches, and a company store for employees. The house in the back is the one Cooper owned. The small building is the doctor's office, and the other is a Methodist church. There was a train station, school, doctor, and a cemetery. Many structures remain today. The brick building under the Norfolk Southern Railroad trestle was the most modern company store in the area when it was built in 1926.

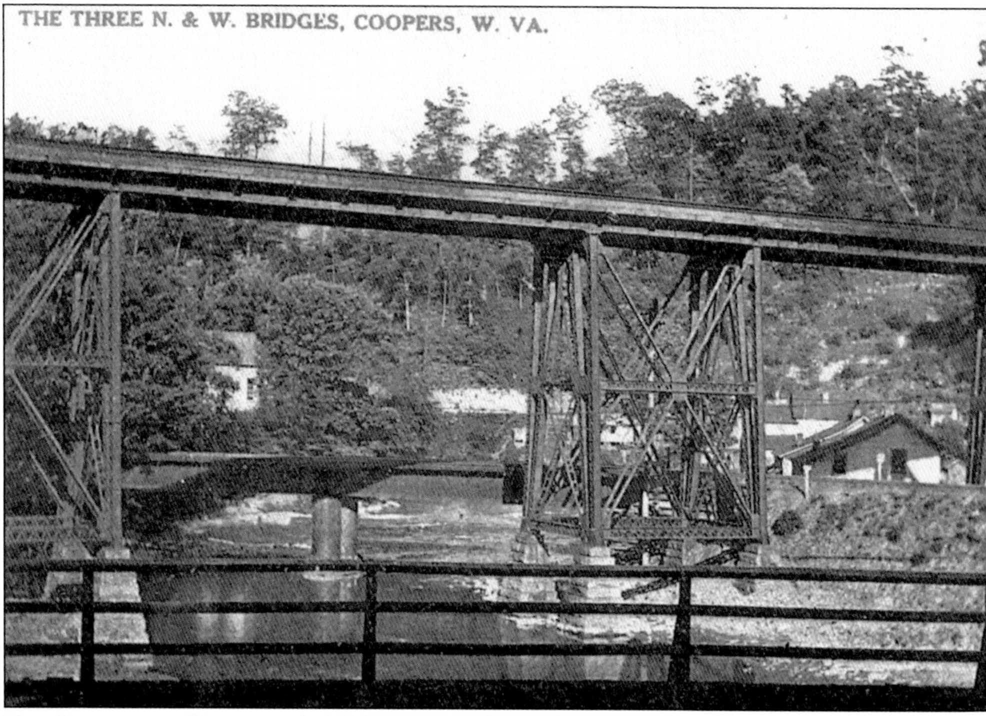

The Bridges of Coopers. A 1929 postcard shows the original trestle used to access the first railroad tunnel for rail access to McDowell County and on to Ohio. On the left is Mill Creek Church. The houses to the right are Mill Creek company houses.

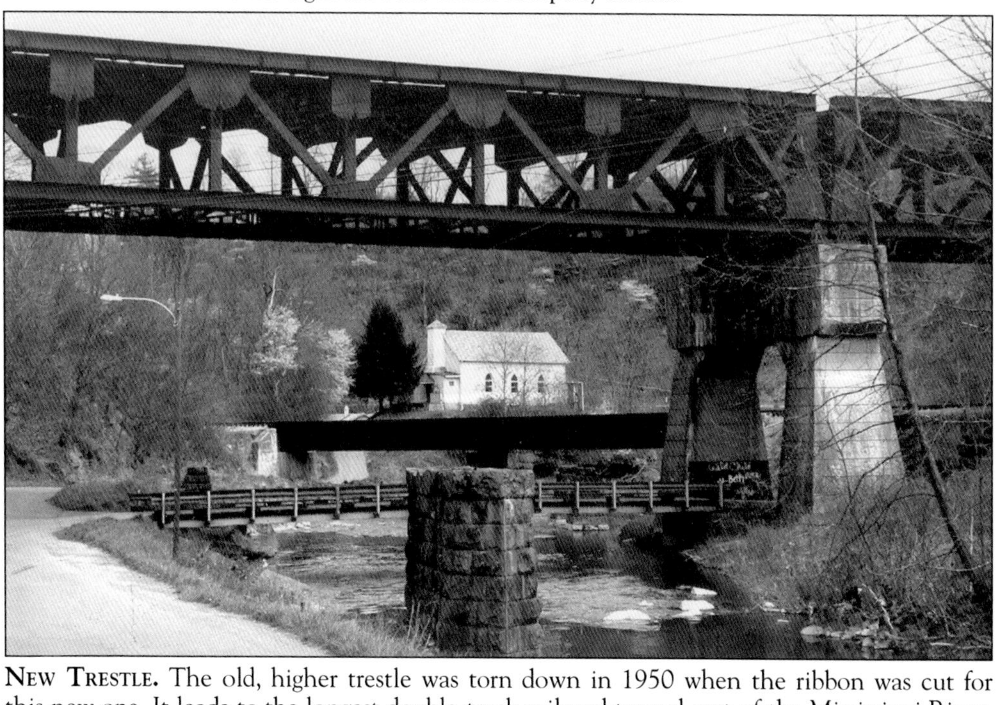

New Trestle. The old, higher trestle was torn down in 1950 when the ribbon was cut for this new one. It leads to the longest double-track railroad tunnel east of the Mississippi River. (Courtesy of Joan Bange Buchanan.)

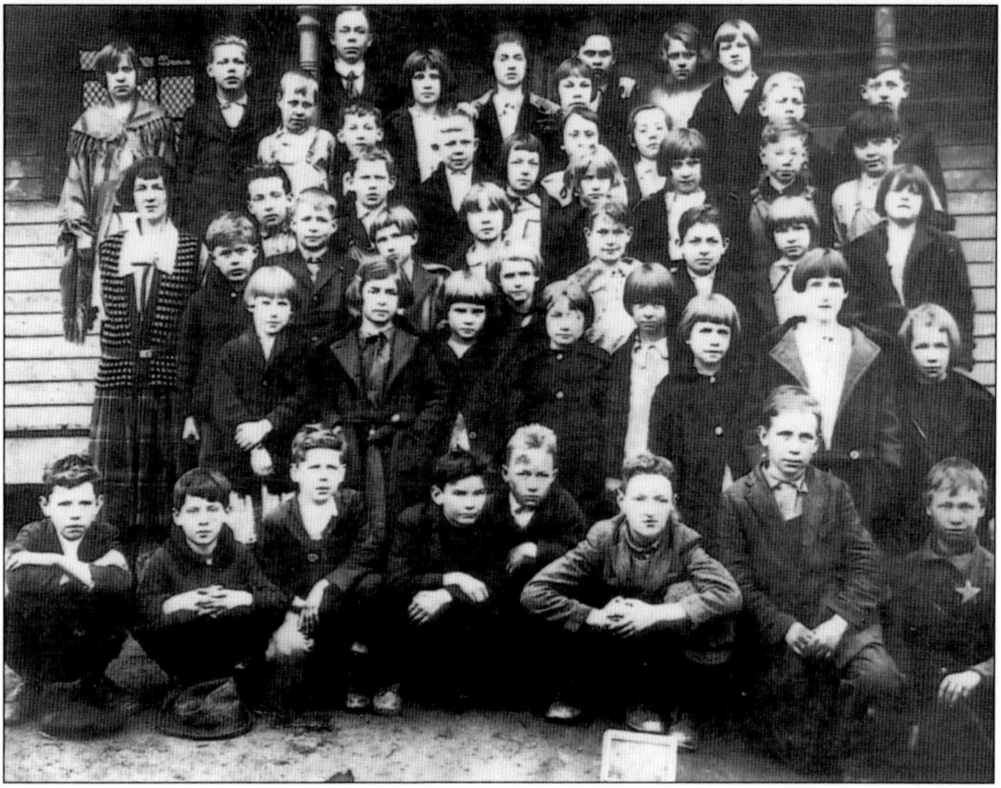

School Time. The third- and fourth-grade students are pictured at Coopers School on Shinbrier Mountain *c.* 1924. (Courtesy of Ennice Hill Allen and Elbert "Dizzy" Harris.)

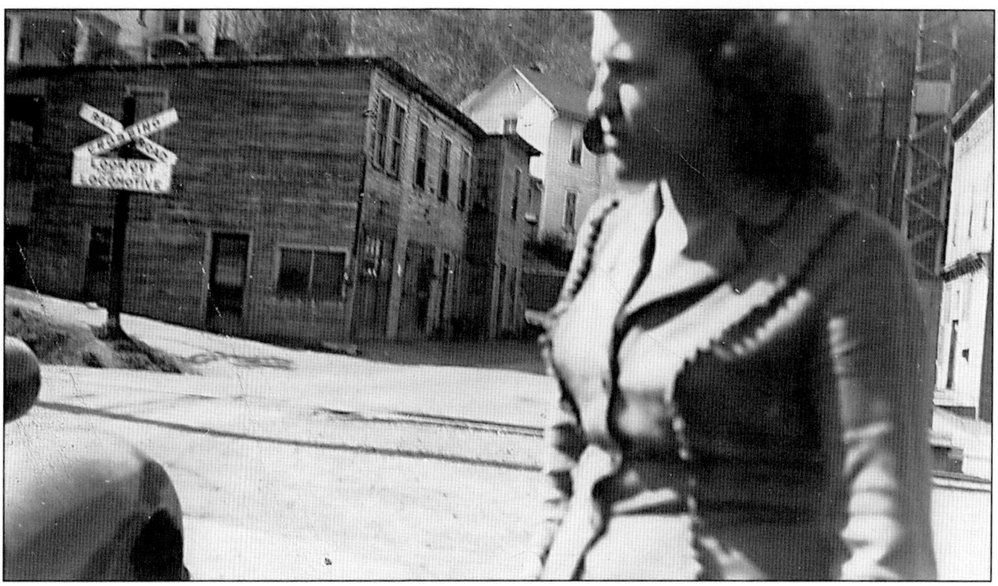

"Ency." Ennice Hill Allen, who supplied the photograph above, is shown here on Main Street when Bramwell was still a busy community. The buildings across the tracks on the left have been gone at least 50 years. The town hall is to the right. (Courtesy of Ennice Hill Allen.)

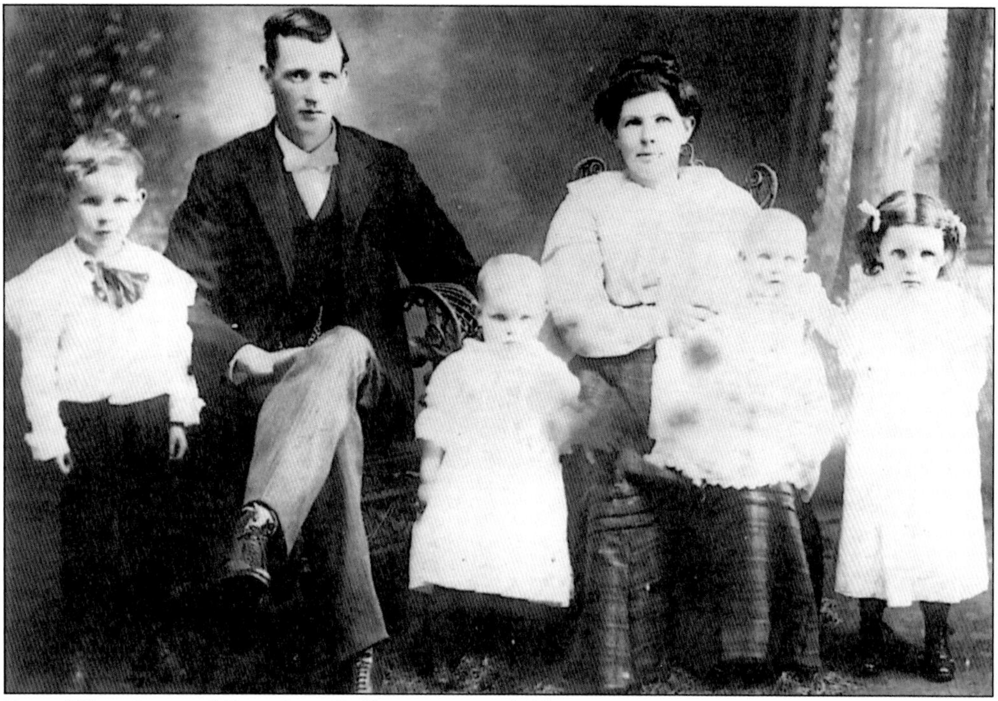

Bell. Elbert Lee and Dora Jane Bell Harris were lifelong residents of Shinbrier. Their children, from the left, are Jesse, Lyndell, John, and Malta. (Courtesy of Edith Harris Butt and Elbert "Dizzy" Harris.)

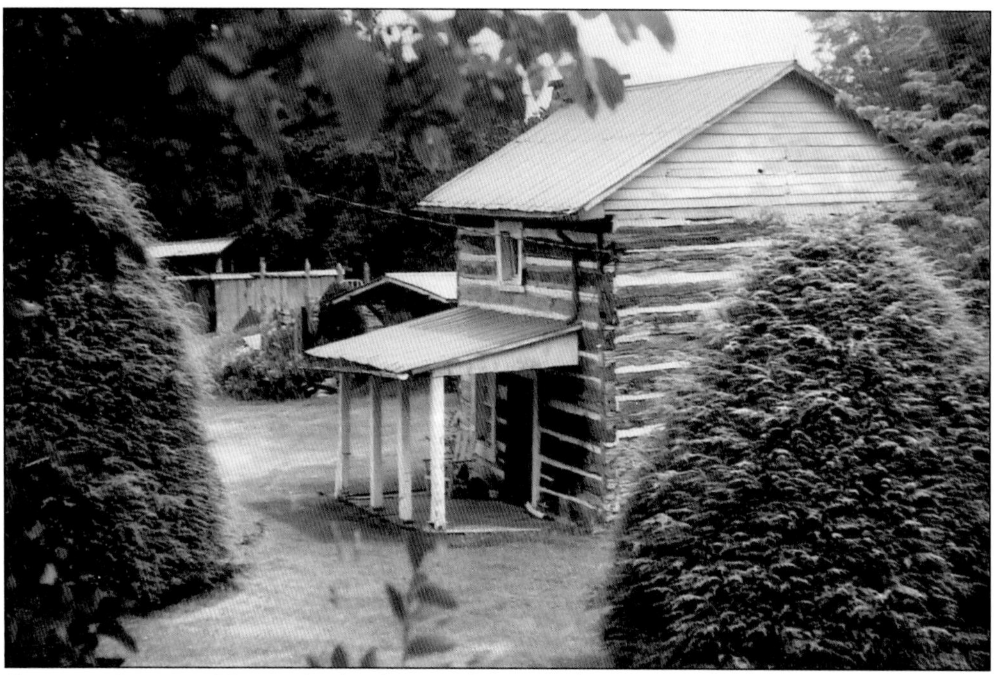

Original Settler. This is the log house of Isaac and Nancy Bell. It was built on Shinbrier Mountain on land Bell received from the United States government for service in the War of 1812. (Courtesy of Wade Wilburn and Elbert "Dizzy" Harris.)

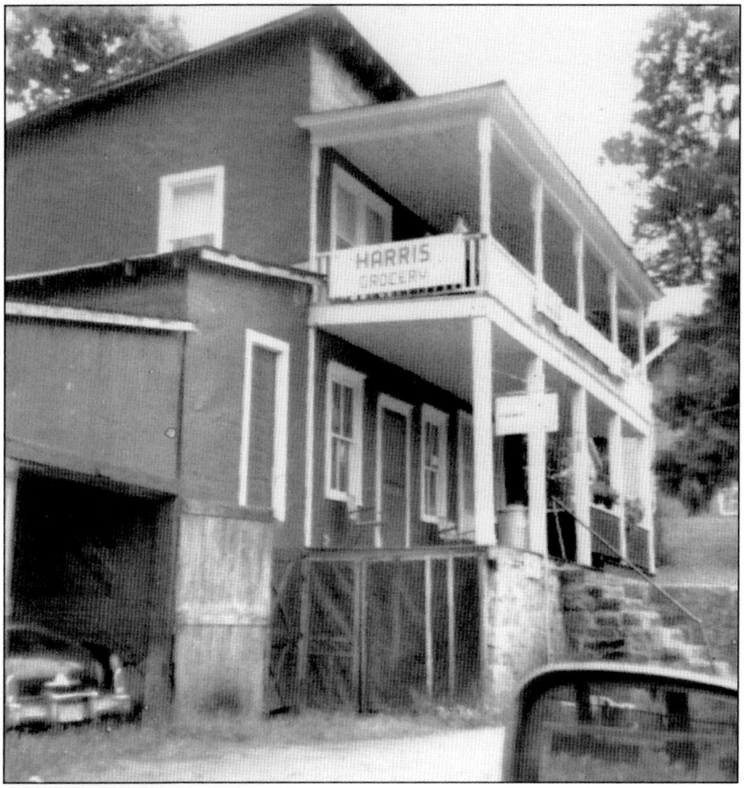

Shinbrier Landmark. Harris Grocery at Shinbrier was built in 1924. It was operated by the Miller family. (Courtesy of Warren Butt and Elbert "Dizzy" Harris.)

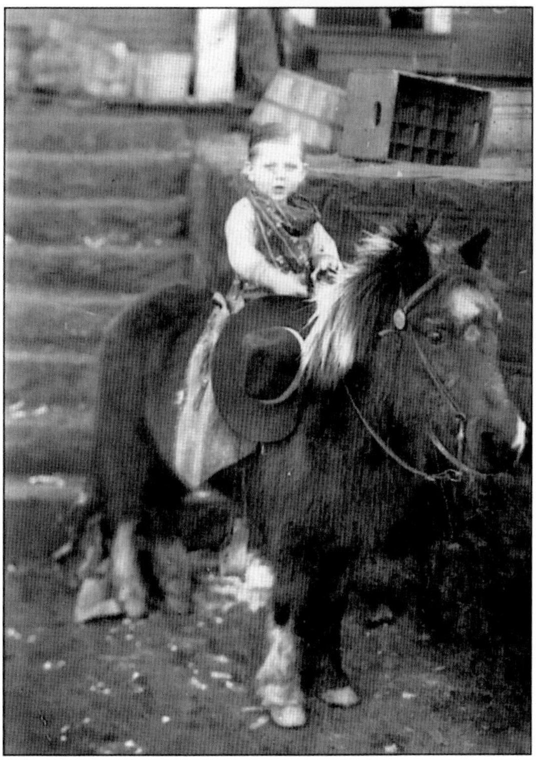

Pet Pony. Elbert "Dizzy" Harris rides his pony in front of the Harris Grocery in Shinbrier about 1942. (Courtesy of Wade Wilburn and Elbert "Dizzy" Harris.)

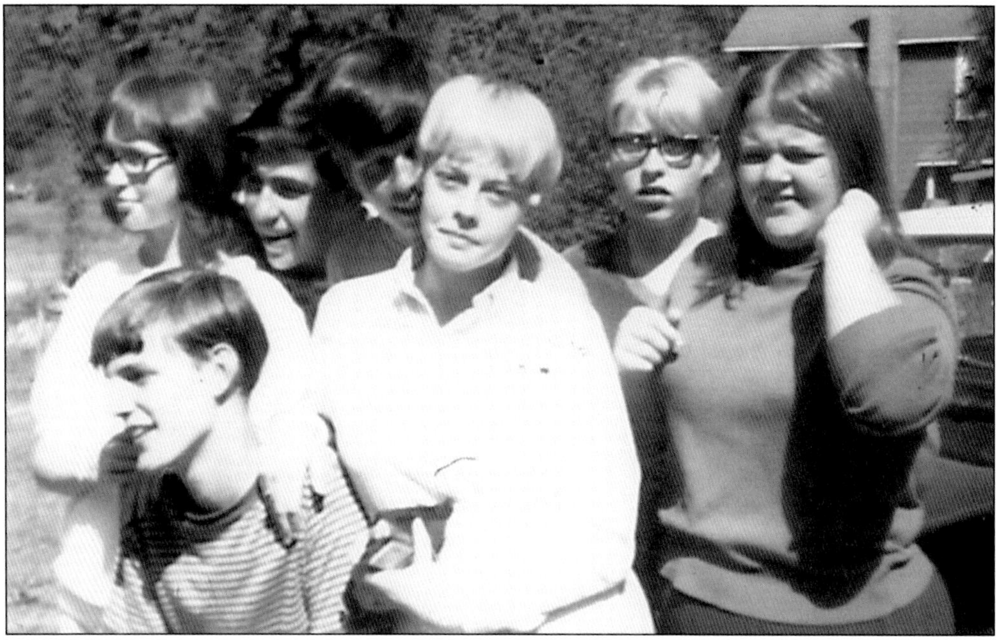

SHINBRIER KIDS. Bramwell High School was where their days were spent, but after school, they gathered near their homes in Shinbrier. That was the way of life in 1966. From left to right are (front row) Johnny Morrisette, Martha Lynn Fudge, and Jeannette Barber; (back row) Diane Buckner, Calvin Green, Dennis Buckner, and Lorraine Corner. (Courtesy of Virginia Buckner.)

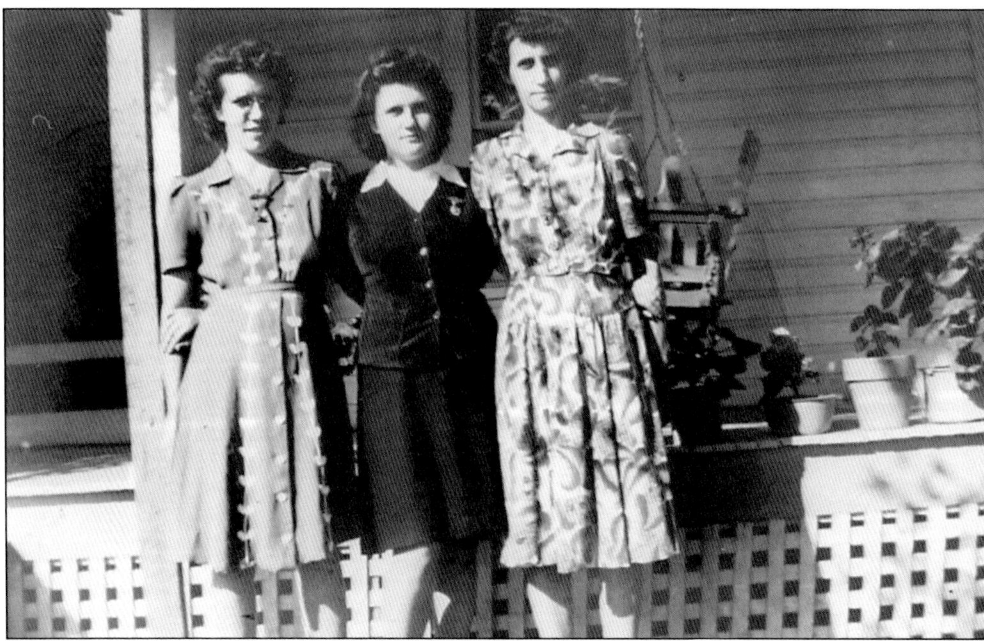

SUMMER, 1941. "We got together at my Shinbrier house the last peaceful summer before World War II," said Virginia Buckner in describing the Sunday these three Hill sisters had their picture made. She is on the left, Elizabeth "Ibby" Hill Tabor is in the middle, and Myrtle Hill McFadden is on the right. (Courtesy of Virginia Buckner.)

GONE FISHIN'. "We went fishing at Blue Hole, and look what we caught!" says Evelyn "Sissy" Williams. The Blue Hole at Shinbrier was a popular spot for swimming in the early days of the town. It was located in a bend in the Bluestone River with very deep water. The course of the river has since been altered, so only fishing is possible. From left to right, Sissy Williams holds the fish with Randy Dean Gibson, Sherman Wayne Bell, and Keith Williams, pictured in the summer of 1972. (Courtesy of Shirley and Randy Gibson.)

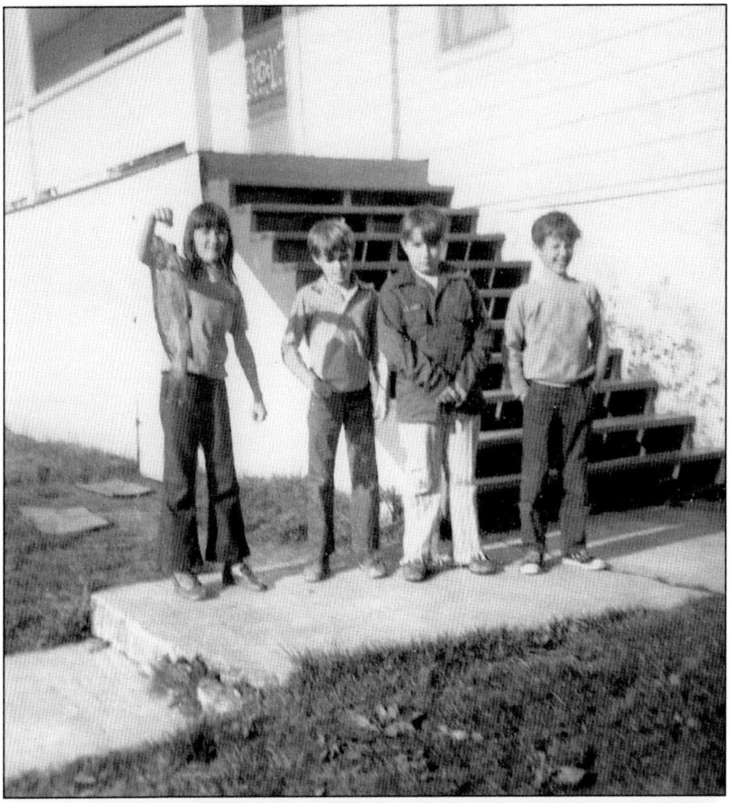

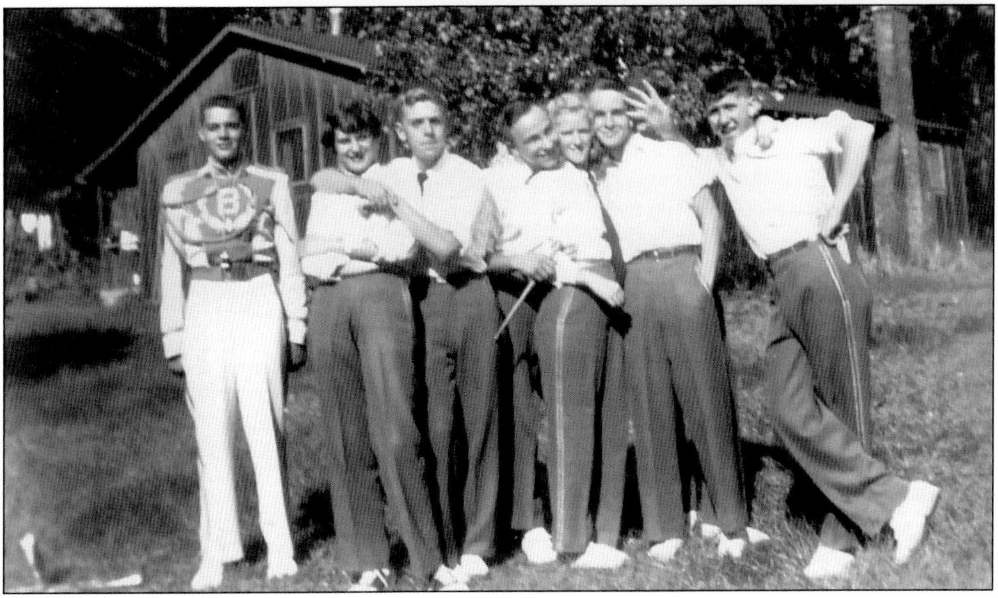

FUND-RAISING. Bramwell High band members spent an afternoon c. 1955 covering all parts of the community, asking for donations for an important field trip. Taking a break for Judith Davidson to make their picture, from left to right, are drum major Jewell Tyree, unidentified girl, Roger Goins, Billy Duff, Judie Allen, Walter Clark, and Buzzy Dawson. (Courtesy of Judith Davidson Gilley.)

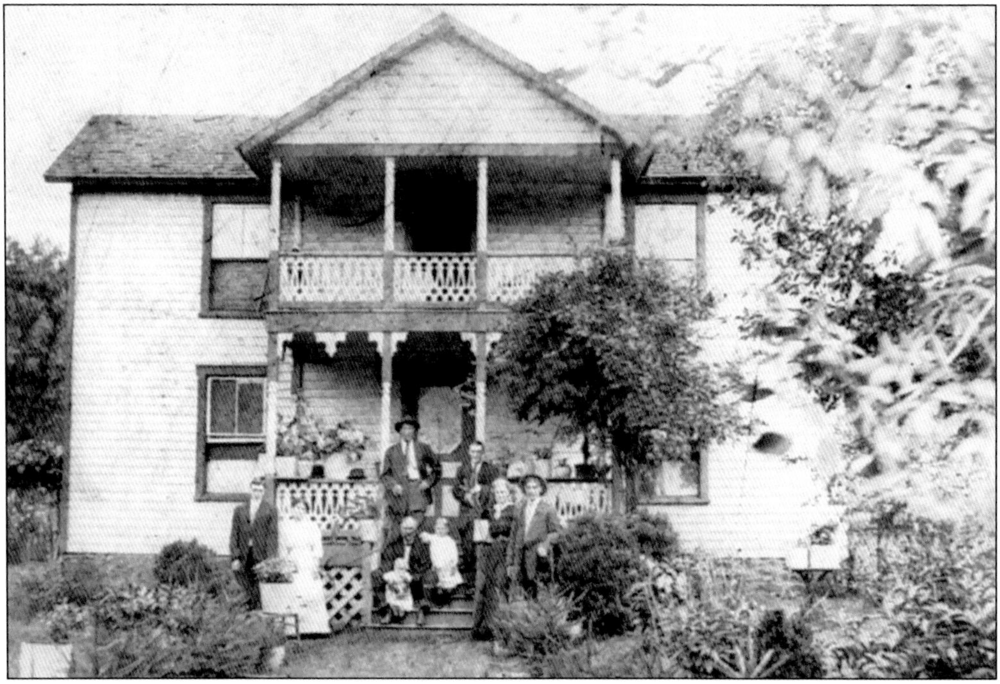

FAMILY MATTERS. An unidentified family poses on the porch of their home on Coopers Mountain before 1900.

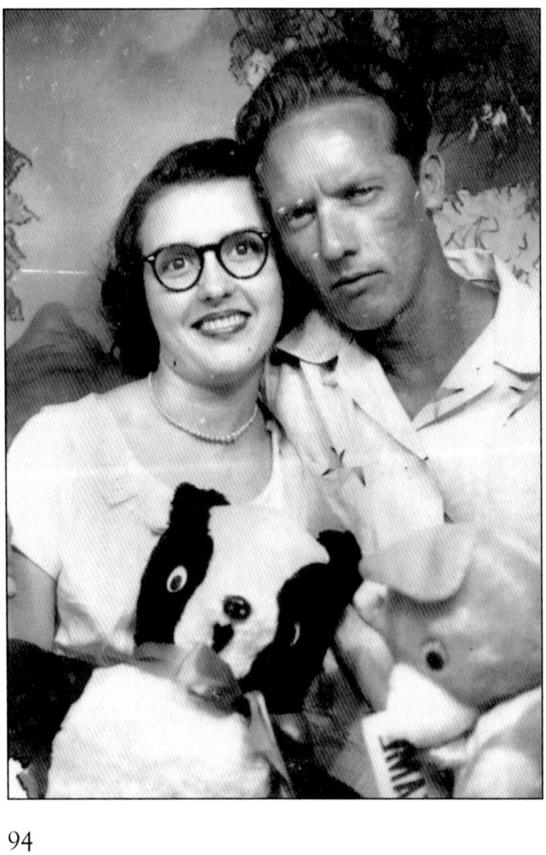

EVENING AT THE CARNIVAL. Ella and Ed Williams of Shinbrier take a break and spend an evening at the carnival. Their children and grandchildren are Shinbrier natives and attended the Bramwell schools. (Courtesy of Evelyn "Sissy" Williams.)

Millionaire Mascots. Sporting events were always supported, whether the game was football, baseball, basketball, or tennis. The crowds came from all over Bramwell and surrounding communities. There were fans and cheerleaders alike. Even youngsters were involved. In 1964, two mascots helped cheer the Millionaire team on to basketball victory. David Talley (left) is the young Millionaire and Jonni Stoker, the cheerleader.

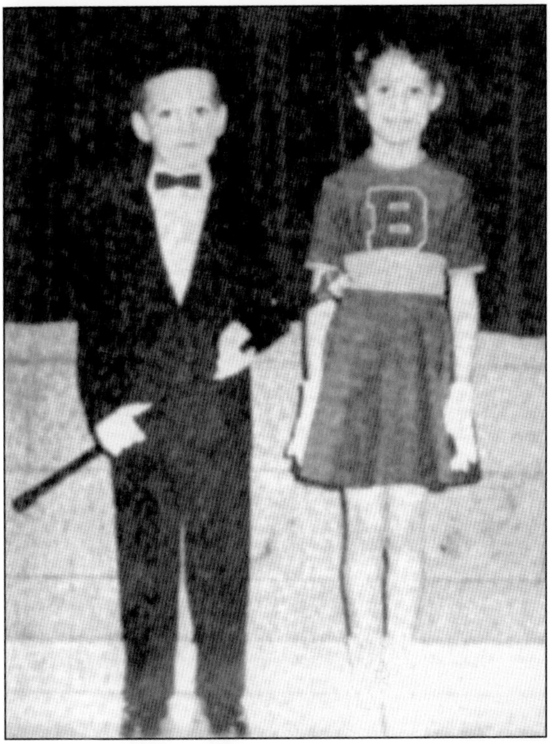

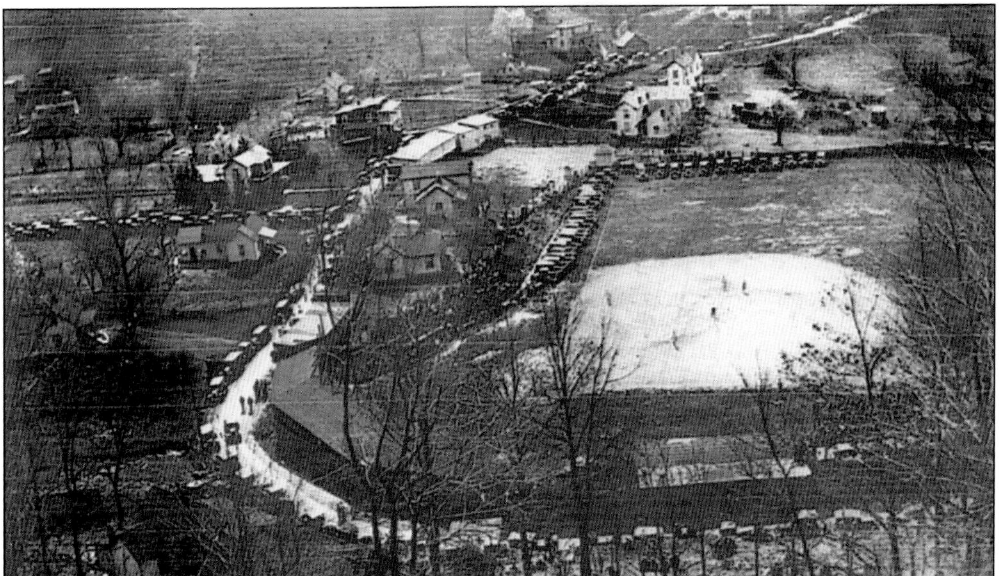

Not Your Average Baseball Game. All coalfield towns' "coal camps" had baseball teams, which competed with other camps' teams. The team from Bramwell, the town of millionaires, was a cut above the rest. The field was provided by the Cooper family of Mill Creek Coal & Coke Co. Some professional teams, including the Cincinnati Reds, traveled by train to play the Bramwell team. The Reds stayed at the Bluestone Inn on Main Street. Crowds came out for the games, as this c. 1930 photograph shows. (Courtesy of Elbert "Dizzy" Harris and Marlene Moran Houchins.)

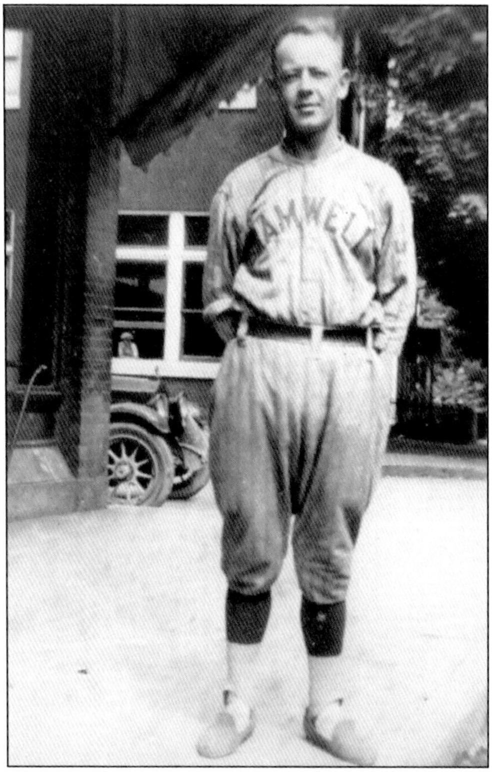

Millionaire Player. In the late 1910s and early 1920s, many local businessmen loved to wear the uniform and play a Sunday game with the Bramwell team. (Courtesy of Joan Bange Buchanan.)

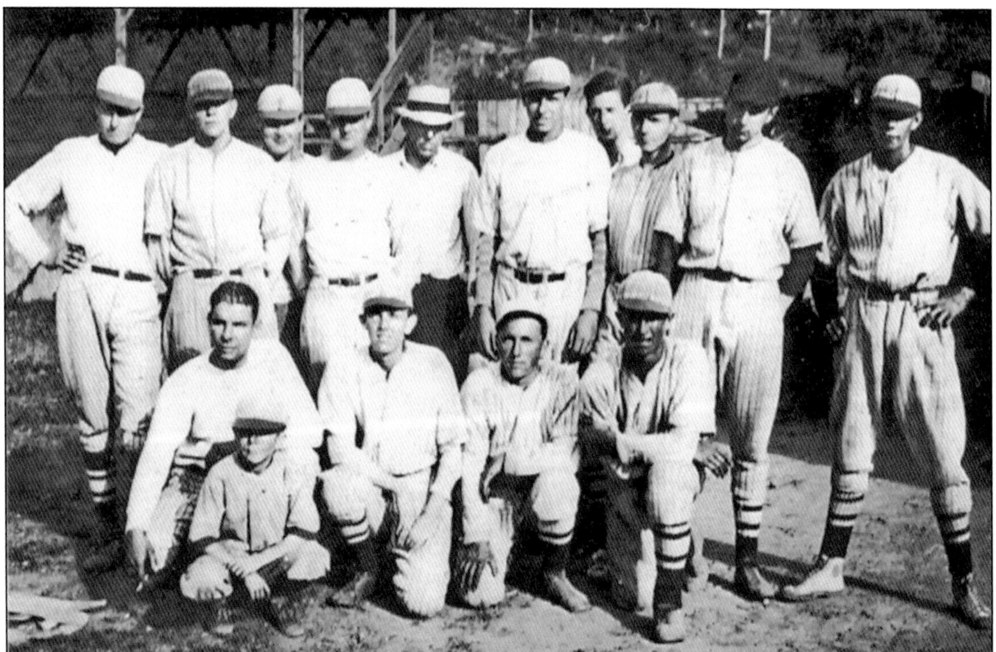

Bramwell's Professional Baseball Team. In this photograph of the team, about 1920, the only identified player is John Mundy, the second baseman standing on the right. (Courtesy of Dr. Wilson Tabor.)

Seven

IMAGES OF BRAMWELL

To me, the greatest attribute of Bramwell
was not the stately mansions
which I took for granted,
but the precious people.

— J. Marion Bryant, M.D.

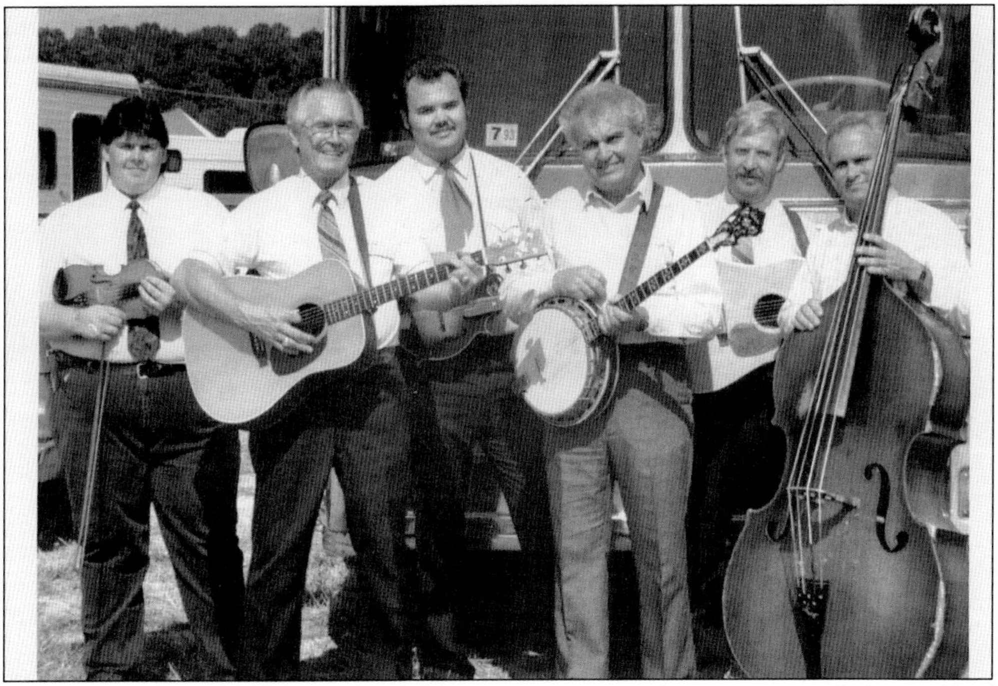

BRAMWELL'S BLUEGRASS LEGENDS. Melvin and Ray Goins have entertained the world of bluegrass music for more than 50 years. Starting at home, playing for round and square dances in the Bramwell High School gym, they climbed the ladder of bluegrass success. They have played on the Grand Ole Opry stage and have been inducted into the Bluegrass Hall of Fame. Melvin was named Morehead State University (KY) Appalachian Treasure, among other recognitions. Melvin is the only bluegrass performer to appear on the cover of Smithsonian magazine. In this promotional photograph, Melvin is second from the left, Ray is fourth. Their baby brother, Conley, is on the right. (Courtesy of Melvin Goins.)

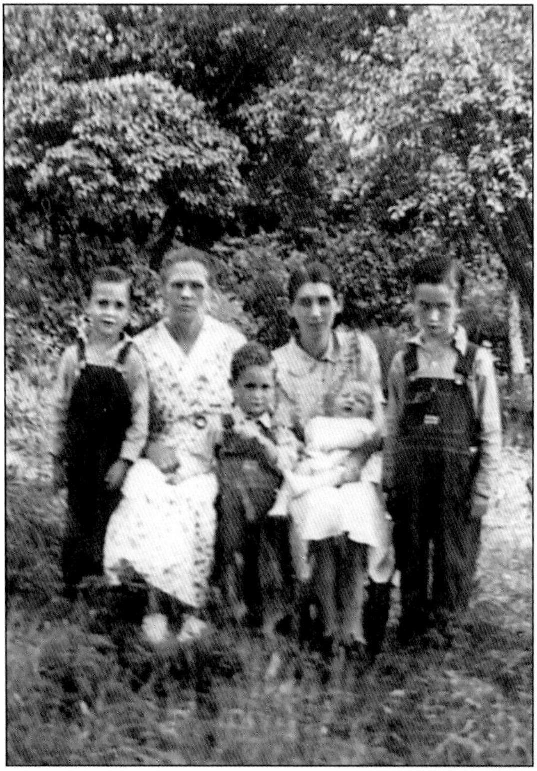

Goins Brothers. Melvin and Ray Goins grew up making music. From left to right are Ray, grandmother Bettie York Goins, Walter, mother Pearl Dillon Goins holding baby Roger Earl "Slick," and Melvin. Two younger brothers of Melvin and Ray were named Lester and Earl after their music idols, Flatt and Scruggs. Their younger brothers play in the group, Goins Brothers Second Edition. (Courtesy of Kelly Lester "Flat" Goins.)

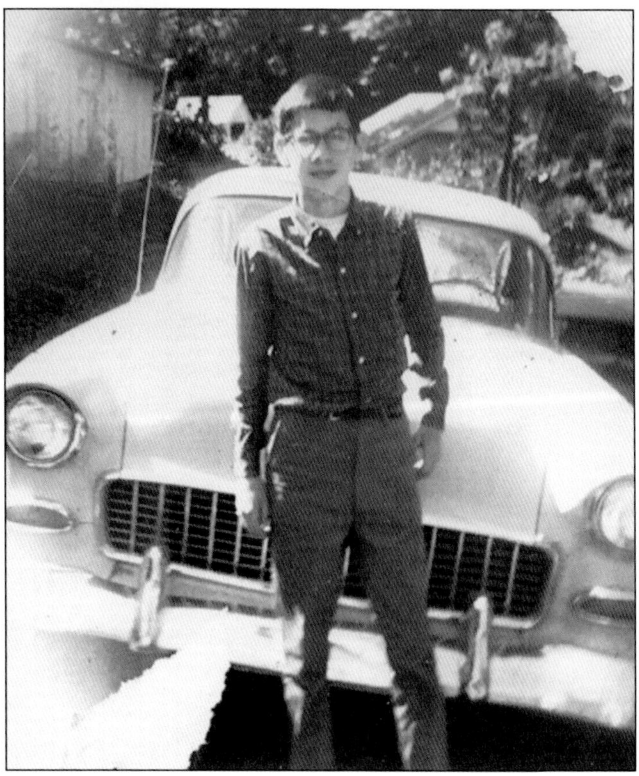

Little Brother. Kelly Lester "Flat" Goins and his 1955 Chevy are pictured *c.* 1965. (Courtesy of Kelly Goins.)

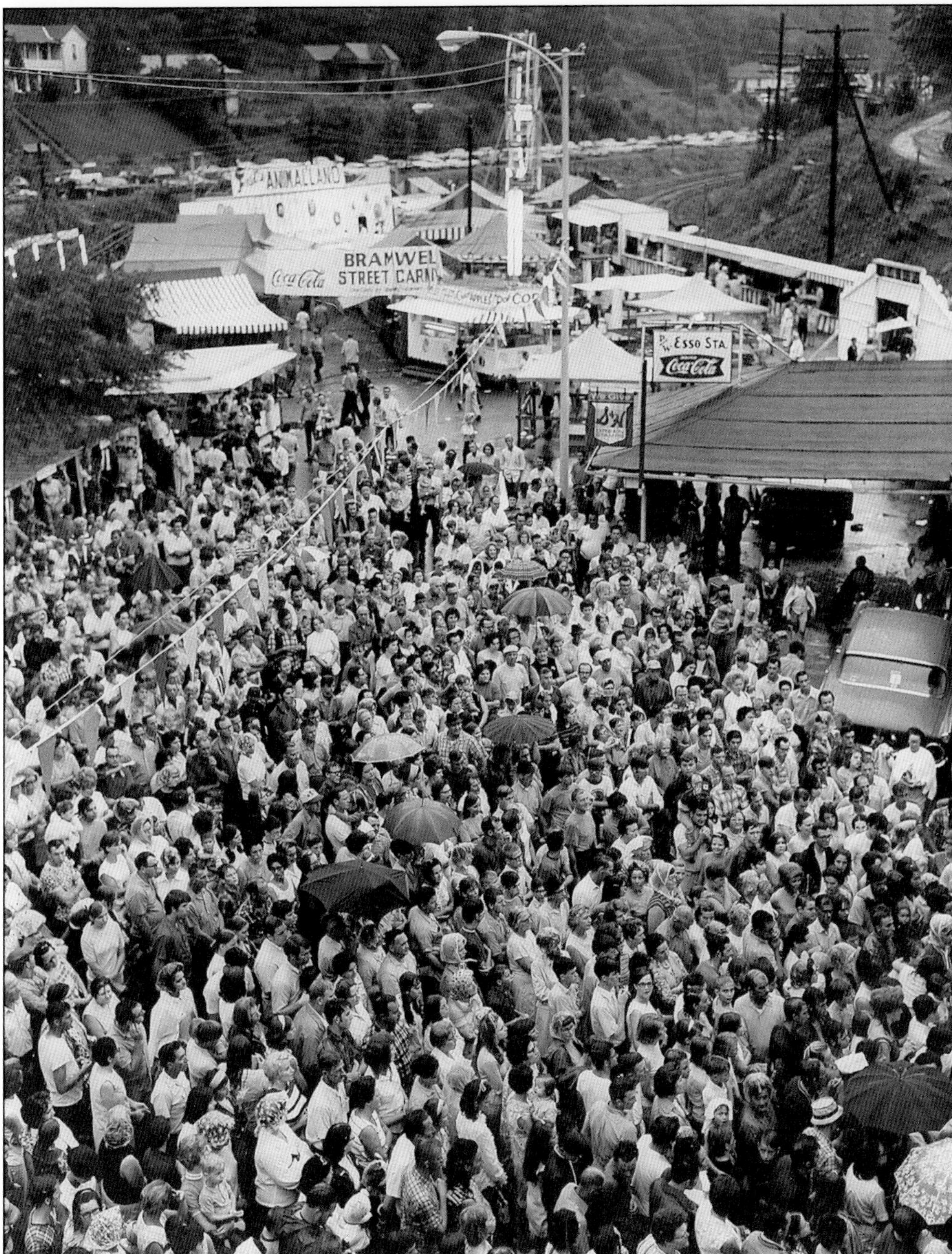

BRAMWELL STREET FAIR. Started in 1967 by the Bramwell Kiwanis Club and ending in 1994, the annual Bramwell Street Fair was the first and most successful of all small town fairs in West Virginia. In this 1968 photograph, only a portion of the thousands who came to hear Loretta Lynn are pictured. (Courtesy of Richard Painter.)

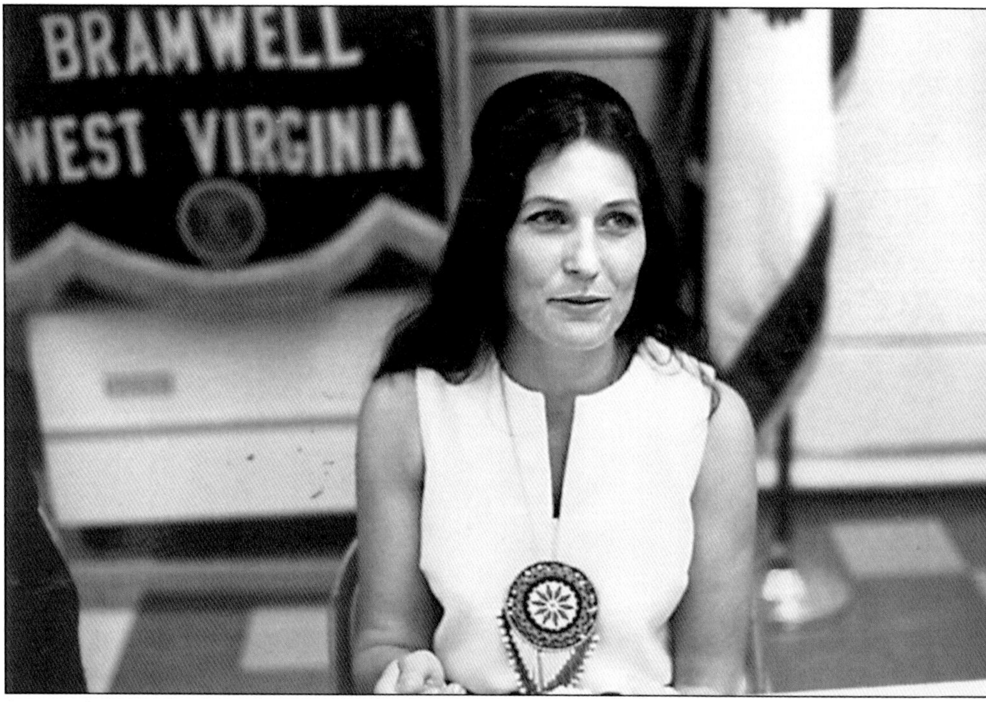

SHOW STOPPER. Loretta Lynn was entertained by the Bramwell Kiwanis Club before her performance at the 1968 Bramwell Street Fair. (Courtesy of Glenn and Louise Scott family.)

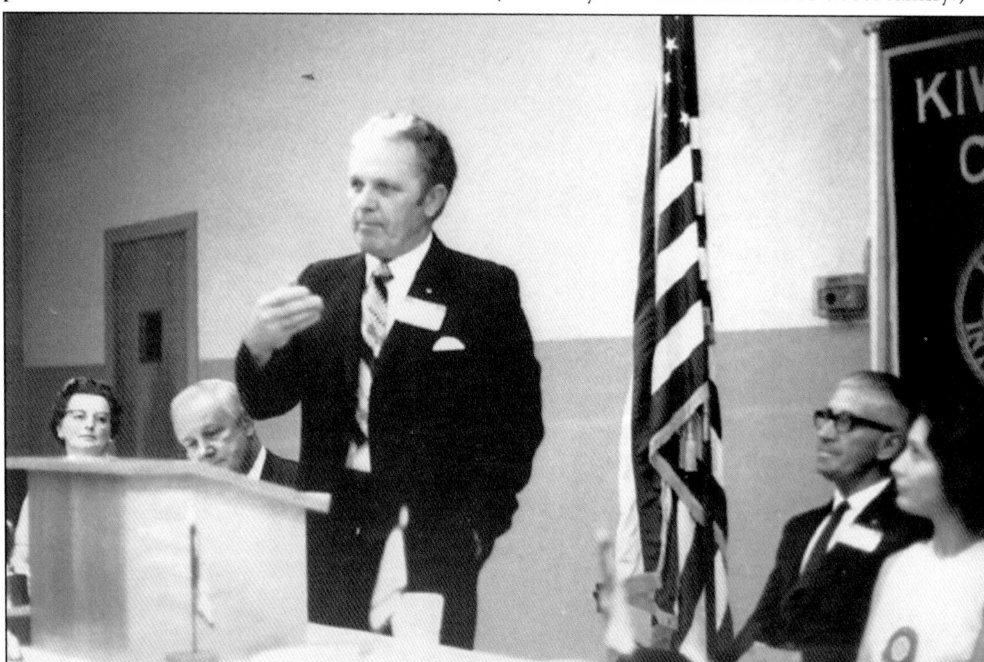

SPECIAL GUEST. With Louise Scott, West Virginia governor Arch Moore, Ralph Cowan, and Loretta Lynn looking on, Glenn Scott introduces the special guest. (Courtesy of Glenn and Louise Scott family.)

TWITTY. Glenn Scott, the father of the Bramwell Street Fair, watches as Conway Twitty autographs his 8-by-10 glossy for a fan in 1973. The country music performer is assisted by his daughter. (Photo by Vernon Fields, courtesy of Glenn and Louise Scott family.)

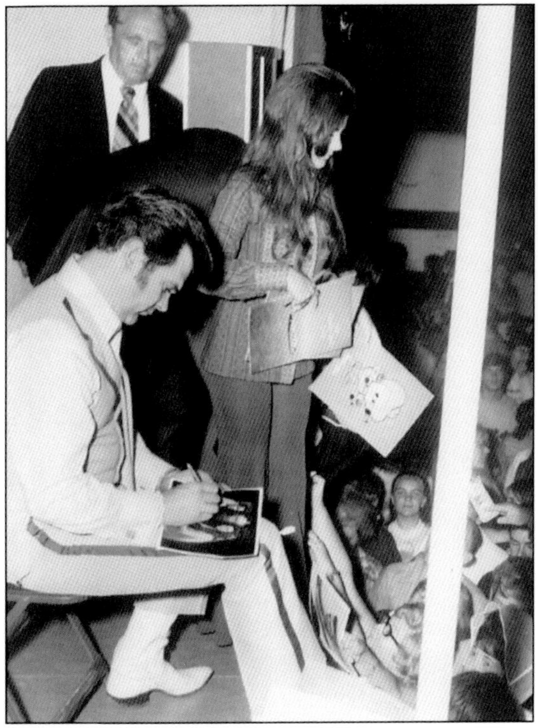

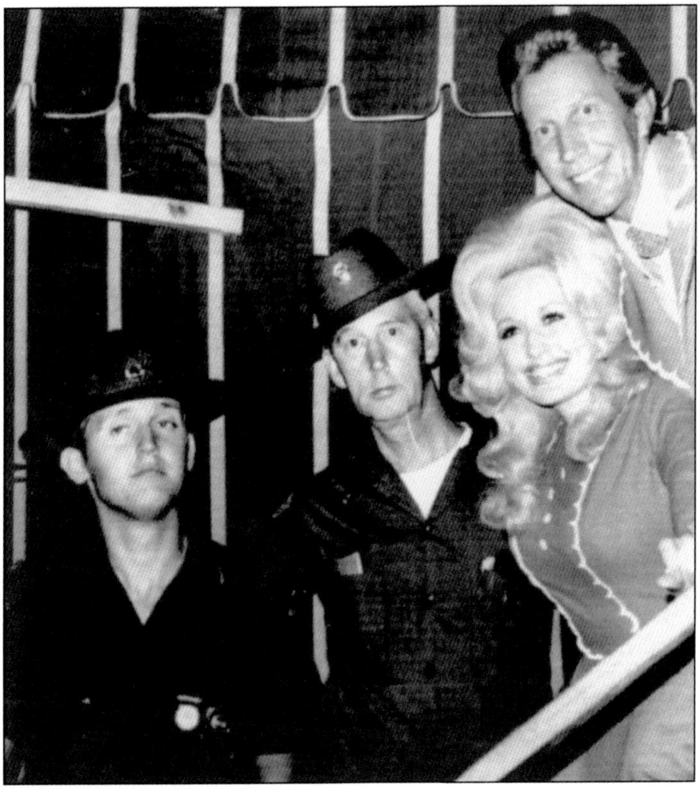

DOLLY AT BRAMWELL KIWANIS STREET FAIR. West Virginia State Trooper "Mack" McCarty and Richard Painter, one of the legendary police chiefs in Bramwell, appear to be very serious about their duty of protecting stars Dolly Parton and Porter Wagoner. (Courtesy of Bibbi Dawson Sigmon.)

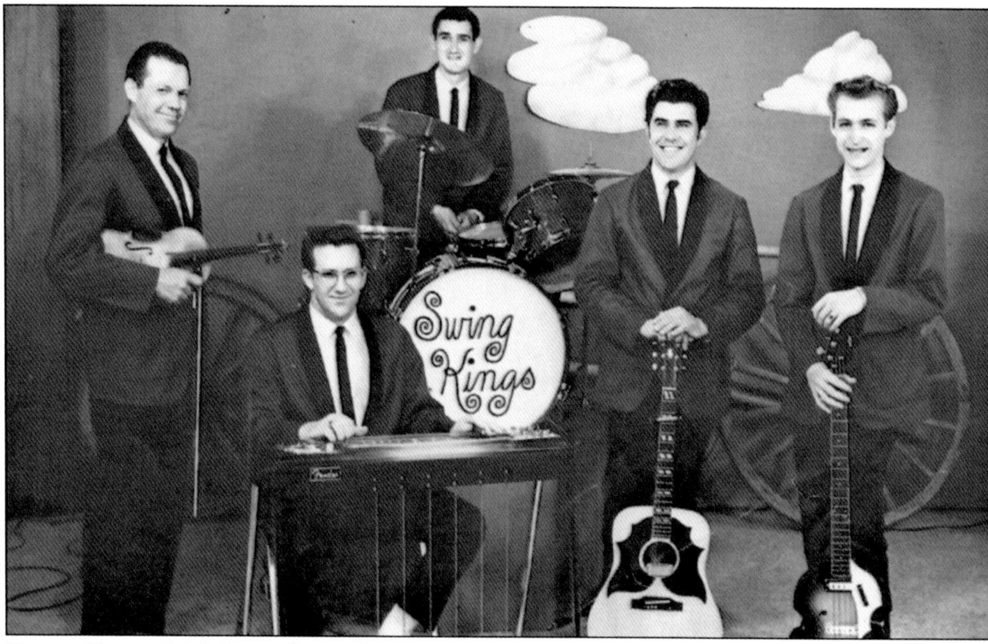

SWING KINGS. Mel Street began his country music career in Mercer County. He performed with the "Swing Kings" until he hit it big with his signature song, "Borrowed Angel." After going solo, Mel returned from Nashville to perform at the Bramwell Street Fair. The band members, from left to right, are, Ray Morgan, Buddy Pennington, Donnie Goins (a brother to the bluegrass Goins Brothers, pictured at the beginning of this chapter), Mel Street, and Ronnie Cochran. (Courtesy of Elbert and Polly Street.)

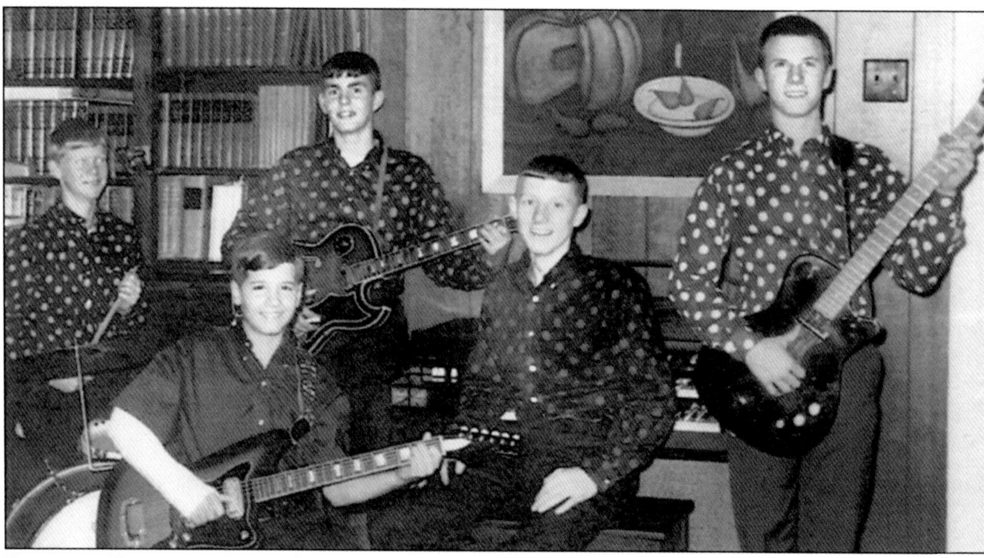

ROCK 'N ROLL. Bramwell had its own teenage band during the era of "garage bands." In the millionaire town, the Chaparrals had their own music room for practicing. They performed for school functions and on weekends at the Corner Shop in the old Bryant-Newbold Pharmacy building. In front is David Bowman. Behind him in polka dot shirts are Jack Richard Goins, Greg Murphy, Joe Hill, and Nick Hill. (Photo by James Shrader, courtesy of Alma Yon Murphy.)

SHINBRIER'S SINGING SON. Dwight Hill (on right) has enjoyed a successful country music career. A featured performer for the last Bramwell Street Fair, he is pictured here with country music singer, Eddie Arnold. (Courtesy of Dwight Hill and "Dizzy" Harris.)

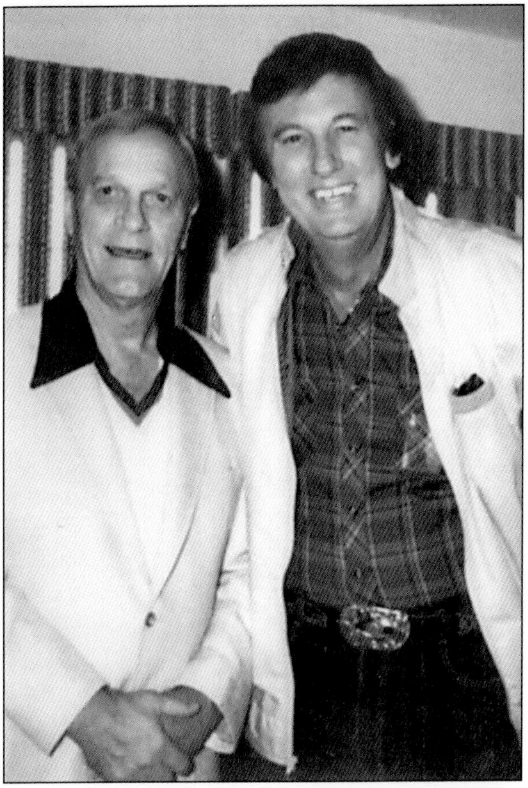

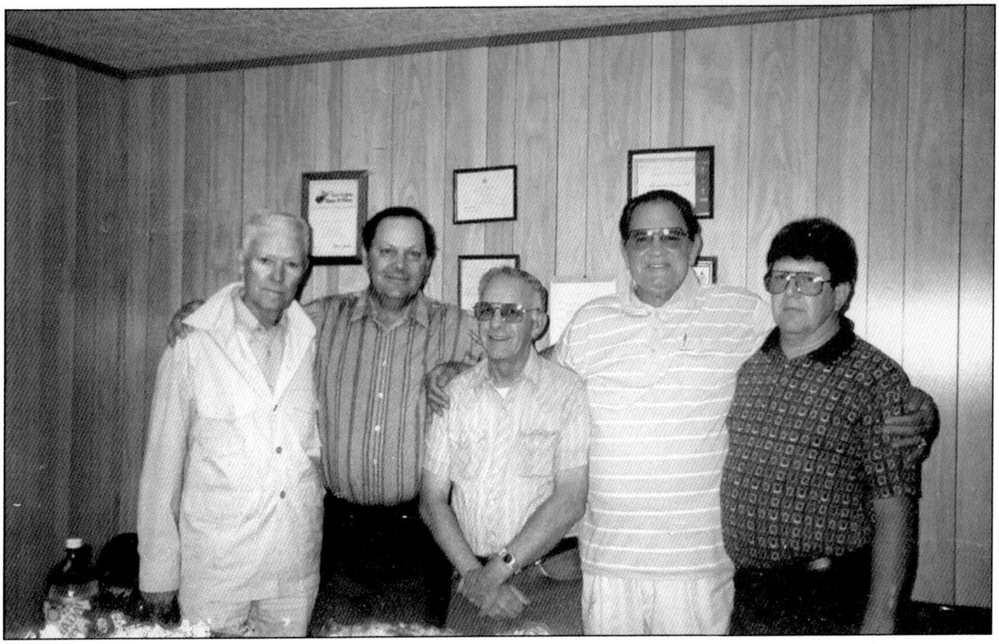

FAREWELL TO KIWANIS. The last meeting of the Bramwell Kiwanis Club was a Sunday in 1994. In its day, the club had been the most successful civic organization in the state. The officers who met to return the charter, pictured here from left to right, are Donnie Allen, Roger Stroupe, John Godby, Lowell Abel, and Jimmy Carver.

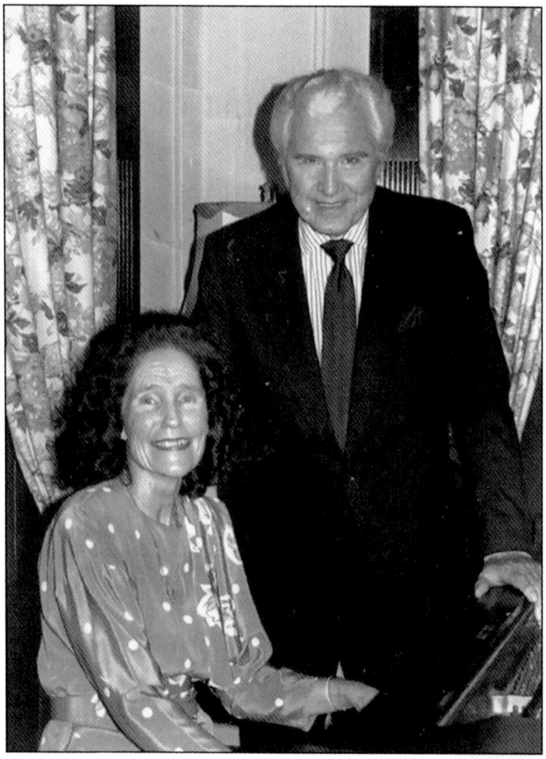

Visitor. In 1995, Broadway singer John Raitt came to Bramwell to visit his childhood friend, Eve Cooper Murphy. The two met in the early 1940s in Hollywood. (Courtesy of Kelly Eller Murphy and Kim Murphy.)

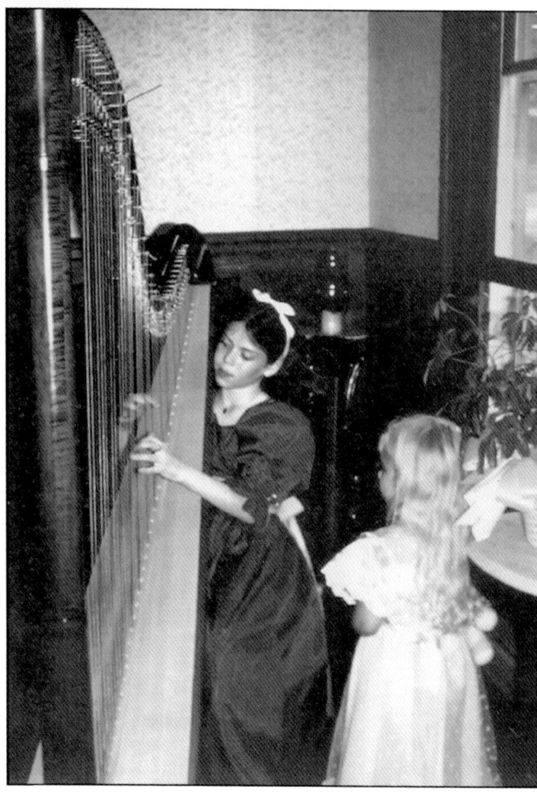

Generations. Harpist Elizabeth Lilly is the great-granddaughter of John B. Perry Sr., second employee of the famous Bank of Bramwell. In May 1986, she played for Amanda Cochran, the fifth generation of women in her family to call Bramwell home. The performance at the new Bluestone Inn was part of the Bramwell Millionaire Garden Club's spring tour. The girls have grown up and the Garden Club tours are a thing of the past, but memories linger in photographs. (Courtesy of John Warner.)

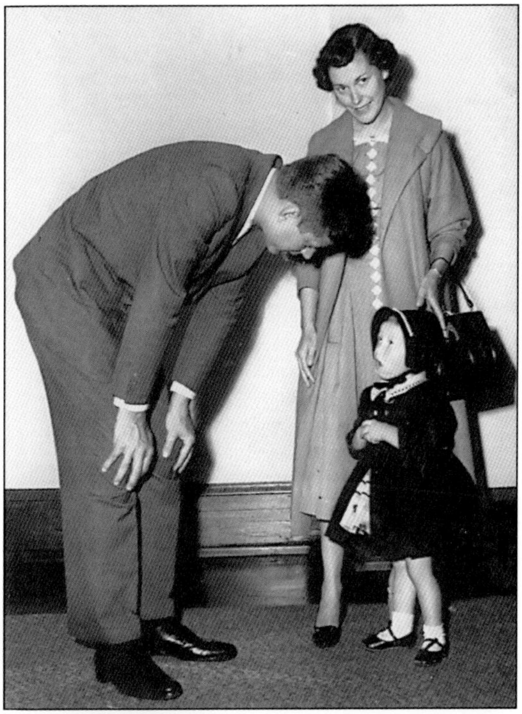

JFK Comes to Town. When Sen. John F. Kennedy was on the campaign trail in 1960, he traveled throughout the state of West Virginia. People from Bramwell still remember his visit to them. The black limousine motorcade drove the long way into town so that more people could see him. A former Bramwell High School student, Helen White Fields, and her daughter, Vickie, will never forget the moment in history when they met our future president. (Photo by and courtesy of Vernon Fields.)

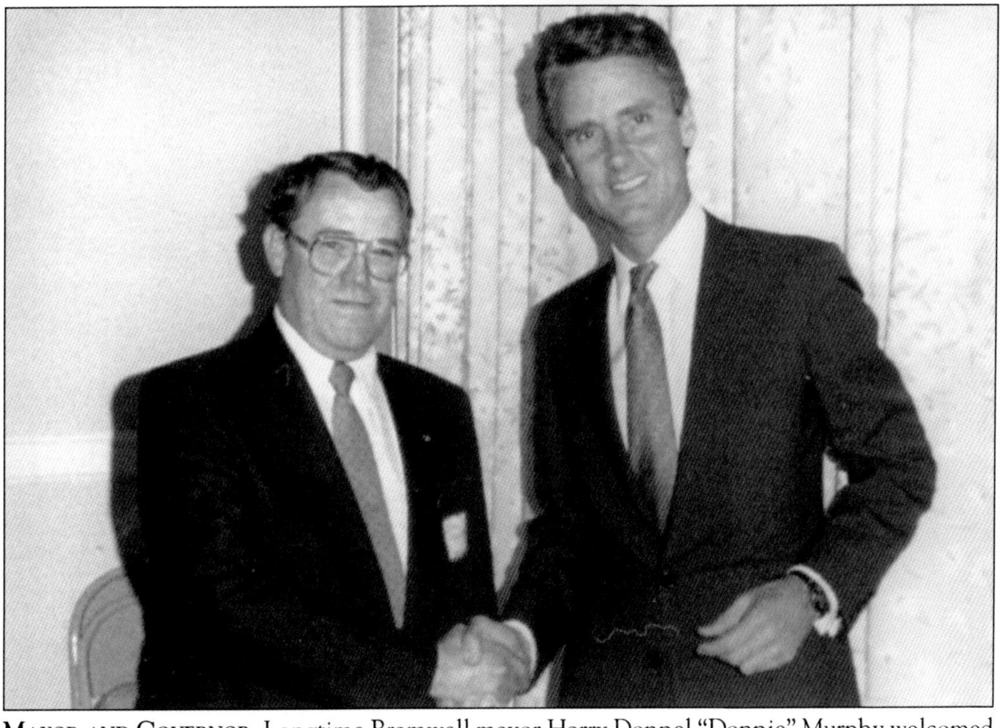

Mayor and Governor. Longtime Bramwell mayor Harry Donnel "Donnie" Murphy welcomed West Virginia gubernatorial candidate Gaston Caperton at a reception for the candidate at Bramwell's Masonic Temple in the summer of 1988. Caperton was later elected governor of West Virginia. (Courtesy of Kelly Eller Murphy and Kim Murphy.)

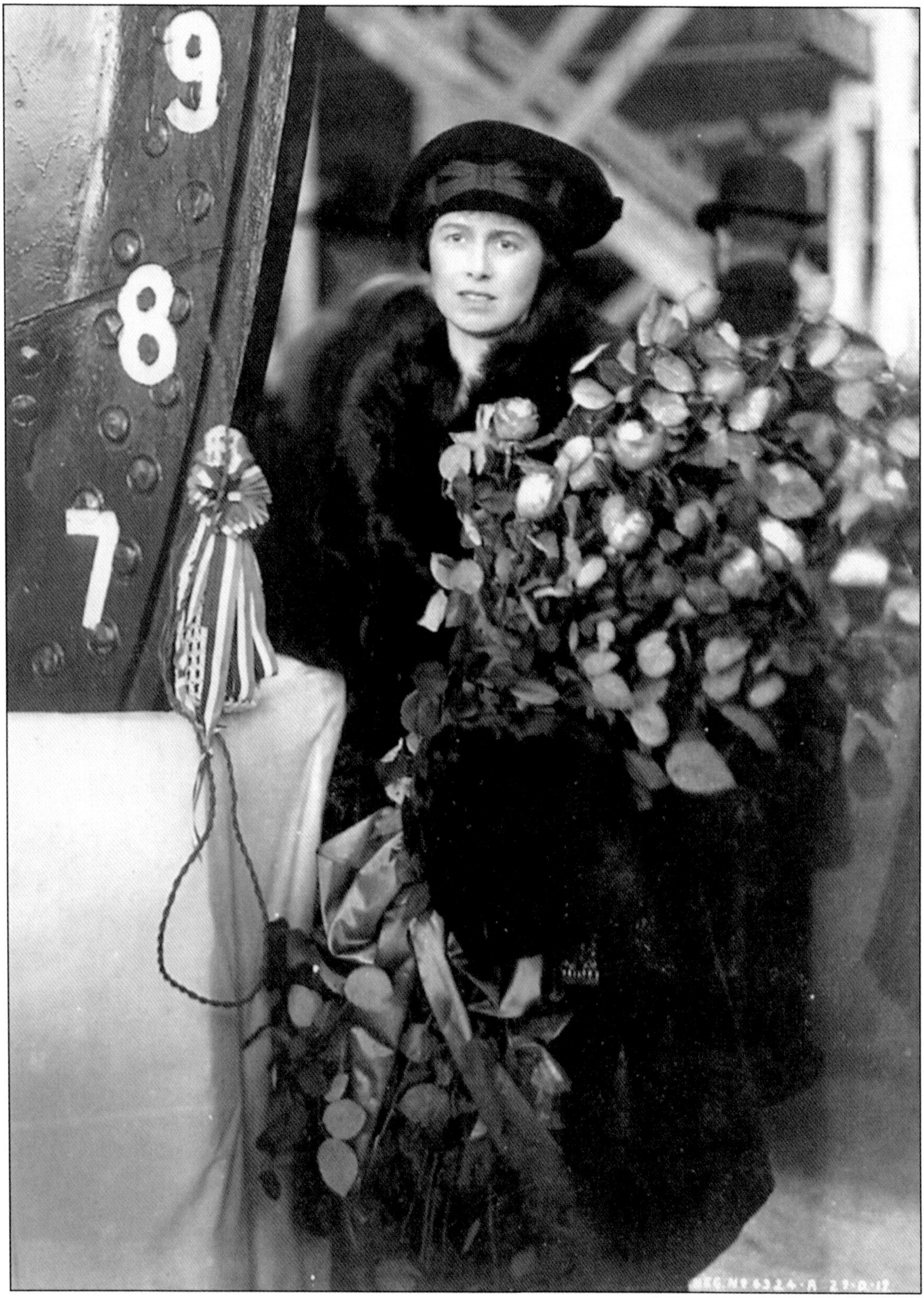

JAMES ELLWOOD JONES. In January 14, 1918, a new collier of the Pocahontas Steamship Line was christened. The place was Camden, New Jersey, and the honor was given to Mrs. James Ellwood "Jimmy" Jones, wife of the Freeman-born son of Jenkin Jones, pioneer coal operator. The *James Ellwood Jones* carried coal between Norfolk and Boston. (Courtesy of Sunny Freeman.)

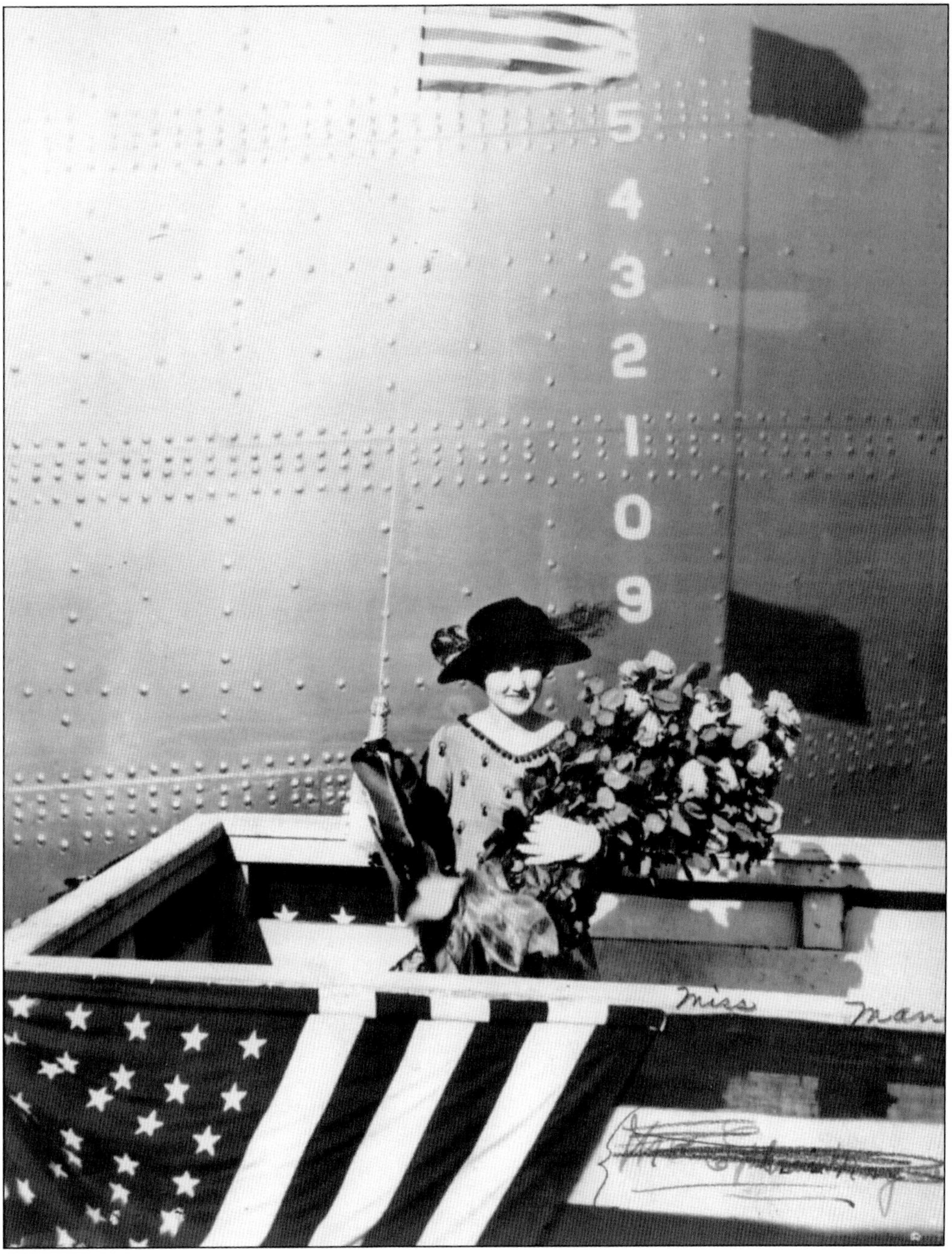

USS *West Virginia*. Isaac T. Mann was living in Washington, D.C., and continued to serve as president of the Bank of Bramwell. His children, Bill and Alice "Peggy," were born in Bramwell and spent their early years in their South River Street home. As the sponsor of the battleship USS *West Virginia*, Alice Wright Mann christened the battleship on December 1, 1923. West Virginia governor Ephraim Morgan was a special guest with Miss Mann at the event. (Courtesy of West Virginia State Archives.)

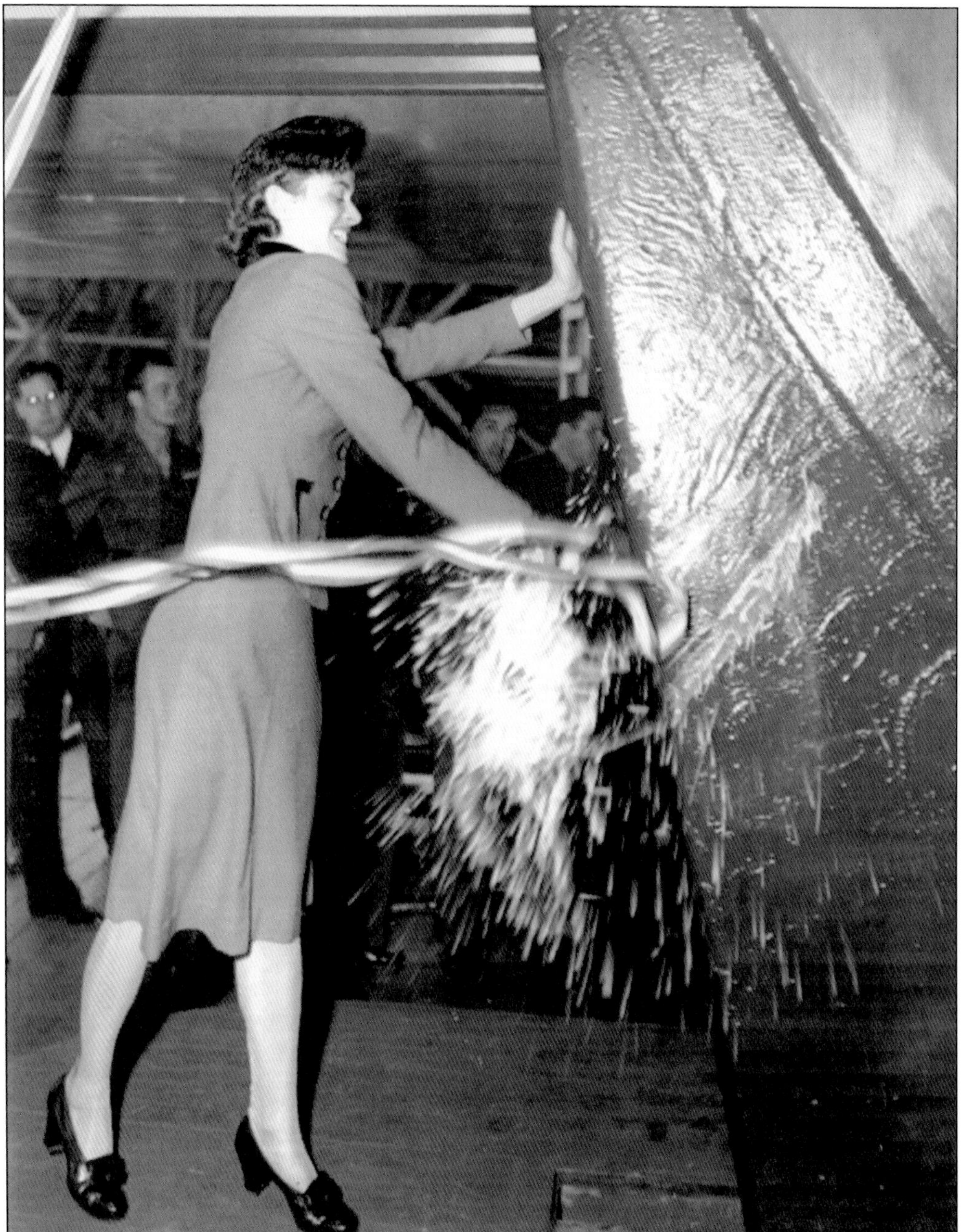

USS GAGE. A descendant of original settler Henry Tabor, Bramwell's Dorothy Tabor Edmunds was teaching school in Portland, Oregon, during World War II. In a contest to sell the most war bonds, she won an invitation to christen the attack transport USS *Gage*. It was April 1, 1944, when she said, "I christen thee USS *Gage*. May God speed you on your mission" and broke the bottle of champagne on the ship's bow. (Courtesy of Dorothy Tabor Edmunds Graham and Henry Edmunds.)

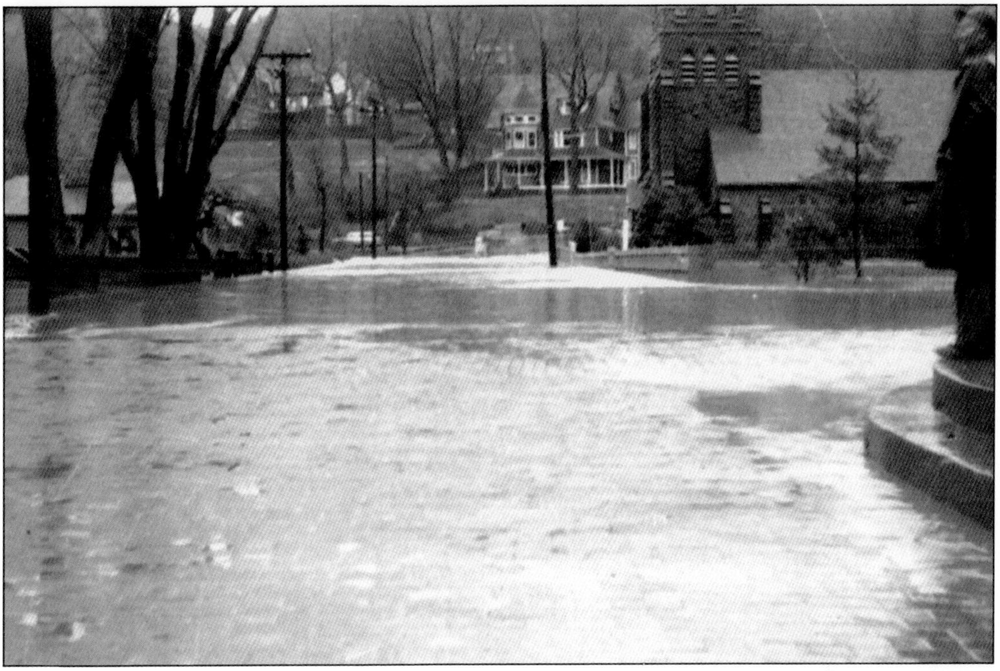

The Rains Came. January 1957 was the month it didn't snow. Instead, it rained and rained some more. On the 29th, the Bluestone River came out of its banks and flowed down Main Street (shown here) and other streets as well.

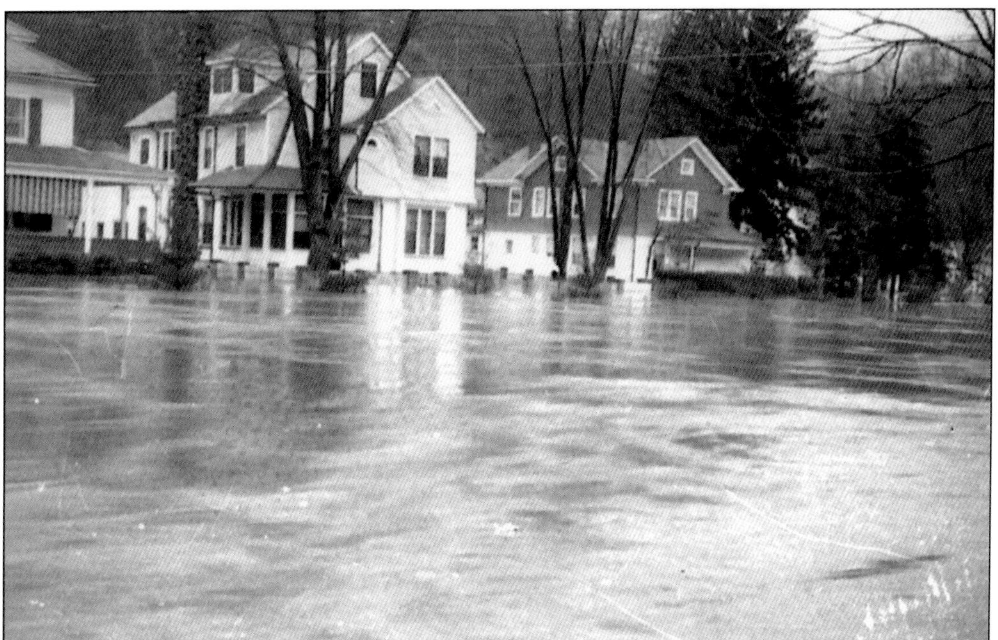

The Great Flood. The river rose until it was in basements and first floors of all the houses along the horseshoe bend.

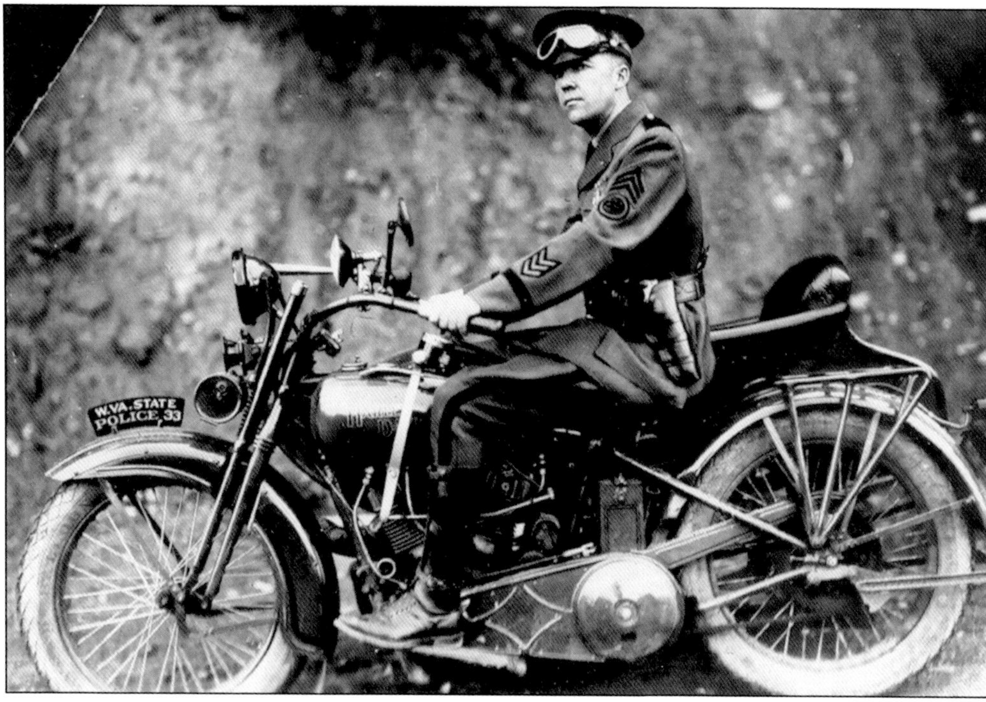

THE LAW. Bramwell Hill's connection to the West Virginia State Police was a Harley Davidson in 1933. Walter Creasy zoomed up the steep mountain on the bike. A sidecar was connected on the right. (Courtesy of Helen Shupe Painter.)

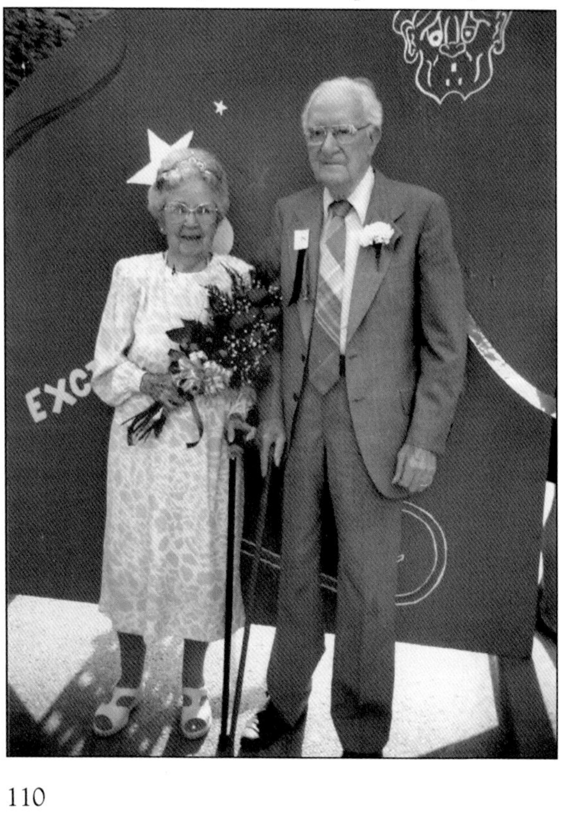

BRAMWELL'S ROYALTY. Queen Mollie and King Walter "Punch" Clark were honored at the silver anniversary celebration of the Bramwell Street Fair in 1992. They were pillars of the community and of the Bramwell Kiwanis Club.

KEESLING GARDENS FOUNDERS. Dr. J.C. Newbold, Hazel Sale Keesling, and Everett L. Keesling seem to be enjoying the spring rhododendrons. (Courtesy of Linda Keesling Beggs.)

A PLACE TO VISIT AND REMEMBER. In 1953, Everett L. Keesling and his wife opened their magnificent gardens to the public. During the ten years it was open for business, the show of almost 20,000 azaleas and rhododendrons attracted thousands to Bramwell. Keesling expanded the playhouse Isaac T. Mann built for his children but left the beautifully landscaped grounds intact, adding to them. The house sits beside a large man-made pond he filled with water lilies. The Mann children and friends used it for swimming and boating. (Courtesy of Linda Keesling Beggs.)

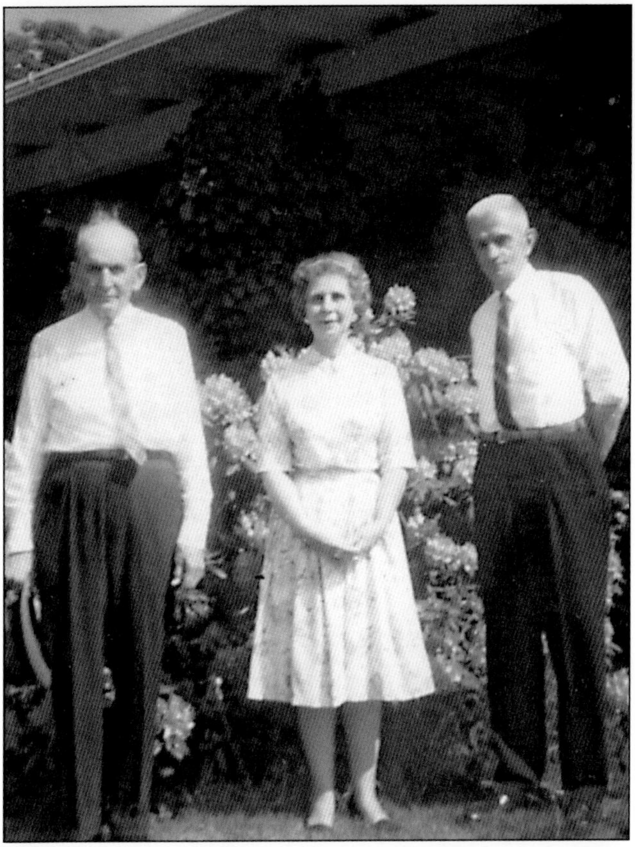

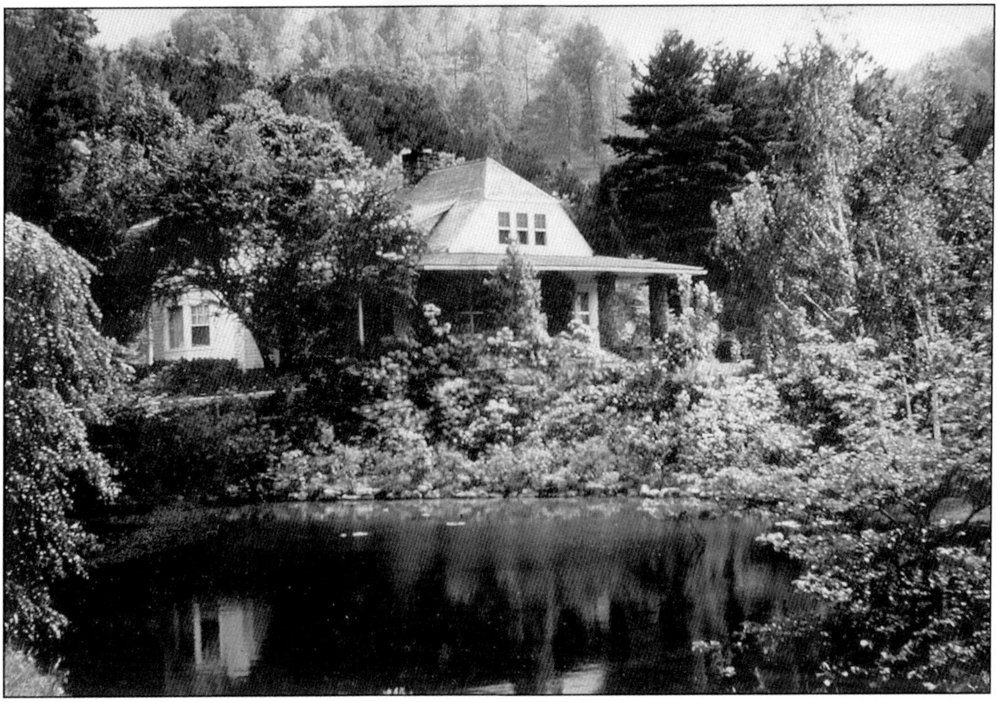

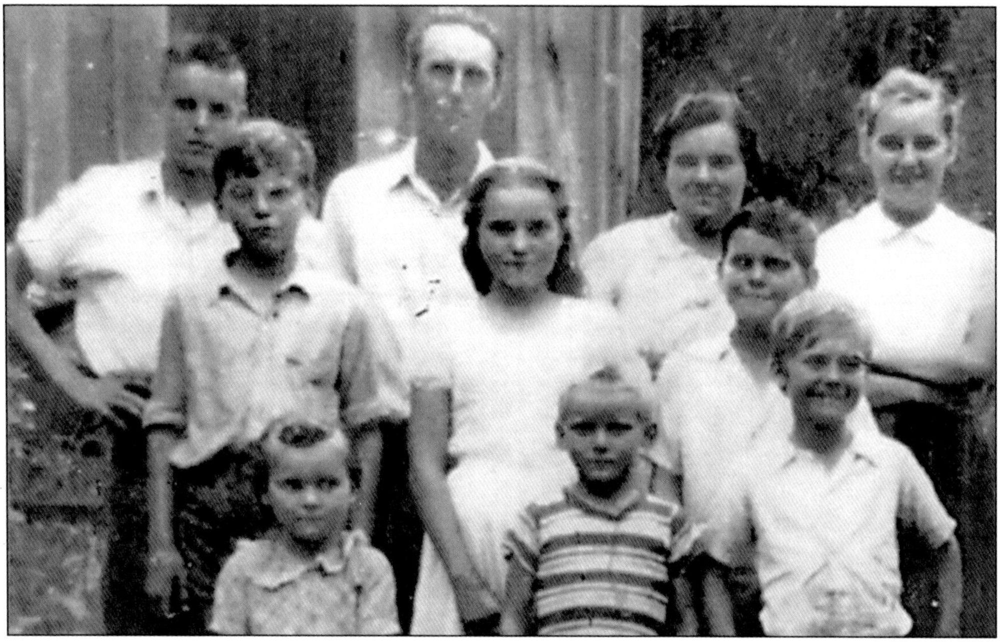

Second and Third Generations. Woodrow Cook and Virginia Sparks Cook spent their lives in Bramwell. From left to right in this 1952 photograph are (front row) Edna, Junior, and Jesse; (middle row) Bill, Betty, and Johnny; (back row) Giles, father Woodrow, mother Virginia, and Mabel. Woodrow, Virginia, and all their children attended Bramwell Schools. (Courtesy of Edna Cook Keller.)

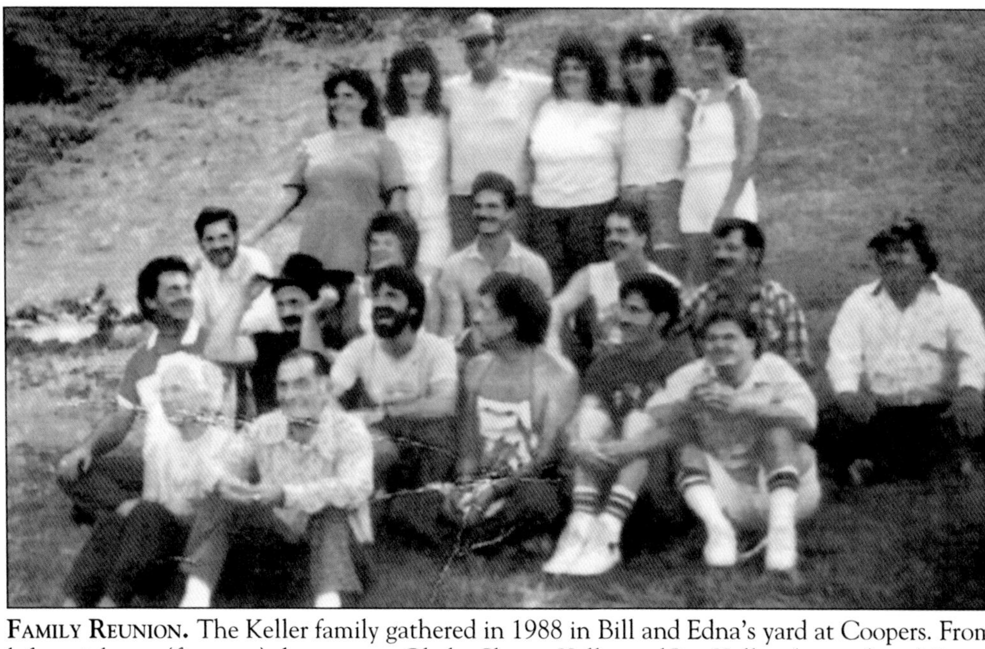

Family Reunion. The Keller family gathered in 1988 in Bill and Edna's yard at Coopers. From left to right are (first row) the parents, Gladys Skeens Keller and Jim Keller; (second row) Ernie, Alfred, Aubrey, Joe, Lacy, and Rufus; (third row) Doug, Jackie, Danny, John, Ernest, and Frank; (standing on the fourth row) Carol, Diane, Bill, Coremae, Verta, and Sue. All eighteen Keller children attended Bramwell Schools. (Courtesy of William "Bill" Keller.)

Eight

It's Bramwell High School

Memories that linger,
Constant and true.
Memories we'll cherish,
Bramwell High School, of you.
—from "Dear Bramwell High School" by David Richardson

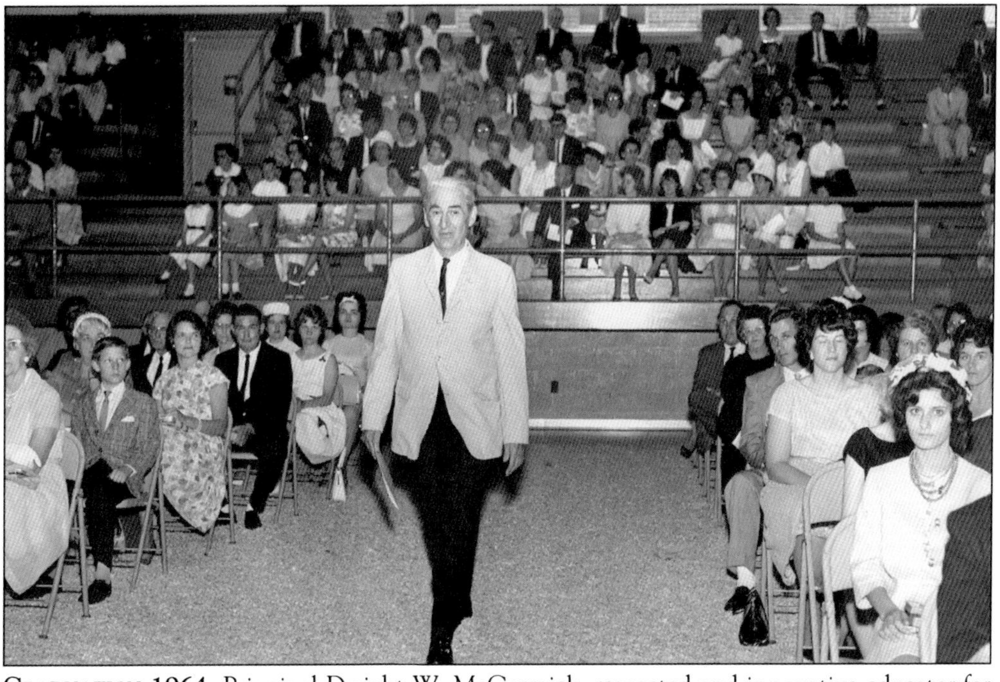

Graduation 1964. Principal Dwight W. McCormick, respected and innovative educator for several generations of Bramwell students, presides over the first graduation in the new Douglas J. Sexton Gymnasium. Mr. McCormick was principal for more than 30 years, during which he administered a superior educational facility while fostering a strong sense of community and family identity within his students.

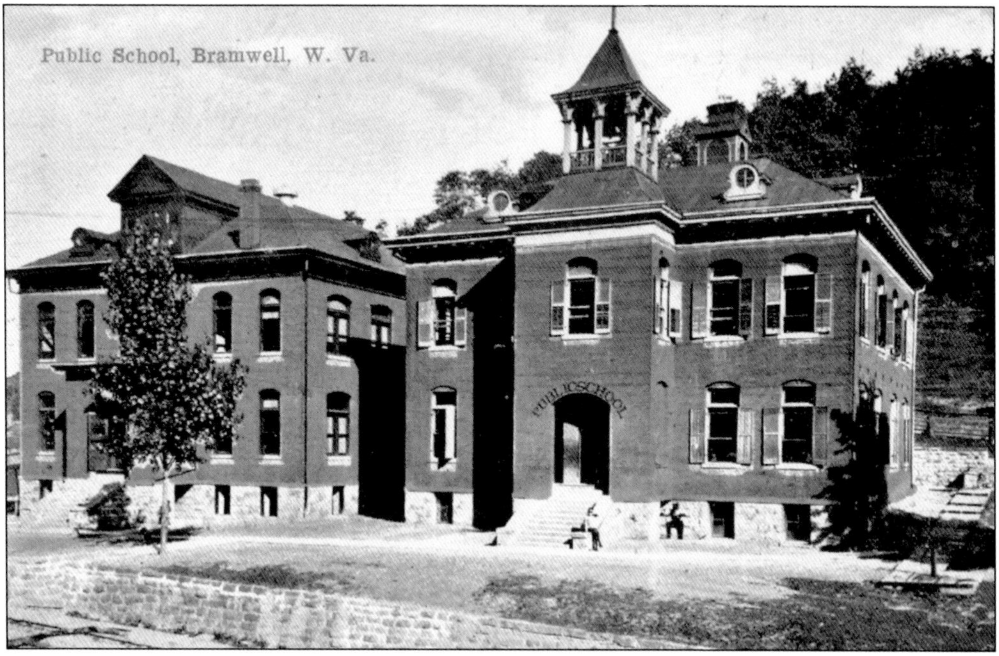

FIRST SCHOOL BUILDINGS. The structure on the right was built before 1908 as Bramwell Graded School. The second building to its left was added soon thereafter. This postcard, published by the Bryant Pharmacy, was postmarked August 25, 1911.

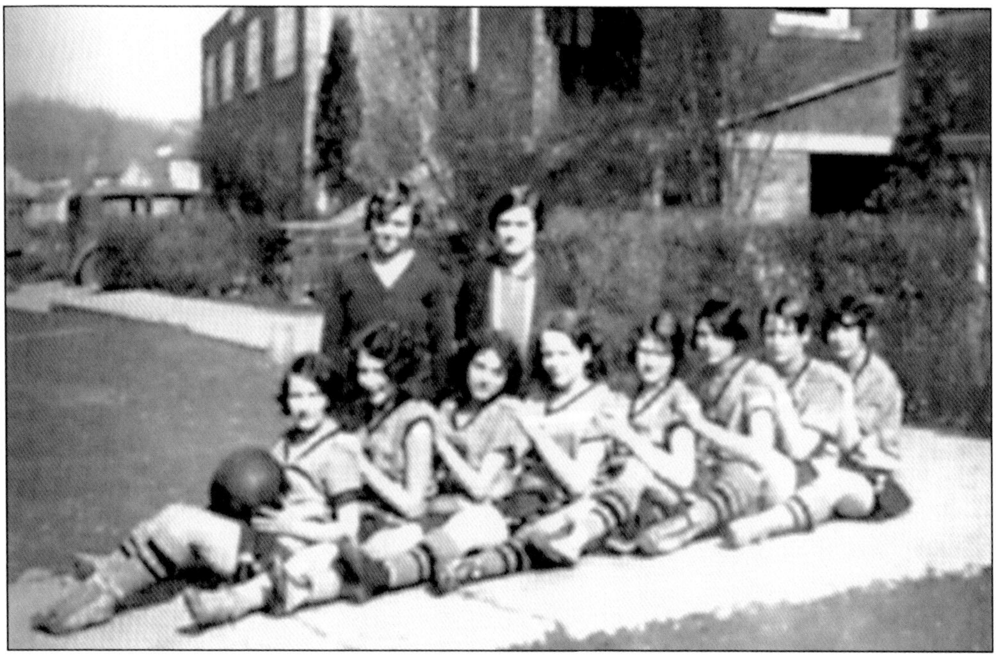

GIRLS' BASKETBALL TEAM. The members of this c. 1930s team were, from left to right, Frances "Penny" Witt, Marie Hill, Kate Osborne, Katharine Hewitt, Emily Lee Hale, Eva Pasley, Mamie Hill, and Helen Ellison. Standing are the coaches, Miss Frable and Miss Hardy. The building on the left is the c. 1930 grade school. The high school building behind the girls burned in 1933 and was replaced by a new structure in 1934.

Schoolhouse Hill. Fourteen-year-old Katherine Hewitt strikes a pose on Bluestone Avenue across from Bramwell High School in 1930. She later taught school at Bramwell High School and retired before the last Millionaires graduated in 1991. The entire Bramwell School complex closed permanently in 2004, 70 years following the construction of the high school building. (Courtesy of Katherine Hewitt Barringer.)

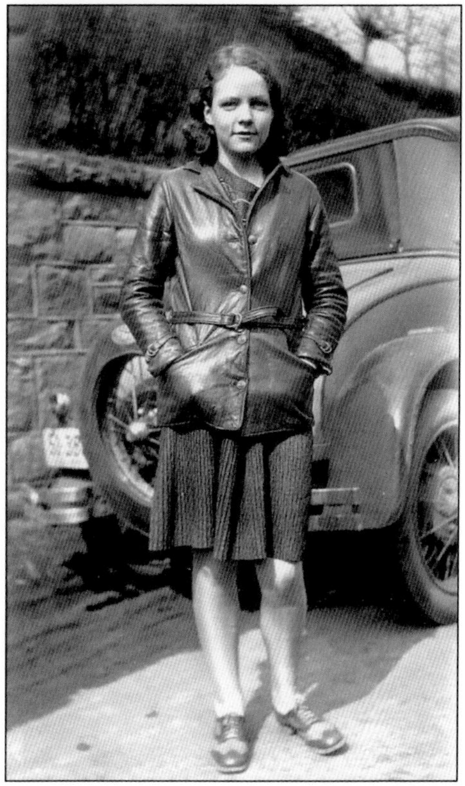

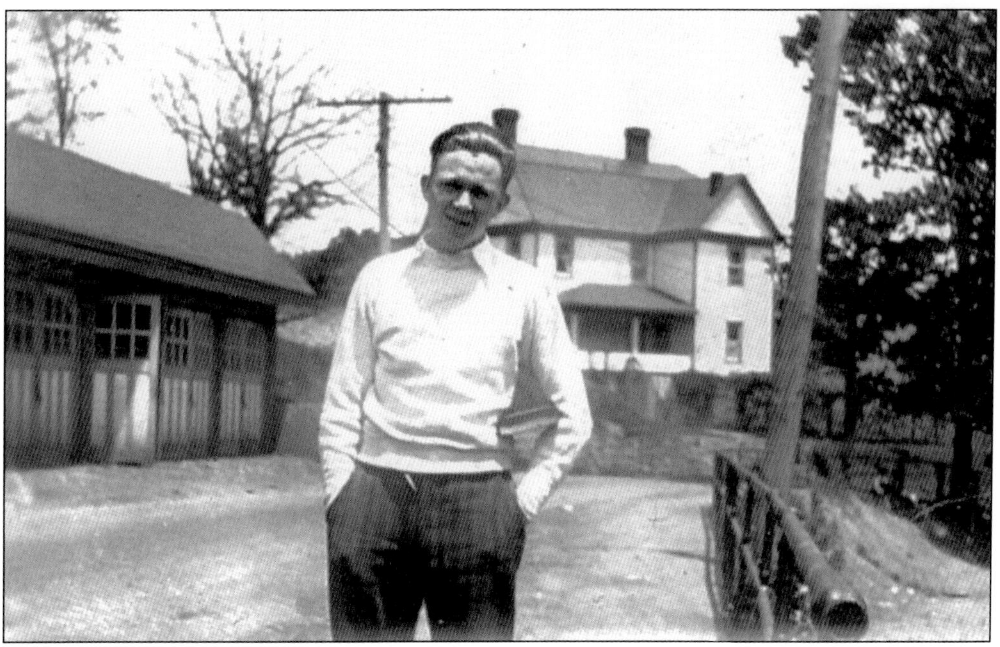

Bluestone Avenue. Standing on the sidewalk in front of Bramwell Elementary School is Stewart Maxey *c.* 1935. In the background is the home of Bethuel Moore, original partner in the Buckeye Coal & Coke Co. operation, and Minnie Moore, a well-known teacher in Bramwell. (Courtesy of Lava Yost Staton.)

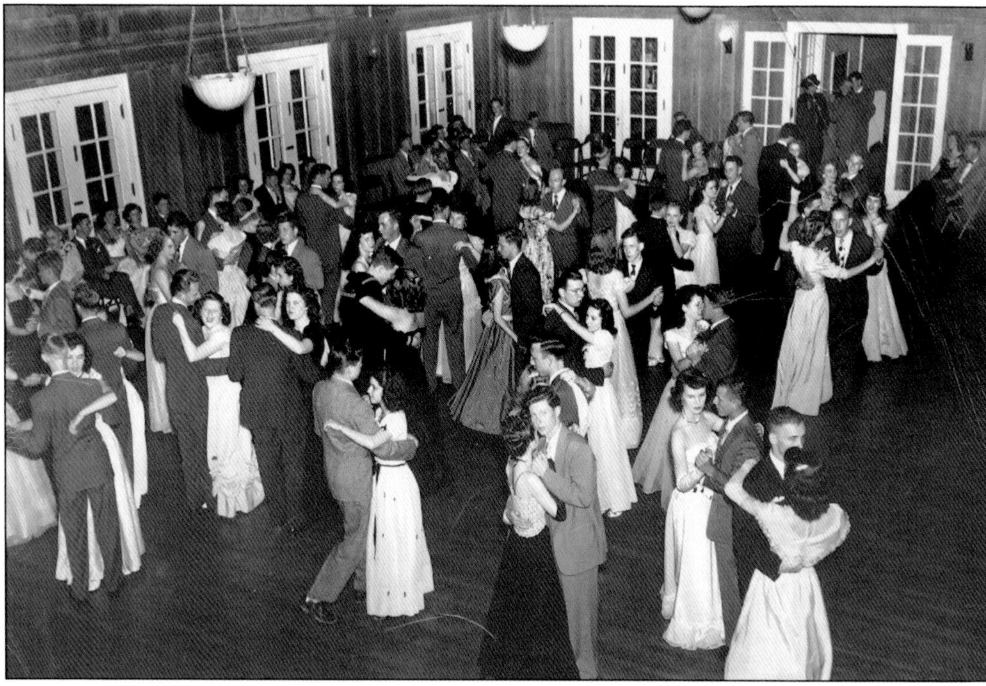

Prom Night. Bramwell High School proms were held at the Bluefield Country Club for many years, and this 1949 dance was no exception.

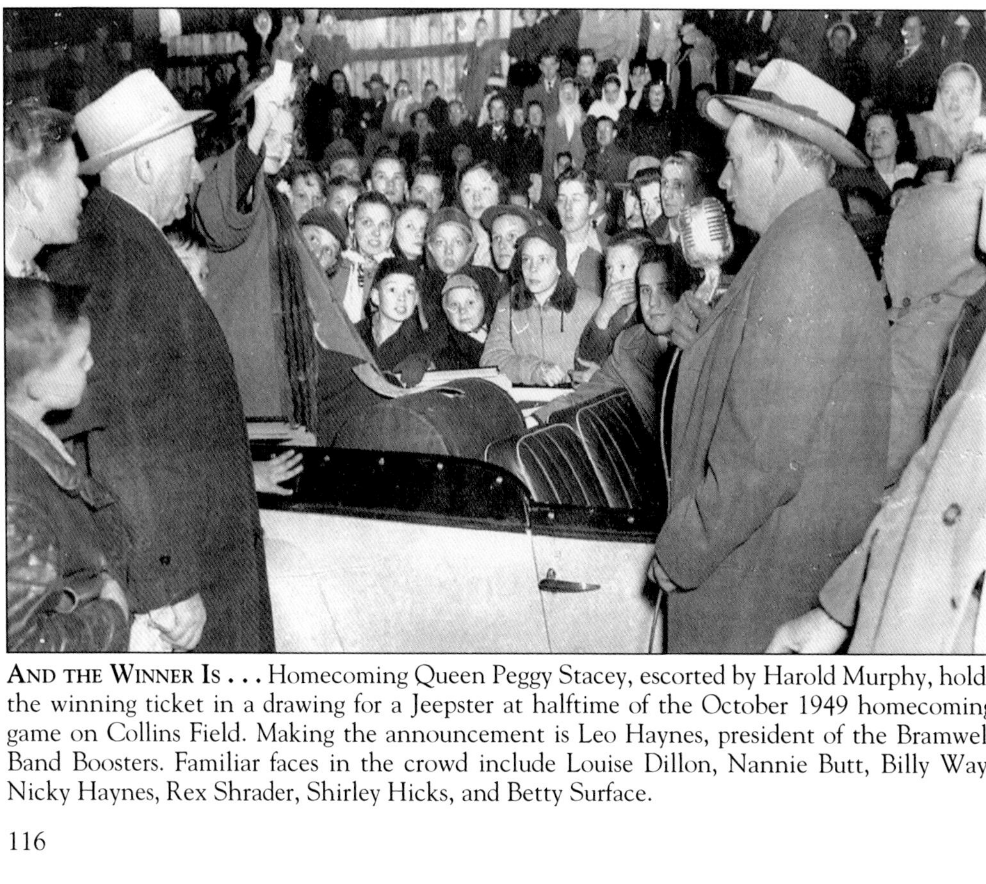

And the Winner Is . . . Homecoming Queen Peggy Stacey, escorted by Harold Murphy, holds the winning ticket in a drawing for a Jeepster at halftime of the October 1949 homecoming game on Collins Field. Making the announcement is Leo Haynes, president of the Bramwell Band Boosters. Familiar faces in the crowd include Louise Dillon, Nannie Butt, Billy Way, Nicky Haynes, Rex Shrader, Shirley Hicks, and Betty Surface.

BHS CHEERLEADERS. Showing off their letter sweaters in 1947 are Billy Dawson, kneeling in front of (from left to right) Jenny Lee Painter, Donna Lee Hurst, Peggy Stacey, and Grace Stacey. (Courtesy of Eve Cooper Murphy.)

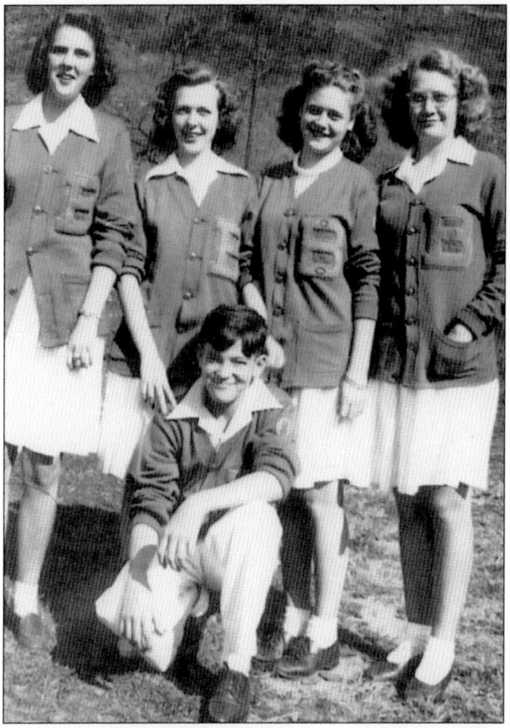

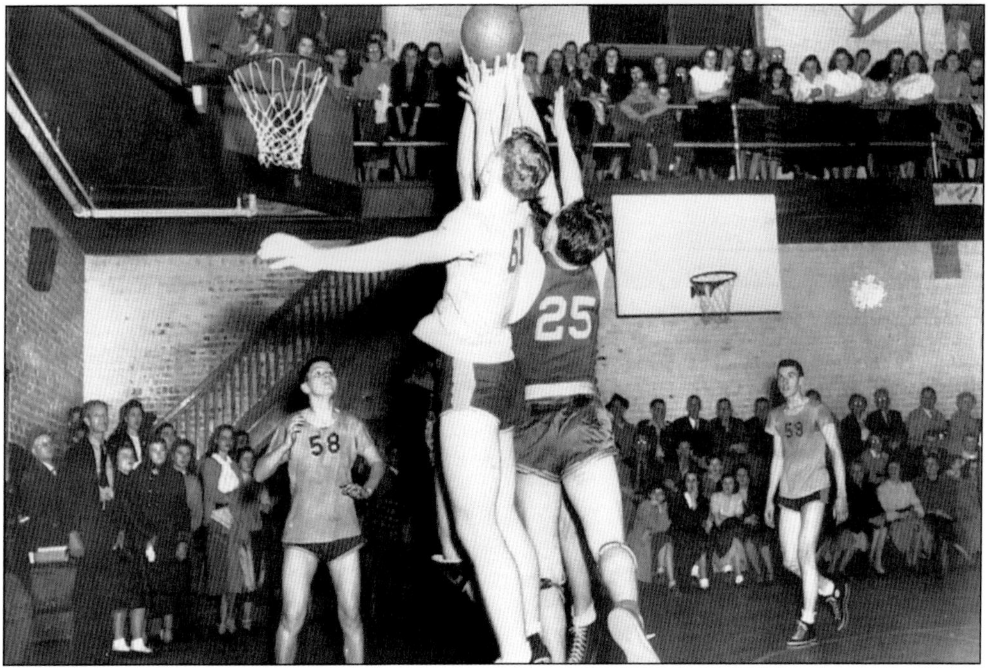

REBOUND. James "Soybean" Shelton, number 61, goes for the rebound in front of a packed BHS gym in 1949. Bleachers around the floor were accompanied by a balcony on three sides. In addition to serving as a sports venue, a stage at one end of the gym also made it the site of pageants, plays, operettas, and other school programs during the years before a new gymnasium was built in 1964.

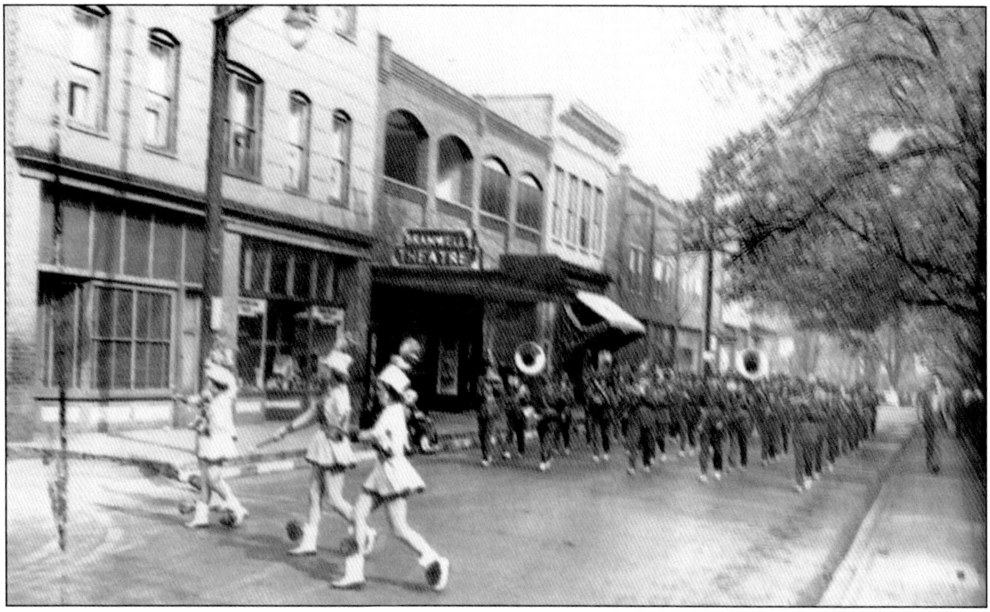

MAIN STREET PARADE. A busy commercial block in downtown Bramwell provides the backdrop for this October 1952 homecoming parade photograph. The Bramwell Theatre marquee is easily distinguishable. Mr. David Richardson keeps pace with his band on the sidewalk to the right.

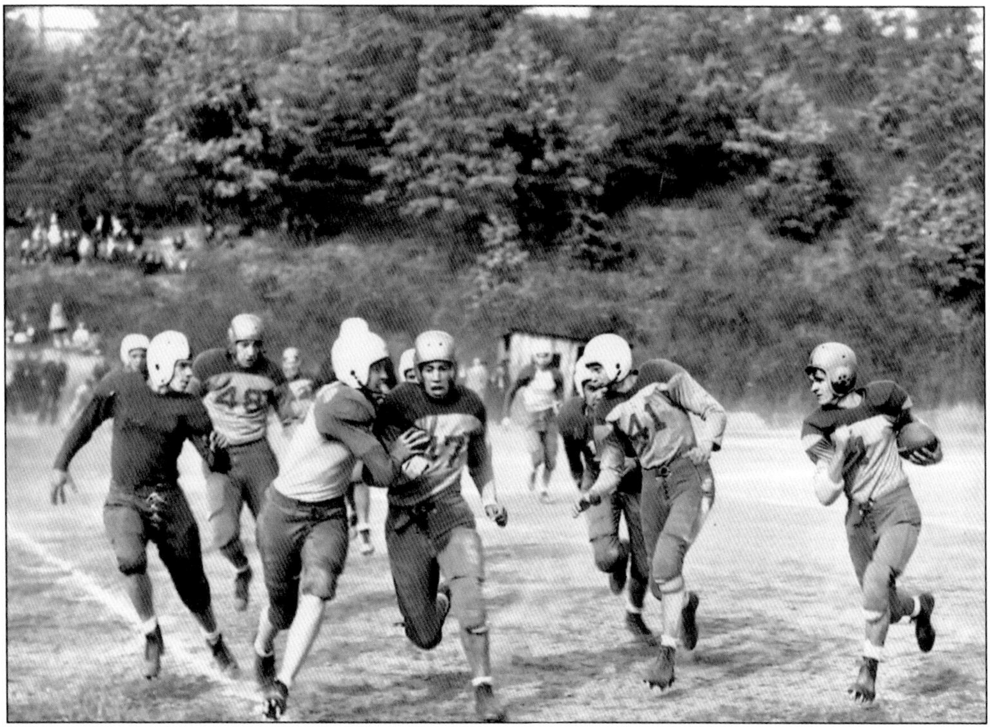

BRAMWELL HOSTS PETERSTOWN. The Millionaires (in numbered jerseys) enjoy home field advantage on Collins Field in this 1952 game on a Saturday afternoon. Bill Epperson carries the ball as his teammates block. Ray Vest is number 48. The football fence is visible in the upper left corner of the photo, and the small building is the restroom.

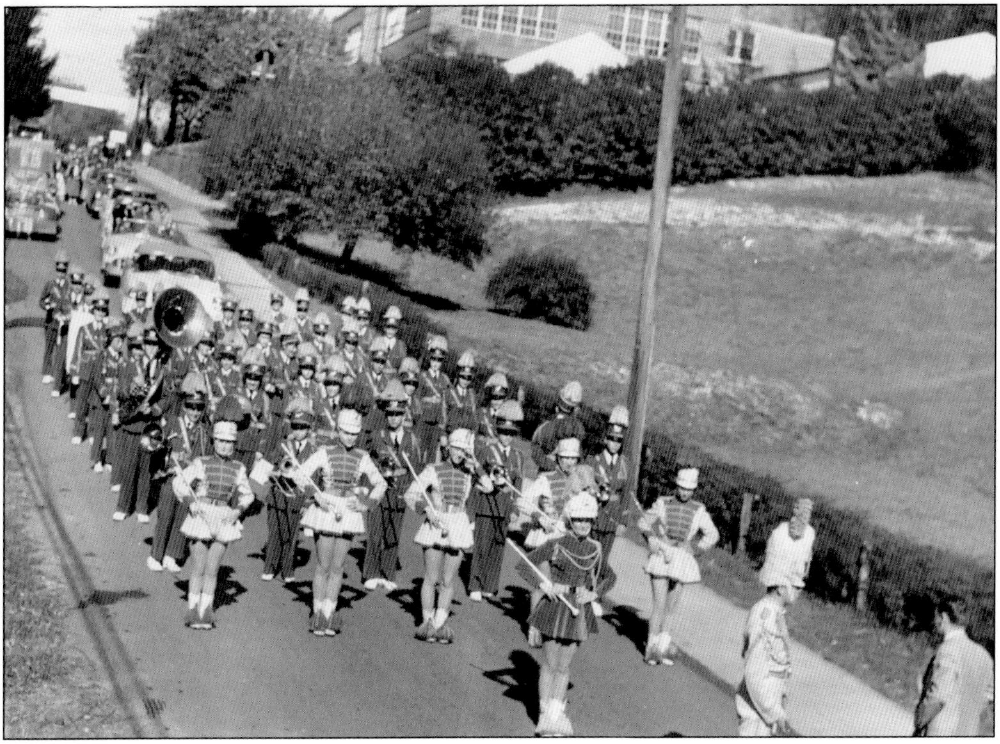

Bluestone Avenue Parade Route. The BHS band begins its 1954 homecoming march toward downtown Bramwell from the high school, the third floor visible above the trees. Mr. Richardson, lower right, confers with Jewel Tyree, drum major. Head majorette is Norma Jean Dawson. Other majorettes, from left to right, are Jonnie McNulty, Ann Clark, Judie Allen, Carol Scott, and Fern Williams.

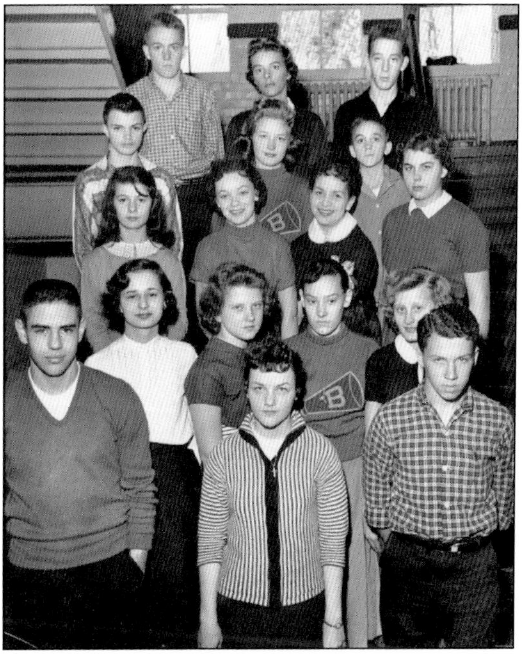

Student Council, 1958. Students from grades 7 through 12 represented their classmates as members of the student council. From left to right are (first row) L.E. Gross, Wanda Godbey, and Walter Williams; (second row) Brenda Meade, Mary Katherine Hill, Joan Tuell, and Patty Rae Caldwell; (third row) Margaret Newman, Judy Hall, Joyce Dowdy, and Patricia Estep; (fourth row) Dorwin Byrd, Billie May Morgan, and Larry Synan; (fifth row) William Bevins, teacher Sue Young. and Bobby Jones.

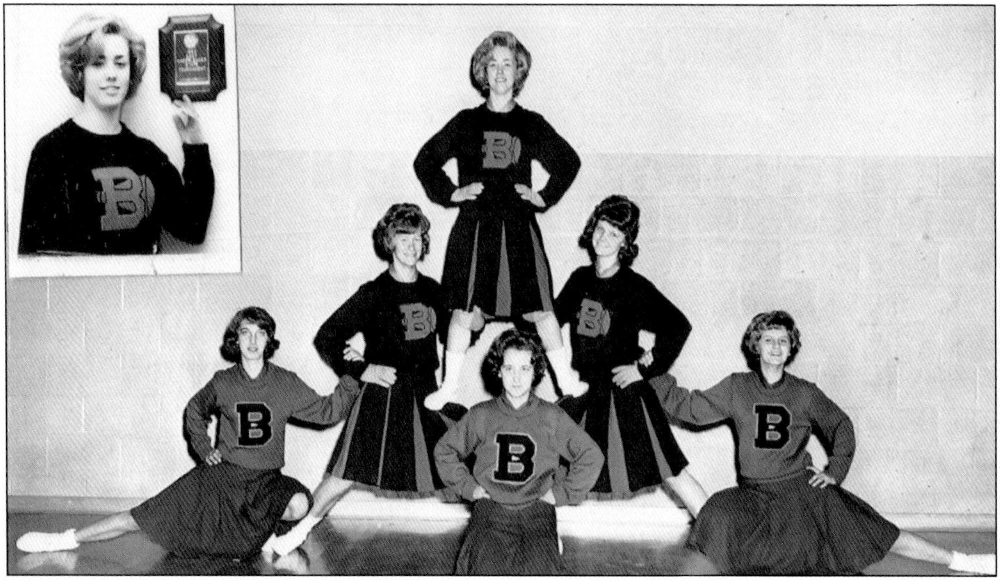

"Upstate" 1965. Millionaire basketball teams competed in the state tournament a total of 11 years, beginning in 1965 with a trip to Charleston, or "upstate" for the southern teams. That year, Bramwell was defeated in the semifinal, but Don Pierce and Joe Lambert were named to the All-Tournament Team. These 1965 cheerleaders were the first BHS squad to support their team at state level. The junior high team, from left to right, is (first row) Carol Rethford, Elaine Turner, and Janie Sparks; the high school cheerleaders are (second row) Ellen Goins, Sarah "Bibbi" Sigmon (captain), and Judy Williamson. Bibbi was also named best cheerleader (inset). She continues to be a Millionaire cheerleader by serving as a founder and organizer of the annual Bramwell Millionaire Homecoming Weekend since 1988.

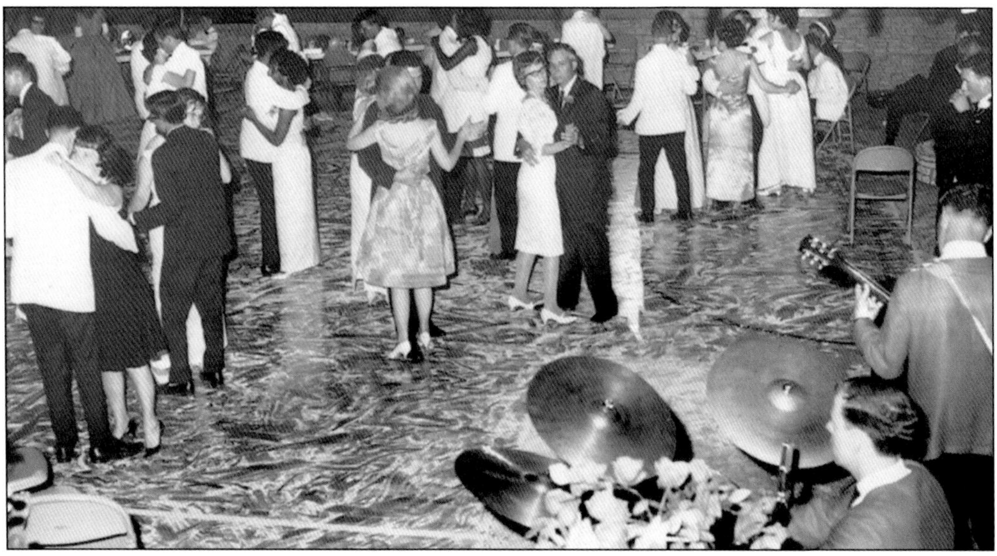

Junior-Senior Prom, 1966. A number of BHS proms were held in the new school gym after its construction, as this 1966 photograph illustrates. Facing the camera in the center of the photograph are business teacher Carol Hurst and her husband, James "Ken" Hurst. Mrs. Hurst served her students as a hardworking and greatly appreciated junior class sponsor for 11 years. (Photo by Jim Graham.)

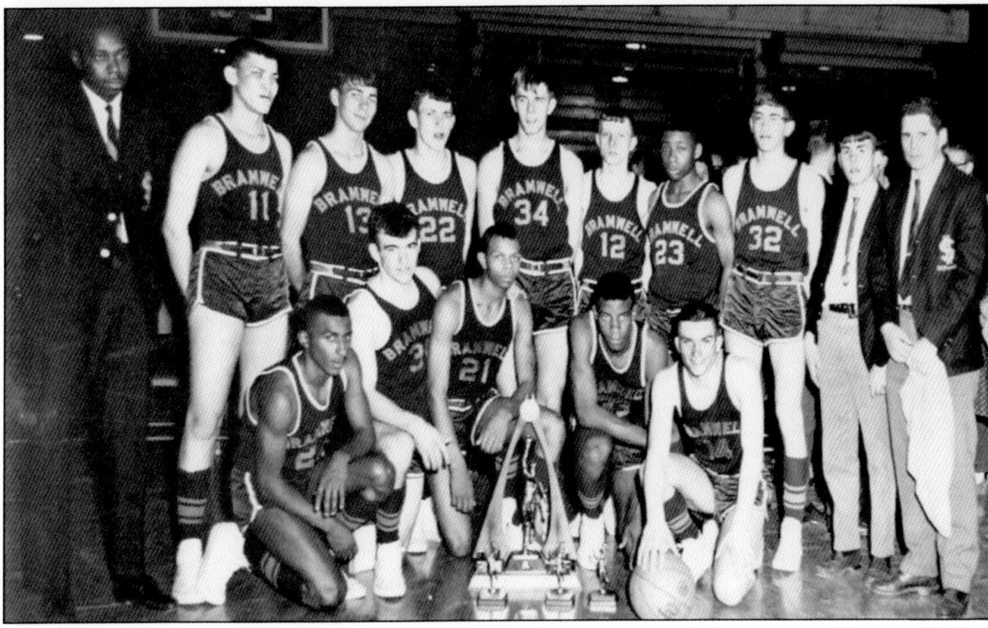

FIRST STATE CHAMPS! The 1967 Millionaires made history, not only by winning Bramwell's first Class A state basketball championship but also by doing so as an undefeated team with a record of 26-0. The Millionaires also set a record that still stands for greatest margin of victory in a championship game by defeating Bethany 86-49. The members of the 1967 dream team were, from left to right, (kneeling) Ricky Stores, Charles Davidson, Dennis Hood, Tommy Gravely, and Bill Pierce; (standing) Asst. Coach Charles Phelps, Wayne Hodges, Everett Frost, Johnny Harman, Mickey Spicer, Joe Hill, Oscar Miller, Paul Porterfield, manager Greg Murphy, and Head Coach Bill Norton. Bill Pierce, Ricky Stores, and Tommy Gravely were named to the All-Tournament Team.

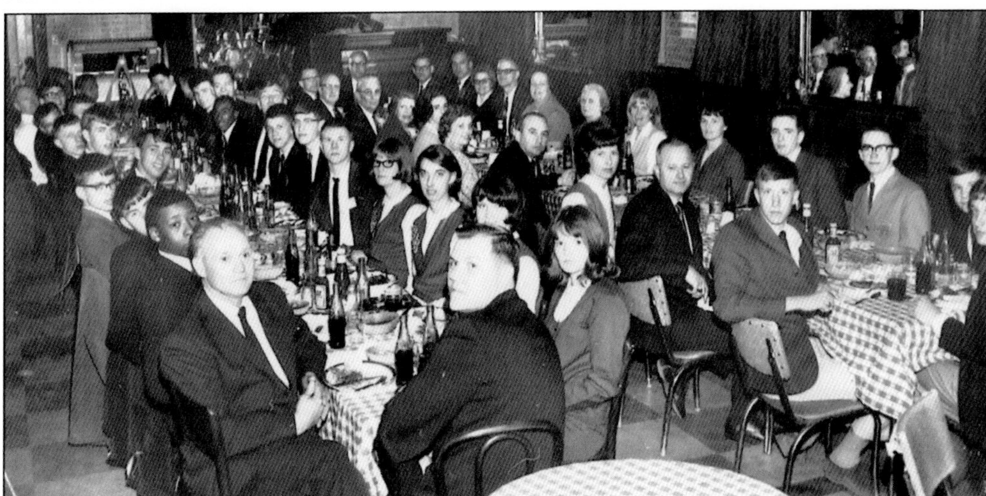

BASKETBALL BANQUET, 1967. The guests at this celebration dinner in March honored the championship team and cheerleaders. Members of the next team to engage in state tournament action in 1970 are seated at the table on the right and include Ken Jones, Jay Barringer, and David Bowman. (Photo by Mantini's Studios.)

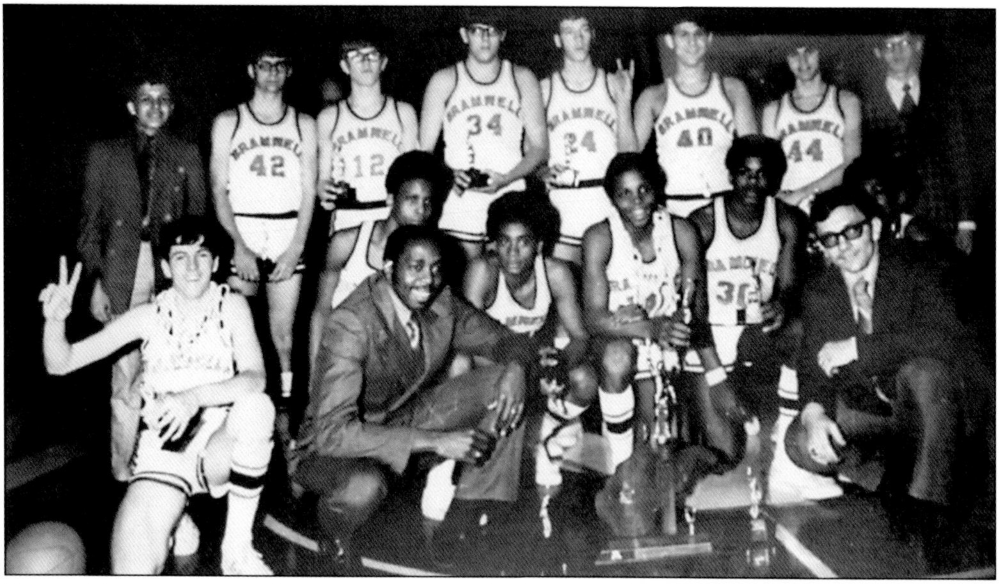

Repeat Performance. After a heartbreaking 61-56 loss to Hedgesville in the 1970 state final, the Millionaires came back in 1971 to win the championship over Hamlin 58-40 and ended their season with a 19-6 record. Team members pictured here are, from left to right, (kneeling in front) Head Coach Charles Phelps and Asst. Coach Lonzo Kennedy; (kneeling behind) Terry Brown, Emmanuel Fuller, Robert Gammon, Donald "Dino" Martin, Melvin "Butch" Cosby, and William Webb; (standing) manager Phillip Baugh, Joey Griffith, Donnie Carver, Ed Lee Pasley, Bill Wells, Wayne Bailey, Edward Richardson, and manager Charles Donald "Donnie" Brummett. Terry Brown, Dino Martin, and Butch Cosby were named to the All-Tournament Team.

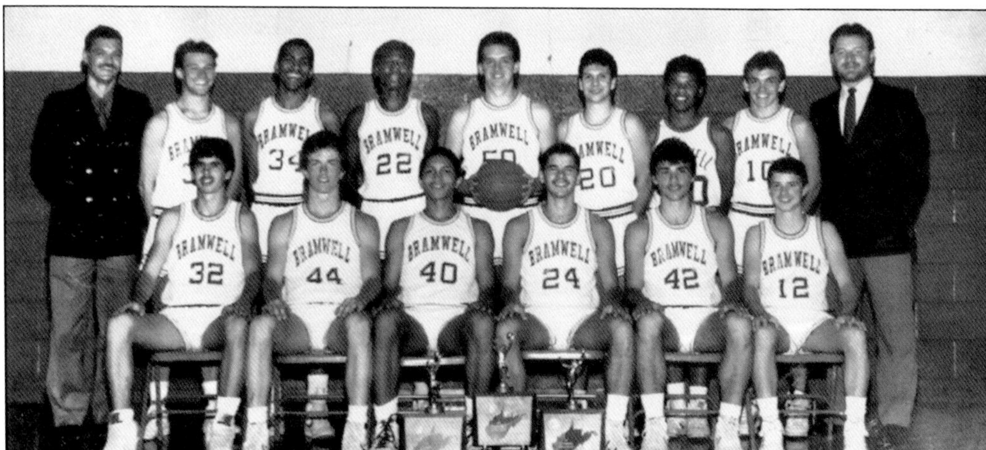

The Sweetest Gift. The undefeated 1987 Millionaires went upstate for the third straight year. They met Paden City, also 26-0, for the title. The Millionaires suffered a 71-61 loss. The 1988 team promised to win the trophy for Bramwell's centennial. Their 25-2 season ended with an 85-54 championship victory over Hamlin. Most of the 1987 team (above) returned for the 1988 season. Pictured from left to right are (front row) Scott Goins, Shawn Jenkins, Lamont Woods, Allen Baldwin, Sean Riffe, and Chris Shoemaker; (back row) Coach Robert Wray, Brain Rutherford, Donald Robinson, Anthony "Boobie" Walton, Terry Akers, Billy Stroupe, Steve Collins, Roy Rice, Asst. Coach Dale Lee. Named to the 1988 All-Tournament Team were Woods, Goins, and Jenkins.

Nine

Epilogue

"Oh, Bramwell was really something then," Ed Pasley sighed,
As he looked at the past with a heart full of pride.
We've more to remember, more stories to tell,
But for today, we bid you farewell.

—Lou Stoker

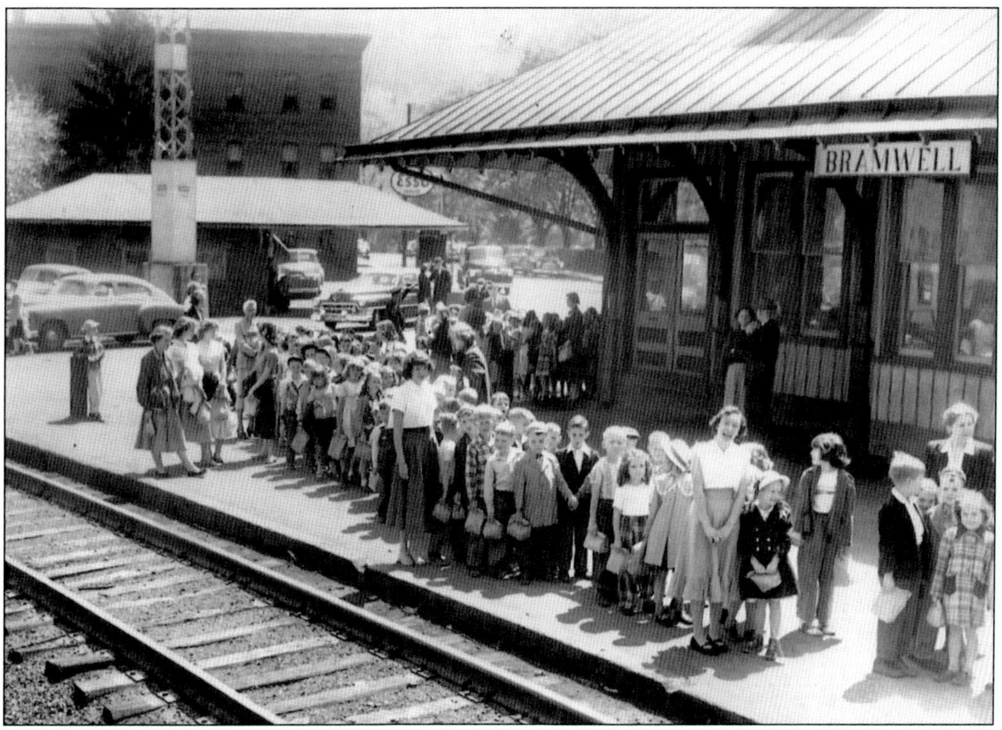

Last Passenger Train. It was April 30, 1952. More than 300 grade school children from Bramwell Grade and High Schools wore their new Easter outfits to school that day. They paid their 58¢ and carried their packed lunches in little brown bags as they walked the half-mile to the train station. A staff photographer from the *Sunset News* recorded the memorable day.

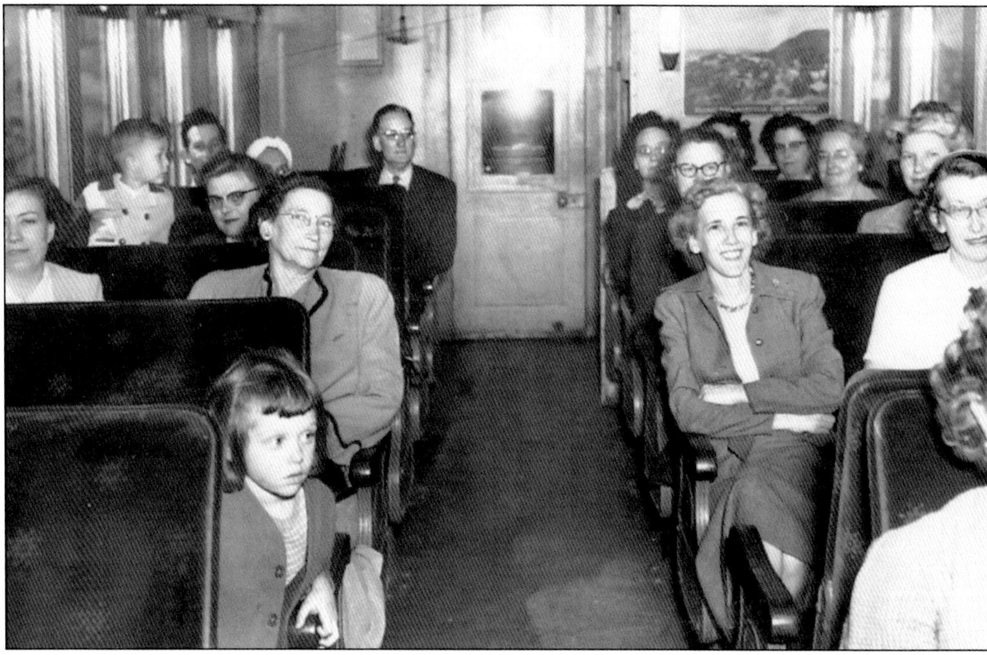

Last Train Riders. The coaches were filled when the special train traveled from Bramwell to Matoaka for one last passenger train ride. From the left are Lillian Shrader, unidentified, Kathryn Hill, Mrs. McKinley Stacey, Leonard Cole, unidentified, Marie Tabor (glasses showing), Dea Peraldo Hughes, Faye Shrader, Alice Cole, Thelma Lamanca, and Helen Mitchell. (Photo by *Sunset News*.)

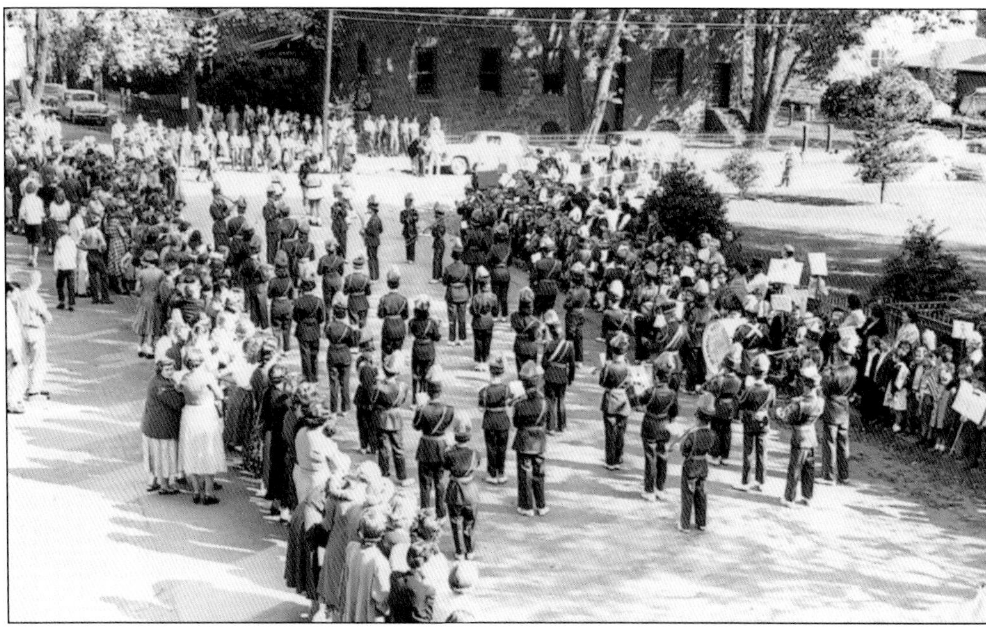

Last Football Homecoming. Bramwell High School's band, under the direction of David Richardson, paraded through the downtown's Main Street in October 1957. It was the last parade for a football homecoming game. The 1957–1958 school year ended football on Collins Field.

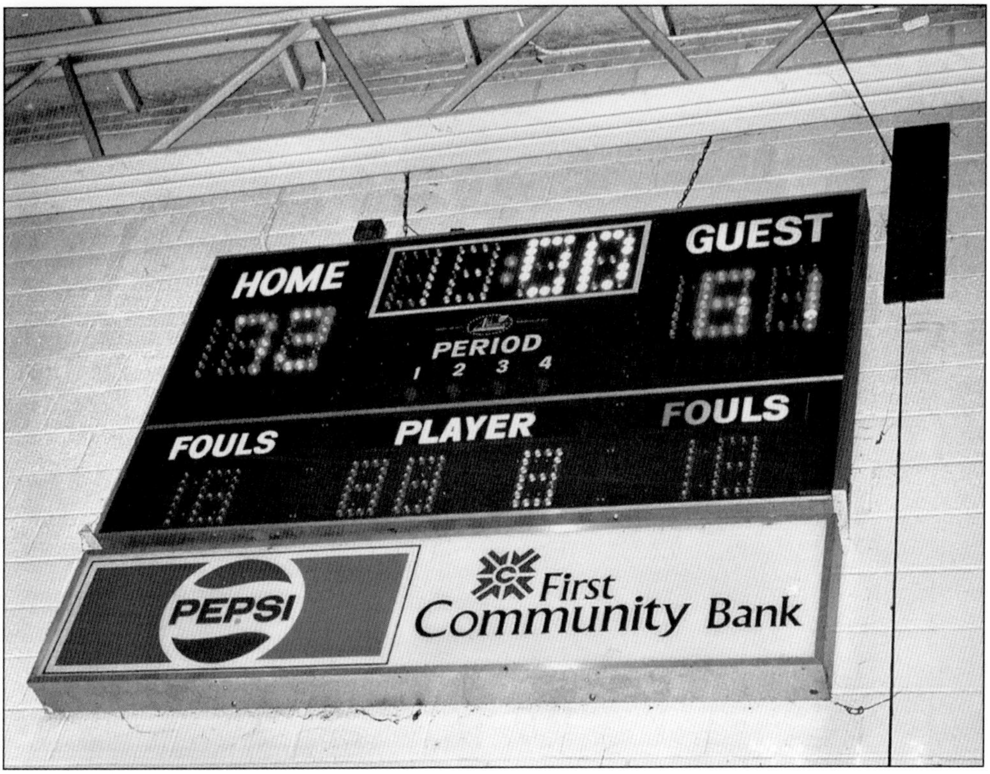

LAST SCORE. This is the score clock with the last score of the last game in the Bramwell High School gym, the "Home of the Millionaires."

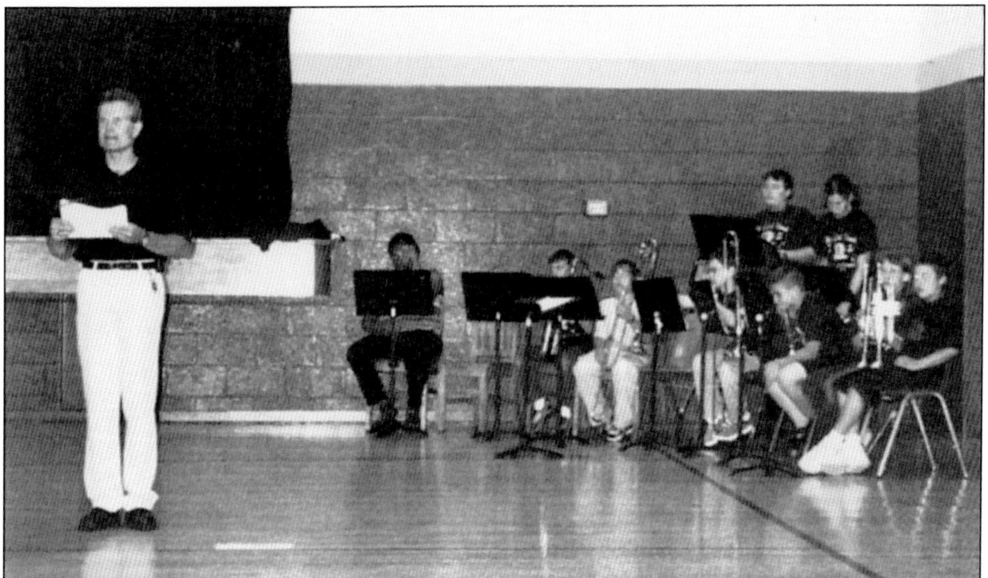

LAST BAND, JUNE 2004. Band director Kim Murphy is pictured with the last band at Bramwell School. Kim was a student of David Richardson, legendary band director for Bramwell High School. (Courtesy of Bibbi Dawson Sigmon.)

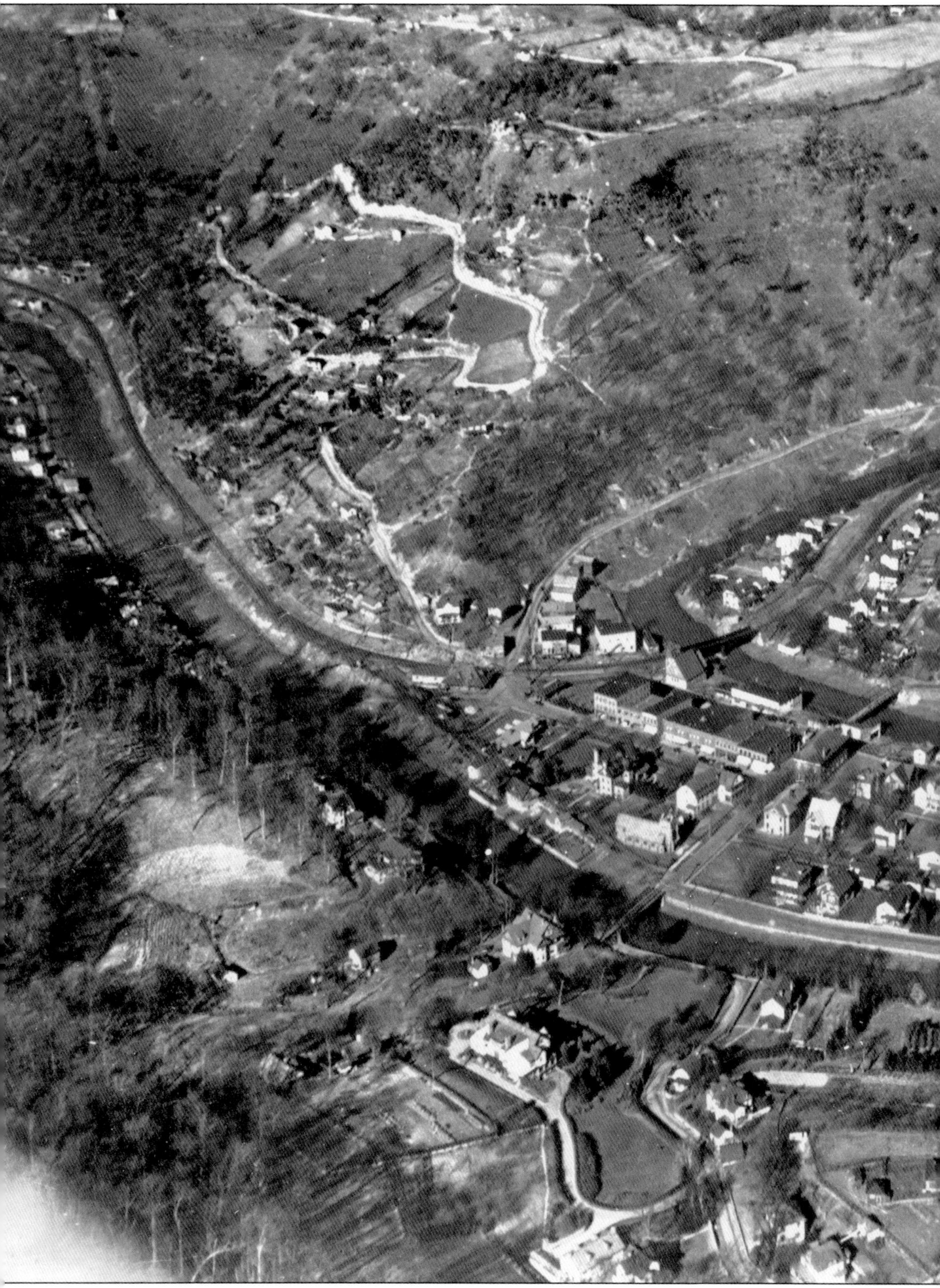

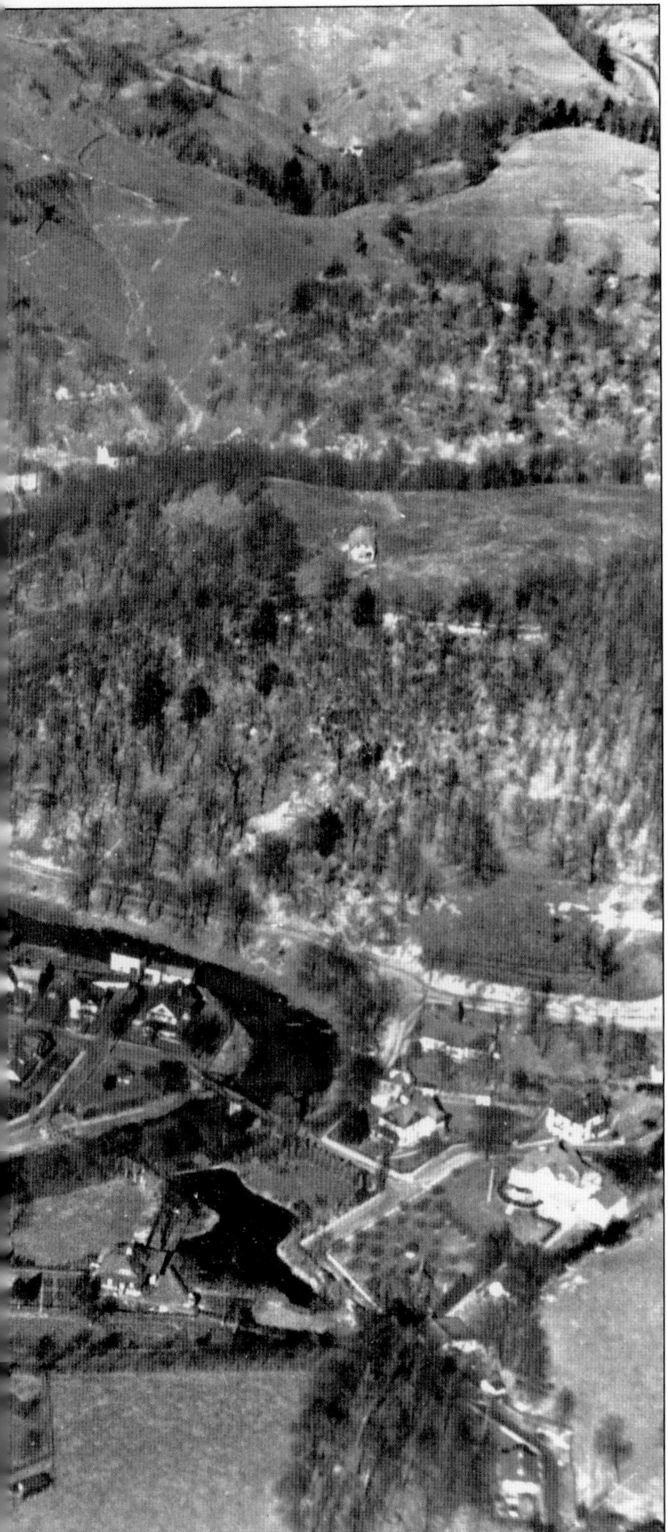

Bramwell From the Air. "You look to the East, the East looks down. You look to the West, the West looks down. And the Bluestone flows all around the town." These words were spoken by a homesick college student in 1920. From this aerial view, we see how the Bluestone River makes its way through the town called Bramwell.

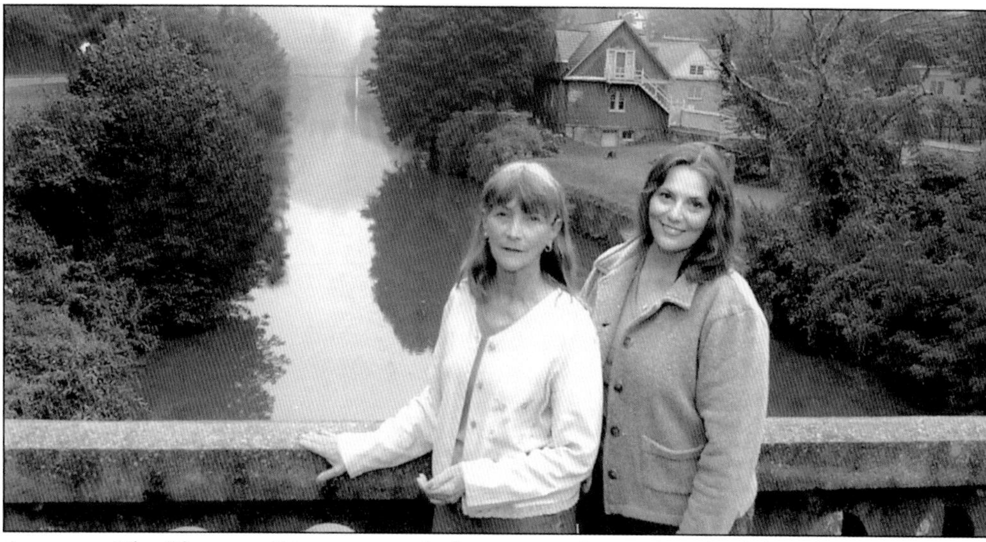

AUTHORS. The Bluestone River surrounds the town and provides a backdrop for Lou (left) and Dana as they write the end to this labor of love. (Photo by John Nelson, chief photographer for *Bluefield Daily Telegraph.*)

BIBLIOGRAPHY

Bluefield Daily Telegraph. Bluefield: Bluefield Daily Telegraph, 1965.

Bluefield Daily Telegraph. Industrial Edition. Bluefield: Bluefield Daily Telegraph, 1896.

Bramwell $tar. April/May 1993. Louise Dawson Stoker: Clinch Valley Press, 1993.

Bryant, J. Marion, M.D. Personal Letters to Author, 1983.

Church of the Holy Trinity Commemorative Booklet, 1924.

Countee Cullen, ed. *Caroling Dusk.* New York: Harper & Row, 1927.

Green Hornet. Bramwell-Bluestone High School Reunion Association Reunion Album, 1977.

Higginbotham, Woody, <http://home.sunlitsurf.com/~woodman/res-a.htm>.

Marshall, Rev. Norman F. Personal Memoir: Unpublished, 1951.

Mercer County Clerk's Office. Record of Marriage. Register No.1, page 109.

Murphy, Eve. *Expressions of the Heart.* Radford: Commonwealth Press, 1994.

Newbold, Dr. J.C. *Travels in the Realm of Poetry: John C. Newbold.* Bramwell, 1971.

Spencer, Anne Bethel. http://www.lynchburgbiz.com/anne_spencer/history.html.

Stoker, Louise Dawson. *Bramwell, A Century of Coal & Currency.* Winston-Salem: Hunter Publishing Co., 1984.

Sunset News. Bluefield: 1952.

United States Census Statistics. 1900.

United States War Department.

West Virginia Secondary School Activities Commission, http://www.wvssac.org.

West Virginia State Archives.